WHEN I WAS A CHILD

WHEN I WAS A CHILD

BY

AN OLD POTTER

WITH AN INTRODUCTION
BY
ROBERT SPENCE WATSON

METHUEN & CO.
36 ESSEX STREET W.C.
LONDON
1903

CONTENTS

CHAP.		PAGE
	INTRODUCTION	ix
I.	EDUCATION	1
II.	WORK AS A MOULD-RUNNER	10
III.	FIRST KNOWLEDGE OF DISADVANTAGE	20
IV.	MY NATIVE TOWN AND ITS SOCIAL CONDITION	27
V.	MY NATIVE TOWN—SOME OTHER SOCIAL ASPECTS	37
VI.	A NEW SITUATION	46
VII.	NEW EXPERIENCES IN A NEW SITUATION	57
VIII.	PAYING WAGES AT PUBLIC-HOUSES	67
IX.	SPECIAL INCIDENTS	74
X.	HAPPY DAYS AND SAD CHANGES	81
XI.	PARENTAGE	86
XII.	A STRIKE AND ITS CONSEQUENCES	90
XIII.	A GLIMPSE OF WORKHOUSE LIFE SIXTY YEARS AGO	99
XIV.	OTHER WORKHOUSE GLIMPSES—A CASE OF DISCIPLINE	109
XV.	BEGINNING OF LIFE AGAIN AT TEN YEARS OF AGE	116
XVI.	THE SUNDAY SCHOOL AND MY YOUNG LIFE	134
XVII.	JOSEPH CAPPER OF TUNSTALL	141
XVIII.	THE POTTERY RIOTS OF 1842	155
XIX.	JOSEPH CAPPER AGAIN	172

CONTENTS

CHAP.		PAGE
XX.	SOME SPECIAL INDUSTRIAL AND SOCIAL CONDITIONS THEN PREVAILING IN THE POTTERIES	182
XXI.	"AN OUT" TO TRENTHAM AT TUNSTALL WAKES	197
XXII.	A CONTRAST BETWEEN THIS AND THE GENERATION OF MY EARLY YOUTH	204
XXIII.	THE PURSUIT OF KNOWLEDGE UNDER DIFFICULTIES	218
XXIV.	LOCAL PREACHERS: HOW I BECAME ONE	230
XXV.	CLOSING INCIDENTS	244

INTRODUCTION

DURING the past quarter of a century labour questions have assumed an importance in all manufacturing countries, which is their just due, for labour is the root-factor in all which appertains to manufacture. In this land such questions have been acute for more than a century. The law, for the greater part of that period, was upon the side of the employers, and its punitive and restrictive conditions were numerous and severe. The result was as unsatisfactory as, with the knowledge which we have gained from experience, we should have expected. Force and servitude can never produce the fruits which spring from love and liberty.

The results were unsatisfactory, both from the moral and the physical points of view. Especially evil were they in their effect upon the children of those who lived by the sweat of the brow. Nowadays, children are rapidly becoming, in the care and thought of the State for the people who compose it, the uppermost consideration. This is only fit and natural, for the future of the State lies in the hands of its children. Thus, however wide may be the divergences of view as to the right plan to be adopted, the education of children has been one of the chief subjects of debate in several sessions of Parliament. Again, the law, in this as in many matters the most efficient protector of the weak, has made provision in several directions to prevent the abuse of youthful labour. Important societies exist to protect children against the cruelty which is not peculiar to any section of the community, and they have obtained special legislation to assist their efforts. There seems to be everywhere movement with the object of still further improving the conditions of child-life.

And yet it is of much importance that we should, as a people, look unto the pit whence we have been digged, and especially so in these very matters. For though much has been done to ameliorate the condition of children generally, yet much remains to do. The steps which have been taken have tended to carry out more fully existing reforms rather than, by widening their limits, to extend their benefits to cases not yet reached. It must not, in this connection, be forgotten that where neglect and misery have been universal, but have been lessened by the amelioration of the lot of those most readily reached, the condition of those who remain unaided is, by the very fact of the reduction in their numbers, rendered worse and more hopeless.

Light upon the past thus becomes of equal importance with light for the present, and tends to project its useful rays into the future. We shall find that we may fairly speak of the progress which has been made in these matters as enormous since, in her "Cry of the Children," Mrs E. B. Browning rather understated the real facts. Only those who are ignorant of the truth accuse her of exaggeration, but many who have been born in brighter times cannot conceive that the poem is, as a picture of actual child-life, somewhat low in tone. They have no idea that in the "forties" the condition of the children employed in our mines and factories was simply appalling; that the cruelties even of domestic slave-drivers in this "country of the free" were so revolting as to make men unwilling to republish the evidence concerning them taken before Parliamentary Committees. When such people read of the lamentable condition in the present day of young coloured children in some of the Southern slave states they cannot fully appreciate the true meaning of the facts narrated, and in their efforts to remedy the evils which still exist amongst us they are unable to benefit by the knowledge of what was done to remove those of the past.

Here, then, is the value and importance of this book, in which the writer bears personal and invaluable testimony to the actual condition of the infant workers in our darker days. It is of the first importance that we should, whilst there is yet time, obtain evidence of this kind, the simple statement of what a child, who remembers and can embody the memory in words, heard, saw and did in actual life when he was himself one of the countless victims of the hard, heartless, and hopeless, industrial systems under which masters and parents could do as they liked with their own infant workers. We gratefully hail the plain unvarnished tale which the author unfolds in this volume. He is now an honoured minister in one of the most useful sections of the Christian Church, but he was the child of working folk, and was brought up as a potter's boy in the Potteries, and at that darkest hour which precedes the dawn. The story of his young life incidentally illustrates the position and condition of labour generally. It shows the keen interest taken by the poor and needy workers of that day in the social and political questions which their more fortunate successors are too much absorbed in sport to give much attention to. But, above all, it throws a flood of light upon the evil times when many a shrewd observer from other lands found the condition of our working classes so deplorable, their misery, degradation, and suffering, so intense, that they could see the only chance of any possible redemption in a violent revolution.

And the revolution has long been accomplished, but without violence,—and that fact marks the great gulf which happily separates the times in which we live from those of which this book tells.

Perhaps that which gives a special interest to the author's story is that the industry to which he was brought up and of which he tells was one in which, bad and cruel as they were, the conditions of child labour were gentle and mild as compared with those where children from five years of age were condemned to labour fourteen hours per day in the dark and noisome mine, or in the cotton mills. For, in either case, the supply being plentiful and cheap, whether the victims had been hired or bought, it was worth a brutal "butty's" or zealous overseer's while to work the last ounce out of them. We do not thus get an extreme picture of child-life at the time of which he writes, but, as it were, a fair average, which is much more helpful.

Because all men and women who have to do with children should learn what has been in the history of child-life and its relations to labour, so as the better to understand how to deal with that which is and is to be. Here and elsewhere there is room for much improvement. "Ye are members one of another" are words which refer to the constituent parts of the world as much as to the individuals composing the people who dwell in each of them. As this is understood by those peoples they will find that the conditions of children and child-labour in any one part are not merely of interest but of actual consequence to all the rest. There are still, even amongst us English folk, multitudes of bairns to whom life is an unmitigated burden. Upon us they have the claims which the child-slaves of sixty years gone by had upon our fathers. This book is one which should be carefully read and deeply pondered by all who feel their responsibility as citizens, by all

INTRODUCTION

who love and care for children. Its historic interest is great; its pictures of bygone life are vivid and picturesque; it bears the impress of truth upon every line. But, far above all, it paints for us the shameful past, a past which we can never obliterate, and it points out how the old evils began to be overcome, and thus indicates how the lot of the uncared-for children still amongst us may be surely alleviated. It is a simple tale simply told, but the lessons to be drawn from it go deep down into the very foundations of any social life worthy to be so called.

ROBERT SPENCE WATSON

WHEN I WAS A CHILD

CHAPTER I

EDUCATION

MY education, such as it was, was like that of thousands in my day. I went to old Betty W.'s school, and as I had "finished my education" when I was seven years old, I must have attended her school between three or four years. The school was the only room on the ground floor of her little cottage. It was about four yards square, with a winding, narrow staircase leading to the one bedroom above. The furniture was very scant, consisting of a small table, two chairs, and two or three little forms about eight inches high for the children to sit upon. There were a few pictures on the walls of the usual garish sort, blazing with colour, and all the figures upon them in strikingly dramatic attitudes. One small picture was reserved for special distinction, as it was supposed to be the portrait of old Betty's deceased husband. He had been a soldier, and must have attained the rank of colour-sergeant, his stripes and sword being well to the front. The children were duly impressed with the greatness of the personage represented by the little picture. To us he was a greater warrior than either Wellington or Napoleon. He was more real, for while we only heard of these men in a distant manner, here was a visible hero, whose exploits were described by old Betty in tones of awe, and in words of admiration. The children listened with wonder to the never-failing recitals of his courage and valour and deeds, and so it has come about that my first vivid impression of a soldier, and what soldiers did, was got by old Betty's devotion to her husband's memory, and by the aid of her husband's portrait.

The course of education given by the old lady was very simple, and graded with almost scientific precision. There was an alphabet, with rude pictures, for beginners. There must have been something intensely vivid about these letters in the alphabet, for to this day when I see the letters Q and S as single capitals I see them rather as when I first saw them in old Betty's alphabet. I have often wondered whether other people carry the same weird impression of the capitals of their first alphabet. I have an impression, too, that the distinctness of that old alphabet had something to do with the success of old Betty's teachings, for though she never taught writing, her scholars were generally noted for their ability to read while very young. I know I could read my Bible with remarkable ease when I left her school, when seven years old.

Betty's next grade, after the alphabet, was the reading-made-easy book, with black letters, making words in two, three and four letters.

The next stage was spelling, and reading of the Bible. For those successful in these higher stages old Betty had peculiar honours. They were allowed to take the ashes from under the fire-grate to the ash-heap outside the house. This ash-heap was a common meeting-place, as everybody used it, and on its elevation many doughty battles were fought. Whoever among the youngsters could get on the top of it and "hold the fort" against all comers, was considered a victor. Going to the ash-heap, then, meant a bit of sport, and possibly a victory to be talked of in the little school world.

Another honour of old Betty's was to allow a successful scholar to sit on the highest visible stair in the winding staircase leading to her bedroom. It was a rare joy to see and be seen by your fellow scholars from this vantage-point of honour. There was yet another distinction the old lady had to bestow. She taught both boys and girls who were successful in reading how to knit stockings. She was a remarkable knitter herself, and could carry on this occupation with the regularity almost of a machine, while her eyes were everywhere in her school. I knew boys who knitted stockings for their families. They thus learnt reading and knitting, instead of reading and writing.

George Smith of Coalville, who became famous in getting legislation carried to relieve the children employed on brickyards, was one of old Betty's scholars at this time. If the old lady had only known that one of her boys would inspire and counsel lords and gentlemen in Parliament. Yet in her humble cottage began the movement of impulses which should move the policy of the Parliament of England. George Smith knew the work of the brickyards. His own father was a tile-maker on one of these brickyards, and the labour for boys and girls in the open yards, or inside the tile sheds, was monstrously and cruelly heavy. I once worked in a tile shed for a fortnight. I was persuaded by a companion to do so, but the smoke and dust of that shed, combined with the hard and oppressive labour for a child, drove me back to the pot works.

George Smith, humble as his position, followed in the footsteps of Lord Shaftesbury, and followed with a dogged courage which no discouragement ever abated. His humble heroism, the incarnation of his solicitude for the children who suffered, is not the least shining light of the last century. Old Betty had yet another resource for pleasing all her scholars. On fine days the little forms were taken outside her cottage, and placed under the windows. The children had their books, or their knitting, and the old lady, knitting herself incessantly, marched backwards and forwards, hearing lessons and watching work. The joy of the children was that they could see the passers-by, and their mothers, for old Betty's cottage was at "The Bottom," a favourite resort for the dwellers in the neighbouring cottages. These were occasions when the old schoolmistress lapsed into continual smiles, and when her usual rigour, in the matter of lessons, disappeared. In spite of the rigour, however, she was deeply respected by both children and parents. It would be too much to say she was beloved, for there was an air of stateliness and solitariness about her which precluded warm attachment. Whether her stateliness came through her military associations in past years, or whether it was a natural habit, I cannot now say. But for her, as a schoolmistress, it suited well. It impressed the children with a feeling of reverence, and it kept parents from intruding mischievously in the little world she ruled.

Poor old Betty! She was, perhaps, above the average of her class who taught the children of England in those days for a mere pittance, when our rulers were squandering the resources of the nation in less useful ways, and were blind to the wisdom of educating the children of the country. She and her class did two things—they made night schools possible for those who wanted to go further, say, to learn writing and arithmetic; and they made it possible for Sunday school teachers to have less elementary drudgery. But for these two social forces, helping to uplift men who have become "captains of industry" and "architects of their own fortunes," besides wider if less distinctive issues of good, England would have been lacking some of the national greatness of which we are now proud. In a nice estimate of effects in this matter, it would be difficult to say whether the statesmen of those days would not have to stand behind the old schoolmistresses and schoolmasters, who, in their cottage schools, for sparse pay, saved the children of England from the barbarism of absolute ignorance. Compare the lavish resources of Church and State with the pittance received by these old instructors of the young, and then imagine what unenviable backwardness and evil we should have escaped as a nation if those resources had been as fruitful as the pittance. Poor old Betty! I say again. She and her class shine out to me with a richer lustre of true usefulness and goodness to her kind than many whose names are blazoned in the pomp of history. But there was another kind of education going on concurrently with that given by old Betty. I was a Sunday scholar. I cannot tell when I became such a scholar, it lies so far back in the early mists. But I do know this: that old Betty's teaching me to read so early and so well, placed me in front of much bigger boys, and by the time I was six years of age I was in a Bible class. One day I remember the superintendent of the Sunday school, Daniel Spilsbury, came to the class in which I was sitting, and called me out. He took me to the staircase leading up into the gallery of the chapel (for in the body of this chapel our Sunday school was held). We sat down on the stairs, and he gave me a Bible and told me to read certain passages. I did so. The old man smiled pleasantly upon me, and stroking my hair, he told me to be a good boy, and said, the Bible I had read from (an old one without backs) I could take home as a present. Sunday school prizes had not then come into fashion. I may say here I never remember any difficulty in reading or spelling, except, of course, very exceptional and long words in the Bible. We had spelling in our Sunday school in the afternoon, and in my class we had words up to five syllables, but I managed to trip them off easily, while other boys struggled and scowled at their spelling books as if they hated the sight of them. The praise of my success I give to old Betty's method of teaching. But what shall I say of the benefit I got from the Sunday school? To speak of the benefit it has been to this nation would be a joy, and all I could say would fail to tell the measure of its beneficence and inspiration, especially to the children of the poor in those days. To me, very soon, it was a life within my life. In the midst of a life of hardship and temptation, this inner life shed a brightness and a sweetness which always gave me an upward look and an upward aspiration. Sunday was verily an oasis in the desert to me. Whatever the weather on other days, Sunday always seemed to me a sun's day. It gave me the only gladsome morning of the week. I got a washing that morning such as I had not time to get on other mornings. I had poor enough clothing to put on, but my eldest sister always helped me in my toilet on Sunday morning, and my hair got brushed and combed and oiled (with scented oil), so that I always carried a fragrance with me. I have the memory of that scent yet, and when I have met with it since, I know it in a moment.

With this fragrance I always had the feeling of flowers about me.

Though I had gone to my work between five and six o'clock every morning, and sometimes even earlier, and worked until eight or nine at night, I was always ready for school on Sunday morning at nine o'clock. I never remember playing truant but once—one bright summer's afternoon—being persuaded by some boys to go as far as the Old Tunnel, through which the Canal ran. I was so punished, however, in my conscience, I never did it again. The Sunday school, I know, leavened my life from my sixth to my tenth year, and this determined all my future. I had temptations afterwards, some of which I dare not name. Even yet at times I tremble with horror as I think of them. In my daily work, nearly at the beginning of every week, as Mondays and Tuesdays were frequently given up to indulgence, I saw drunkenness and lust in appalling forms in the place where I worked. Some employers were easy about the morals of their workpeople, and winked at the weekly indulgence, if only the week's full work were done. There was no machinery. The men, as they found their own candles, could work until ten o'clock at night and begin at four or five in the morning. The hardship this involved for women and children was never considered by the men nor their employer, who could have restrained it. Amidst these unfriendly and perilous circumstances, the influence of the Sunday school stood me in good stead. It was not so much that I understood all the evil about me and saw into its baleful depths, as that I had an inward influence which gave me an opposite bias and always led me to think of the Sunday school. When this came round again, it was as if I had passed through "a washing of regeneration." Sunday brought sweetness into my life, and lifted me out of the demoralising influences of the working days. I was emancipated from the past week, and when the scenes I had to witness, as on Monday and Tuesday, were fullest of evil I felt strongest, for the spell of the Sunday was then fresh in my soul.

My education then came from two sources—old Betty's school, and the Sunday school.

The former soon ceased to flow directly, but never indirectly, while the latter, Nile-like, has spread its fruitful waters over all my life.

CHAPTER II

WORK AS A MOULD-RUNNER

FROM education to work. This is the proper order of life. There is, of course, always a presumption that the education should be such as to prepare for the work. I need not point out how many centuries it has taken old England to get this presumption into its head. We are only just beginning to talk of technical education, and fortunately the failure of the Chancellor of the Exchequer to compensate publicans for the loss of their licences, has become the means to the first successful effort to provide common and widespread technical education for the people. In a scientific essay on this subject, it would be clearly shown that there is a logical necessity that education should be made to dovetail into the work to be followed in life. But life is not a series of propositions, nor a course of logic, nor a scientific scheme, but very often a medley of facts, which have to get adjusted by rough-and-tumble methods. These facts don't fall into kaleidoscopic adjustment and harmony. Sometimes these never come, and unwedded facts get jumbled on to the end, destitute of any fruitful issues for good. Other facts in other lives get adjusted, in spite, sometimes, of ugly and hostile surroundings, and then we see surprising issues, such as no scheme of education, preparatory to certain work, could have surpassed. But these things are rare, and leave the great mass of life so far unredeemed from the weltering incongruities of imperfect training. May it not be truly said that the world's rulers and leaders have strangely and logically blundered in their methods? Only just now, after all these centuries, is the training of the millions beginning to be felt as a primal necessity for all true and effective human developments.

I began to work, but I could never see in what way my poor little bit of an education could prepare me for such as came to my hand.

This began when I was a little over seven years of age, and it was in this wise:

At that particular time (as I have since found from knowledge, but then found from experience) industrial and national matters, in 1839-1840, had got rather awry.

It is true Queen Victoria had come to the throne after dynasties of confusion, corruption and weakness. She was a bright, pure presence, and her gracious looks and acts carried the promise of a reign whose beneficent depths and heights no statesman then foresaw. We know now she was a remedial and healing influence from the first. In nothing was her solicitude more active than in relief of the oppression of child-workers, and the poverty of the poor. No wonder her goodness, and her sanctified sorrow, made the nation, the empire, and even the world render her such a homage as the mere pomp of monarchs can never command. When the Queen came to the throne, work was scarce and food was dear. The Corn Laws were bringing into play their most cruel and evil results. One of these results was that little children had to compete for the decreasing sum of available work. As no Factory Act applied in the district where I began to work, the work of the children could be used as harsh necessity or harsher greed determined.

We had an old neighbour, a kindly-disposed old woman, full of sympathy for her poorer neighbours, suffering herself, perhaps, a little less than those about her, and so willing to do what she could to help them. She had a son, Jack, who was an apprentice in a "pot-works" as a "muffin-maker." His mother, knowing the poverty of my parents, suggested I should become Jack's "mould-runner." It is necessary to explain that a "muffin-maker" was one who made small plates less than seven inches in diameter. Such a workman needed a "mould-runner." These moulds were a cast of plaster on which the clay was laid in something like the shape of a pancake. The clay was pressed by the wet right hand of the maker upon the plaster mould which was being spun round upon a whirling disc by his left hand. The plate-maker then got a wet tool which he pressed upon the clay, and by this gave the outer surface the required shape. By this tool, the foot-ring of the plate was formed on which it stands when used. When the plate had gone through those processes, the plaster cast on which it had been made had to

WORK AS A MOULD-RUNNER

be quickly carried away by the boy-help into a hot stove close by. Hence the term "mould-runner." This stove was a room four to five yards square, shelved all round at regular intervals, on which the plaster moulds were placed by the boy so that the soft clay plate just made could be dried to a certain extent. In the middle of this so-called stove-room was placed an iron stove full of fire, with a sheet-iron pipe carried into the chimney. It was no unusual thing for this stove and the chimney pipe to be red with the intense heat of the fire. Frequently there was no light in this stove-room but such as came from the glare of the fire. It was the mould-runner's business to place the plaster moulds on the shelves on their edge, slightly leaning against the wall, so as to get full surface heat, and to avoid damage to the soft plate on the moulds.

To enable the boy to reach the higher shelves in this stove-room, a small pair of wooden steps was used. Up these he had to run for all the higher shelves, say one-fifth of the whole number. He had to run to his "master" with an empty mould, and return with a full one to the stove-room. This was properly called "mould-running," for nothing less than running would do. A boy would be kept going for twenty minutes or half-an-hour at a time, the perspiration coursing down his face and back, making channels on both, as if some curious system of irrigation were going on upon the surface of this small piece of humanity. The latest developments of irrigation in Egypt would not surpass that of the "sweat of the brow" and face and back of this boy. When so many dozens of the soft plates had been made, and had attained a certain dryness, the moulds were carried to the " master " to be tooled or " backed " on his whirligig, so as to smooth the outer surface of the plate. They were taken back one by one into the stove-room to be still further dried, so as to shell off from the plaster mould, and then the " green " plates were gathered in " bungs," about two dozen in each " bung," ready for " fetling." This " fetling " was the last process of the day's work, and a comparatively easy time for both " master " and boy, and very welcome, as both were exhausted by the long hard labour of the day. I should say there were regular intervals of change in the work when a " set " of plates had been made, and this interval was filled up by the platemaker and the boy " wedging clay " or making " battings." This " wedging clay " was nominally the work of the boy, sometimes assisted by the platemaker, and the latter made the battings, that is, from balls of wedged or refined clay he made the pancake-like shapes of clay which he had to use in making the next " set " of plates. Wedging clay, for a boy, was as common as it was cruel. What it now done by hydraulic pressure was then done by the bone and muscle of, perhaps, a half-fed boy. He had to take a lump of raw clay upon a plaster block, cut it in two with a piece of wire, lift one half above his head, and then bring it down upon the lower half, to mix them, with whatever force he could command. This had to be repeated till the clay was brought to the consistency of something like putty. Doing such work as this was " rest " from the mould running. Imagine a mere boy, running in and out of this stove-room, winter and summer, with its blazing iron stove, his speed determined by his master's speed at his work. Coarse oaths, and threats, and brutal blows in many cases following any failure to be at the bench at the required moment. Thank God there is no mould-running or wedging now. Mechanical contrivances have done away with these cruel forms of child-labour. But such was the condition of life of thousands of youths "when I was a child," and the great humane Parliament of England, composed of lords and gentlemen of kind and beneficent hearts, never once thought of the little Pottery slaves. Something was done for the children of Lancashire and Yorkshire, but for those of the Potteries, either in pot-works or brickyards, nothing was done till many years after the time of which I write. While Elizabeth Barrett Browning was writing her " Cry of the Children " in heart-piercing words, I, and many other children, were making that cry in heart-piercing accents. That poem comes to me like a sort of poetic autobiography, written not with ink, but with bitter tears. Read that poem, and you have the inner history of English children sixty years ago as it could only be given by the sympathy and imagination of a great poet. Some poetry is truer than any " chronicle," however realistic.

> " But the young, young children, O my brothers,
>   They are weeping bitterly ;
> They are weeping in the playtime of the others,
>   In the country of the free."

But the lords and gentlemen of our district were deaf, and dumb, and blind. This mould-running, then, was my first employment. What affinity there was between it and my learning to read the Bible with ease at old Betty's school I never knew. No legislation of that day ever condescended to inform me, either. In fact, no legislation knew of my existence or occupation, and that of thousands of others, except, perhaps, one aldermanic legislator, who, through the glare and glory of city dinners in London, could hardly be expected to think anything of the condition of the children who worked for him in the Potteries. Now, in these hard times of which I am writing, and as I was supposed to be clearly educated and ready for work, Jack's mother proposed that I should go and run moulds for her son. My wage was to be a shilling per week. For this large sum I had to work from between five and six o'clock in the morning, and work on till six, seven, or eight o'clock at night, just as Jack pleased. The earlier hour only applied to Monday night, as the potters had a devout regard for Saint Monday. This saint was the most beneficent patron the poor Pottery children then knew. On the other nights of the week work was rarely ever given up till eight o'clock, and it was followed until between five and six o'clock on Saturday. There was another part of a mould-runner's business, not the pleasantest, which should be mentioned. The poor lad had to get a fire lighted in the iron stove before-mentioned, so that work could be begun by six o'clock in the morning. Woe to the poor wretch who had not got his stove well heated by that time. If this were not so, words and blows fell thick and fast, and rarely did any employer ever trouble himself about this matter. The said employer thought it no part of his business to provide fire for the kindling of the stove fires. Boys had to go prowling about the "bank," as the "pot-works" was called, and pick up what they could of fire or wood. There were the "ovens" in which the pots were baked, one or more always "firing" night and day to bake the "ware" which they held. There were the "biscuit" ovens, in which the ware was first fired, and then there were the "glost" ovens, in which the glaze or enamel had to be burnt upon the pots. These ovens, with their fiery mouths, at regular intervals of space, were surrounded by "hovels," broad at the base and tapering upwards in conical shape, so as to form a sort of chimney for the smoke from the ovens. Boys and girls stealthily peeped through the doors of these hovels, and if the "fireman" was "getting a nap," or absent for a short time, a dash was made with a shovel at an oven mouth. But if the fireman caught such an unlucky wight, the fire would be quickly spilled, and he would be helped further than he had bargained for by an ugly kick. The fireman got exasperated by such an intruder, because he was afraid any disturbances of his fire might endanger the proper firing of his ware, and this was a very responsible matter. His responsibility often made him brutal. There were, of course, instances of rare fun, where a boy's tact and audacity would beat the fireman's utmost vigilance. This fire-hunting went on in all seasons of the year, in sunshine and in pelting storms of rain and snow. Shivering or sweating this hazardous business had to be done, and was done, with mocking laughter in success, or with howling torture in defeat. Every morning brought its peril for the poor mould-runner. I have seen sights of sickening brutality inflicted upon mere children, and yet such was the social callousness of the time that neither masters nor men thought of measures to do away with these cruelties. I remember after I had been working for Jack, my "master," for some weeks, he proposed one day that I should have a day's "play." This was the word used for a holiday. His reason for doing this was that he would save my day's wage of twopence. Poor Jack was no economist, or else he would have seen that if the thing answered for one day, it might just as well answer for every day. He looked simply at the twopence gained, and not at the pence lost by doing less work. So I was sent off to play. I was nothing loth, and leaped at the idea of a day's play. It was in the spring of the year, I remember, and in the free sunshine and with roaming friends I was happy. When Saturday night came I went, as usual, to Jack's home for my wages, for his mother always paid me out of what Jack brought home. He told his mother a very plausible story about my day's "play," in his simplicity making it out, truly enough, that it was no fault of mine. Upon hearing this the kind-hearted old woman placed a shilling in my hand, saying: "Here, lad, take the shilling; it was no fault of thine thou played." Poor Jack! I shall never forget his face at that moment. More than sixty years have gone since then, but I shall never forget his confusion of face. What was worse for Jack was, that in my simplicity I told in the workshop that Jack's mother had paid me for my day's play. This brought upon him the laughter and banter of his shopmates. Jack took it all very quietly, and, to his credit be it said, he never blamed me for this, but I never got another day's play on such welcome terms.

CHAPTER III

FIRST KNOWLEDGE OF DISADVANTAGE

I VERY well remember an incident which touched me to the quick about this time, and made me painfully conscious of the disadvantages under which I was suffering.

I had been sent for some drinking water to a well near the works, situated in the midst of some gardens, called "Woodcock Gardens." It was a place for birds, as the name shows. It was a quiet, restful spot. The day was a Good Friday, and it was one of those days when the balminess of a May day comes before its time.

"Shirley" has told us that there is a day when you feel that that is the first spring day, even though it may come long after spring time has gone. This was such a day, full of sweet stillness and breathing an entrancing promise of better things to come. It was the herald of a coming time for which all nature seemed to long, and which the birds celebrated by a choral outburst of surprised joy. I felt the thrill of the sunshine, I heard the birds with a quiet rapture flooding my soul, and an indefinable gladness pervading my whole nature. There came the dawning sense of a relationship to other and higher things I had never before felt. Yet I had no repining, and never thought it a hardship to go back to mould-running and the stifling atmosphere of the hot stove. But while there, I saw a youth, walking among the garden paths reading a book. As it was Good Friday, and his father's grocer shop was shut up for the day, I suppose he had the leisure to do as he pleased. Now, I had acquired a strong passion for reading, and the sight of this youth reading at his own free will, forced upon my mind a sense of painful contrast between his position and mine. I felt a sudden, strange sense of wretchedness. There was a blighting consciousness that my lot was harsher than his and that of others. What birds and sunshine, in contrast with my work had failed to impress upon me, the sight of this reading youth accomplished with swift bitterness. I went back to my mould-running and hot stove with my first anguish in my heart. I can remember, though never describe, the acuteness of this first sorrow. I must have got over it, however, in time. It is rare for youths to nurse melancholy. God has been good in endowing them with such abundant resources of healing hopefulness. So, like other boys, with the coming of boyish reliefs, I got over this Good Friday trouble.

Mr Balfour has recently said of the last century it is only the "first third" that "engages his sympathies." That is very flattering to me, for I was born during that "third," and it is pleasant to feel that one's birth-period is canopied by the sympathy of such a brilliant man. But I imagine if Mr Balfour had been born under the grim facts of that "first third of the century," if his youth had been beaten down and impoverished by its war and Corn Law policies, and if he had had to work in a pot-works for twelve or fourteen hours a day, that part of the century would not carry such a philosophic, because a distant, halo. That first-third of the century was the grimmest and cruelest period for child workers in English history. The new greed for the rapid increase of wealth, developed by our advancing industry and commerce, was rampant and largely-unchecked in its industrial methods. Fortunes were piled up on the pitiless toilings of little children, and thousands of them never saw manhood or womanhood. Their young life was used as tillage for the quick growth of wealth. I don't suppose these facts entered into the purview of Mr Balfour, or I am sure a man so tender and cultured would have lessened some of his glowing admiration for the "first third of the century."

But philosophic statesmen cannot be expected to look at the mean and sordid details which would interfere with brilliant generalisations. After all, facts are not always brilliant. As there are "Mean Streets" in great cities, so there are squalid facts which spot the glory of the nineteenth century, and especially its "first third."

The place at which I began to work was rather a noted one, on account of the character of its owner. He was what was called "a master potter." There were "masters" all over a pot bank in those days, for every man who had anyone working under him was a "master," and so this exalted distinction of "master potter" was reserved for the employer. This particular employer was as perfect a human bantam as ever strutted before his fellows. He was a bachelor, and so remained all his life. He was a small man, but always did his utmost to look his full height. He walked quickly, daintily, and mostly on his toes, with a conceited springiness in every step he took. He always wore a very tall beaver hat, with broad brim, so that while to others he looked a small piece of overshadowed humanity, to himself he seemed to look as tall as most other men. Besides this tall hat, he always wore a dress coat, with its tails unduly long. These coat tails were probably made to serve the illusion that he was taller than he really was. When moving at a leisurely pace, or when standing with anyone, his hands were placed under the said coat tails, and every now and then he would jerk these upward, and, with his bantam aspect, you seemed to expect him to crow just at that moment. He had withal a falsetto, squeaky voice, so that if he had crowed there would have been no shrill challenging note. And yet, he was always challenging, while his ordinary expression was something between screeching and raving. His eye, shadowed by the brim of his big beaver hat, was always sending forth menacing flashes. He esteemed few men as his equals, and only to these was there shown a forced blandness. For all others there was the fierce glitter of the eye, or the harsh, querulous voice. The least thing which disturbed him made him almost hysterical. He had an insufferable contempt for all beneath him, and his workpeople were to him as ninepins, to knock down in whatever fashion he pleased. In those days, in whispers and in loud oaths, he was called "a little tyrant," but such was his vanity, the word little would have stung him more than that of tyrant. In the time of which I am writing, cruel hardship and want prevailed in the town, but this man's name was never mentioned in connection with any effort of relief.

It is no libel to say he was a strong Tory in those days. There was nothing of which he was prouder, for his party was formed by the "gentlemen" of the country. For a Whig and a Chartist he had about an equal abhorrence. They stood to him in the relation of cause and effect. To him, if there had been no Lord John Russell with his Reform Bill, there would have been no Fergus O'Connor and Chartism.

Besides being a Tory he was an ardent Churchman. These two things went together inseparably with him, and were as natural as the stars and the firmament. They were from the beginning, and would continue to the end. As may be easily imagined he was no historian, and no philosopher. He was made of clay, like the pot figure of a man, and just as the one was shaped by the plaster mould in which it was formed, so the other was rigidly shaped by the circumstances of his life.

As a Churchman he was most diligent and devout—every Sunday morning. Nothing would keep him from church on Sunday morning. In his hysterical manner he would recite prayers and creeds and collects, and sing psalms. In the same hysterical manner he would bespatter curses upon his fellows, if occasion served, as soon as he left the church. He went to church dressed in his very best—his way of making broad his phylactery. His bantam strut, and his jerking of his coat tails never performed such ostentatious manœuvres as on his journey to church. He would stay at the communion most punctiliously; but this was a matter of common knowledge—that he always went direct from the church to his works. The reason was that, usually on Sunday morning, an oven had to be drawn. The ware, having been fired, was taken out of the oven. If anything had gone wrong in the oven, or the men had the misfortune to displease him in any way, he would prance and curse and scream as if he had been an untutored Red Indian rather than a professed English gentleman and Christian. These ovenmen were forced by his greed often to draw ovens before they were properly cooled, the men sometimes as red as turkey cocks with the heat of the oven, from which they were taking the fired ware in saggers, shaped like earthenware bandboxes. Perspiration would flow down their faces and the bared upper part of their bodies. As they came out of the ovens in turns, they would be obliged to breathe the outer air through flannels. It was a Plutonian horror to be seen in England on a Christian Sunday. Still the sight of such endurance and labour never touched this man's proud and flinty heart. No grace remained upon him of his Saviour's name or service. He was a master potter now, and this only, and all other things in heaven and earth were forgotten.

CHAPTER IV

MY NATIVE TOWN AND ITS SOCIAL CONDITION

THE town of T——, where I was born, is built on a long hillside. It slopes upward from the south to the north, the north standing in close proximity to a mining district, bordering on Cheshire, and the southern part of the town tailing off towards the town of B——. The western side of the town was the most built upon, though in later days the eastern side has become more occupied. Looking from this western side, there was at that time a little valley, through which a tributary of the Trent ran. I have often caught Jack Sharps in the tiny stream, and gathered buttercups, daisies, and lady flowers on its banks. In spring time the flowers were most abundant in the fields lying in the valley. In the midst of them stood Chatterly Farm, then a farm of some consequence, as it mainly supplied the town with milk. It was, too, a centre for Sunday wanderings, especially in spring and summer, for the heavy workers of the town, where they got refreshing supplies of milk and curds and whey. Poor "Billy Brid"—a half-daft cowboy or cowman lived at the farm.

Who will ever forget his small figure, his half-opened eyes, and his self-possessed merry whistle? Why he was called "Billy Brid" I never knew, and can only suppose this "dub" was given him owing to his persistent whistling. Birds abounded near the farm, and through the valley, which was uninvaded and as peaceful as Arcadia itself. On the other side of the farm, and rolling southward, was a well-wooded hillside, called Braddow Wood in the common speech of the time. This wood was divided by the same common speech into the Big Wood and the Little Wood. The Big Wood was a home of birds and rabbits, strictly watched by two keepers, who lived in cottages, one at each end of the wood.

Bold was the man or boy who strayed off the footpath leading through the wood. Beside the two keepers were two ferocious dogs, their constant companions, and probably no constable in those days, or policeman now, was such a terror to evildoers.

The Little Wood, however, was the most trespassed upon, for birds' nests in summer and for blackberries in autumn. Blackberries then meant not only a luxury, but meant also less butter and less treacle to be used in the poor homes of the people in the town. Children were encouraged, in spite of perils from dogs and keepers, to invade the Little Wood at the proper season. Happy those who came away with their cans full of the precious berries; but woe to those pursued by keepers and dogs, and whose cans lost their precious treasures in the pursuit.

This pursuing was a brutal business, for little harm could be done by the children in tramping on such rough scrub as the wood contained. But game was sacred then, even rabbits, and rather than these should be disturbed a useful and wholesome fruit was allowed to perish largely on the trees. This lovely, peaceful, and fruitful valley is now choked with smoke and disfigured by mining and smelting refuse. If Cyclops with his red-handed and red-faced followers had migrated upwards from the dim regions below and settled on the surface amid baleful blazes and shadows, a greater transformation could not have taken place. Huge mounds of slag and dirt are seen now, filling the valley, burning for years with slow, smoky fires within them. Poor Chatterly Farm stands like a blasted wraith of its once rural buxomness. The Big Wood is blotched and scarred with heaps of slag in enormous blocks. Where birds once sang in the stillness of its trees, a railway engine now snorts and blows like an o'er-laboured beast, and trucks mangle and jangle with their wheels and couplings. A railway runs through the valley, and it seems a mystery to every observer from the town how the trains find their way through the mound encumbrances which would seem to block the road. Such is the march of civilisation! Such is the progress of industry! And yet people wonder that Mr Ruskin curses these devastations with such passion and with such brilliant invective. Changing Eden to Gehenna may give the outskirts of Gehenna " greater productive power, and maintain a larger population," but there will always be sentimentalists who will prefer Eden in its simpler and smaller life.

If great populations meant more robust manhood, more of "sweet reasonableness" in all the conditions of life, more of virgin humanity, then they might be preferred. But when industrial population means rural desolation there will always be found those who prefer a poor simplicity of life to the rich drudgery and foulness of "growing industries." But when I began this chapter, I did not intend to say so much about the surroundings of my native town. I was intent rather on describing its social condition, and must ask to be excused this digression which has come as the expression of a long pent-up sorrow and indignation.

My first employer was called "Owd Neddy" in whispers when he was near, and in fierce contempt when he was far away. In one thing he was typical of employers of the town, who were few, and this in his absolute indifference as to the condition of the people, with one or two exceptions. Beerhouses abounded, drunkenness was a prevailing vice, making the common and chronic poverty more bitter and ghastly—beerhouses for the common herd, but, the hotel and the "Lamb" were for the gentlemen. "Owd Neddy" was one of the gentlemen, and though he could have indulged himself to his heart's content at home, yet his vanity demanded a social vent, so he was often found at the hotel or the Lamb on the week evenings. Of course, many of his poor helots were working while he was quaffing his social glass, or else that glass would not have been so inspiring. These gentlemen exhibited their inferior tastes, especially at the fag end of an annual Wake. When the bulk of the people had spent their money in fun and fury, and in riotous living, these gentry and publicans would subscribe for sack-races, for eating boiling porridge, for eating hot rolls dipped in treacle, suspended on a line of string, eight or ten competitors for a prize standing with gaping mouths, swaying bodies, and their hands tied behind their backs. Then as dusk came on, and the excitement flagged, these "gentlemen," with their glasses of whisky, sitting at the second-storey windows of the hotel or the "Lamb," threw shovelfuls of hot coppers among the frantic crowds. And so the revelry and devilry continued till darkness and exhaustion dispersed the silly and misguided multitude. This was the sort of life I witnessed yearly in the early forties.

We had only two constables in the town then, and they were both cobblers as well as constables. The time of bobbies was not yet come. They always stuck to their "last" till they were sent for, whenever their was a row or fight. Perhaps they had less to do with the "last" on Monday, for this was the day when the idle saint got most notice. Colliers and potters rarely worked much on Monday, and, with drink plenteously imbibed, free fights were very common. Pugilism and dog-fighting were then in much favour, these succeeding the cock-fighting of a previous generation. In every street where there was a beershop, there would probably be a couple of men stripped to the waist, pounding at each other in regular fisticuff order, till they battered each other black and red, or else a couple of bulldogs would be devouring each other amid a howling ring of brutal men. Sometimes the women would scream at these sights, and the constable might hear them, or some women would run to tell him what was going on. If not engaged elsewhere, he would come hurriedly, not with the modern bobby pace, and as soon as he was seen there was a cry raised, "The constable is coming." That cry never failed to disperse a crowd. Fighting men would pick up their clothes and run as if for life. Backers of dogs would rush the mangled animals away or carry them in their arms. There was a potency in the word "constable" which I have never seen in the word policeman. But we live in progressive times.

I said the cry of "Constable!" never failed to disperse a crowd, but I saw it do so once. There was a riot among the colliers. This had sprung from a strike. These men had marched to a colliery with the purpose of destroying whatever they could touch on the pit bank. While engaged in this work, a cry came that "the constable was coming." And so he did, and expecting, as usual, that the crowd would disperse, he boldly ran into the thick of it. But nobody gave way. Nobody was afraid. The men were too numerous and too grimly in earnest, and so when the constable attempted to hinder their destructive work, two or three of the men seized him and carried him to a large water pit, and threw him in as if he had been a dog. Doglike, the poor constable tried to swim to the bank. I stood on that bank full of curiosity and fear, and when the constable was coming to the side a collier got a rail and shoved him back. This cruel treatment was continued till the poor fellow was nearly exhausted, and as drowning was a near issue, a humane cry of protest was raised. The brutal collier threw down his rail, and the nearly drowned constable was allowed to creep out and crawl off home. The constable away, the work of destruction was completed. Everything destroyable on the pit bank and in the engine-house was destroyed.

Night fell upon the scene of havoc, and then the roaring, savage multitude dispersed. That was the end of it, for no arrests had been made, and no witnesses were forthcoming. Strikes in those days were sternly brutal outbursts, only equalled by the merciless tyranny and cruelty of those who provoked them.

Writing of this matter of strikes, reminds me of a trades-union meeting I once attended before I was ten years old. How I got to that meeting I have quite forgotten, as I have forgotten how I got to the pit bank riot, but the meeting itself remains a fixed memory. I don't remember the language, but I have never forgotten the sentiments expressed. The meeting was held in the club-room of a public-house. Perhaps about a hundred men were present. The door, I know, was locked, for such a meeting was then illegal.

The unjust restraint gave fierceness to the tone of the speeches, and led to loud declamation against the tyrant rulers of the country. The principal speaker was the editor of *The Potters' Examiner*. He was a man who had espoused the cause of his fellow-workmen, and so got advanced to this responsible position. He was a vivid and rousing writer, and fluent and fierce speaker. On this particular night he stood on a table to address his audience. The men were pale, and had an exhausted look before the speech was delivered, for most of them had worked twelve to fourteen hours that day, and probably not one of them but had felt the pangs of hunger. But the speech soon changed the colour of their faces. Every drop of blood they had seemed to rush into their faces. Their exhaustion disappeared with startling swiftness. Flushed faces were seen everywhere, and wild demonstrations of approval of the speech came in quick response to its telling points. References were made to the men's poverty, the wretchedness of their homes, the want and sickness of their wives and children. These were contrasted, with awful emphasis, with the well-fed tyranny they had to endure and support. Luxurious homes filled with light and plenty and music were contrasted with the hovels in which they lived, often fireless, but for the cinders picked from the cinder heaps of the pot banks, their children crying for food, and their wives groaning in their helplessness to relieve their wants. Their manhood, their rights were appealed to ; their God-given rights and the callousness and indifference of the Church were denounced in words that might have been dipped in gall. I remember well the aching tumult in my own heart after this meeting, the sense of a malignant confusion of all things. Yet I remember, too, the flowers in the valley only a few hundred yards away from that throbbing centre of passion. I thought also of the singing of the birds in Braddow Wood, but here were men yelling with hate of those they regarded as their oppressors. I knew these things meant two different worlds—one belonging to the God and Father, about whom I read every Sunday in the Sunday school; and the other world, belonging to rich men, to manufacturers, to mine-owners, to squires and nobles, and all kinds of men in authority. These I supposed made the world of men what it was, through sheer badness in treatment of all who had to work. "It was a childish ignorance," but it served to fire my heart with hatred towards all who were well-to-do. The editor finished his speech hoarse and exhausted. His wearied and half-famished hearers were exhausted too. After a short and feverish sleep, these wretches would have to be on their way to work by five o'clock next morning. Through such ploughing and sowing, wet with tears and tilled with blood, we have come to the better harvests of organised labour in these days.

Those pale-faced workers have vanished, their storms of passion sobbed themselves out beneath the stillness of the untroubled stars, but "their works do follow them." We glibly talk of "better times," but this hurrying and superficial generation seldom thinks that these times are richer for the struggles and blood of those who went before them, as the early harvests of the plains of Waterloo were said to be richer after the carnage of the great battle fought there.

CHAPTER V

MY NATIVE TOWN—SOME OTHER SOCIAL ASPECTS

WE sometimes hear of "horse-play," but the thing itself is now very rare. When I was a boy, on Saturday and Monday nights, owing to the fact that work was seldom followed on those nights, horseplay was a common incident in the dark season of the year. There was no gas in the streets then. This dispeller of mischief and ghosts had not then come into the available "resources of civilisation." Horse-players and ghosts have nearly become extinct since gas spread its illumination in our streets. In the dark streets and alleys and entries of sixty years ago both were rife. A ghost was seen almost every night in some dark and lonely spot. Horse-players were felt and heard, but were more invisible than the ghosts. The ghosts frightened folks, but never touched anyone. The horse-players both touched and frightened. Poor old Betty, my ancient schoolmistress—how often there was a log of wood tied to her door handle, and then a gentle misleading tap given at her door, as if some friendly neighbour wanted to get in, and instead of this, when the knock was attended to, the rough log tumbled in with danger to her limbs. Sometimes the log would be tied to the door, and the door itself partially fastened, so that when old Betty came to it in response to a friendly inquiry, the log would tumble against the partially opened door, and the old lady, mistaking it for a drunken man, would lecture and scold the log for its bad manners, and threaten that unless it went home to its wife and children she would fetch the constable. This gave the brutal merriment sought by a number of brutal listeners. Woe to the man who interfered, unless he was a constable himself.

Woe to the man, too, who had a cottage whose chimney could be easily reached, especially if he lived alone. There was a schoolmaster lived near old Betty's, who had a living room apart from his schoolroom. He taught the bigger boys who could go during the day, but as these were few, his school was busiest in the evening. He was not an old man, but reputed to be very clever, a born gentleman, but a drunkard who had wasted his substance in riotous living. Many were the times when the poor fellow's chimney pots were stopped up by mischievous marauders, and he and his scholars choked by smoke, or forced to leave off their work. When they got outside they were assailed by the jeers of their tormentors, who fled into safety in the darkness of the surrounding streets.

These were forms of mischief which, however annoying and troublesome, never called for the intervention of the constable. Between law and order in these smaller matters there was a wide gulf. So long as there was no personal violence, and no destruction of property, there was left a wide margin for mischief and brutality. In the change which has taken place, perhaps it may be said that gas in our streets has helped to remove disorder of this kind, as well as promote civil and educational advancement. People talk of the rudeness in our streets nowadays, but they would be rather astonished if they got a taste of the brutal and annoying mischiefs of the days when gaslight did not cast its civilising illumination, and when popular education was a ghastly spectre of what we see to-day. Hooliganism was then common.

Another proof of the low social condition of the time was found in the way idiotic and half-mad people were allowed to go abroad. We had several of these in our town, but "Soft Ben" and "Suck Thumb" I remember particularly well. Poor Ben was a young fellow eighteen to twenty years of age, and always wore a coarse blue pinafore. This gave him the outward semblance of a little boy, combined with the build of a man. This, along with a painfully idiotic face, made him look a human monstrosity, provocative of mirth and humour. The times he was most to be seen was when children were going to or coming from school, and the pot-works stopped for meal times. Whether his appearances there were prompted by an instinct for boys, I cannot say, but he was always about when the children were about. Their love of fun and mischief were used to goad "Soft Ben" to run after them. It cannot be supposed that he was particularly hurt by being called "Soft," but the call seemed to madden him. He dashed first in one direction and then in another. All this was regarded with mocking glee by the adult bystanders, but woe to the youngster whom Soft Ben caught. What with fright and punishment his yells were hideous, and no one knew what that punishment would have been if the bystanders had not gone to the rescue. Ben never resisted adults, so the victim was dropped whenever they approached.

"Suck Thumb" or "Billy Suck," as he was sometimes called, was another idiotic wanderer. He would be from twenty-five to thirty years of age. His particular weakness was always gripping his coat collar near his chin, by which to hold his thumb in his mouth, as if it were the most delicious lollypop. If you seized his hand and pulled it from his coat, you would see a poor little shrivelled thumb, almost sucked away. The fun was partly to see this little thumb, and partly to irritate "Billy," for as soon as he felt the thumb out of his mouth he would make a violent dash at it with his mouth to get it back to its welcome receptacle. If it were taken out persistently Billy would get wild, and even dangerous, but just then the fun and fury of his tormentors rose to their height.

The allowance of such revolting sights, and the torture these poor creatures were put to, shows a strange grossness in the moral condition of the multitude sixty years ago. Yet England had thousands of clergymen and ministers. Its

Government was supposed to be the noblest fabric of law and order and liberty. The great Reform Bill had been passed, and commerce and wealth were rapidly increasing. The schoolmaster was not yet abroad, and whether since he came, his "ruler" has ruled these things out of sight, is a question I must leave others to determine. These things may have had no more relation than the Tenterden church steeple and Goodwin Sands, but the coincidence, at the least, is suggestive. The churches and Parliament didn't work the change alone. Have the schools helped the merciful issue?

I don't know whether the winters were always severe in a meteorological sense, but in my memory of what I saw and felt I should say they were. The lower half of our market-place stands out vividly in my mind in those wintry seasons. The lower and upper halves of the market-place were divided by what was called our Town Hall. This was a quaint little building, where the stipendiary magistrate, Bailie Rose, ruled as the Jove of the Pottery district. He was certainly a terror to evil-doers, but only a terror. When he had committed a prisoner to gaol, the poor wretch was first taken to a damp, dark, foul den under the Town Hall. Anyone "taken up by the constable" was incarcerated in this black hole till he was taken before "his betters." The lower half of the market was considered the most important, and hence the busiest part of it. The Town Hall faced it, the hotel was on the north side and the Lamb on the east side. In front of the Town

Hall, just at the bottom of its flight of steps, was placed "the stocks" for the tipsy fellows who had given trouble to the constable. Many poor fools have I seen sitting there for weary hours, sent there by the magistrates, and tormented by onlookers. If the magistrates had been sent there as often as they went tipsy from the Lamb, the stocks would have been kept busy. But every constable in those days was smitten with a judicious, if not with a judicial, blindness. He could never see a drunken magistrate.

All the great events of the town took place, as I have intimated, in this lower half of the market-place. During the severity of winter I have seen one of its sides nearly filled with stacked coals. The other side was stacked with loaves of bread, and such bread. I feel the taste of it even yet, as if made of ground straw, and alum, and plaster of Paris.

These things were stacked there by the parish authorities to relieve the destitution of the poor. Destitution, for the many, was a chronic condition in those days, but when winter came with its stoppage of work, this destitution became acute, and special measures had to be taken to relieve it.

The crowd in the market-place on such a day formed a ghastly sight. Pinched faces of men, with a stern, cold silence of manner. Moaning women, with crying children in their arms, loudly proclaiming their sufferings and wrongs. Men and women with loaves or coals, rapidly departing on all sides to carry some relief to their wretched homes—homes, well, called such. Twenty people

MY NATIVE TOWN 43

of any other time would have made more noise than this hungry crowd did. The silence froze your heart, as the despair and want suffered had frozen the hearts of those who formed this pale crowd. This relief, wretched as it was, just kept back the latent desperation in the hearts of these people. In contrast with the silent patience of the poor recipients was the noisy fussiness and brutal insolence of Bumbledom's officials. This crowd might have been ordained from all eternity to be pale, and pinched, and hungry, so that these pampered blusterers might display their fat paunches and their overblown importance.

It seems strange now that such a sight should have been authentically visible within the realm of England during the last sixty years, but there it was in all its ghastly and tragic awfulness—a spot, aching with the deepest of human pains, and yet treated by the powers that be as a matter of course, like a bitter frost or a destructive tempest. In Cobden's brain and heart lay then a policy which could easily change all this, and bring plenty and gladness in its place. "Tut, tut, tut," said the powers that be, "it cannot be done!" It never would have been done if those powers had not been overpowered by the reason and conscience of the nation. When those poor people were pining in the market-place for bread, there were other lands where food was abundant, or soon could be, with Nature so prolific there. But these treasures were not allowed to come into our country, and fill the mouths of her starving children.

The Tories who inaugurated and sustained this

policy were not, individually, hard-hearted. Perhaps none were kinder when they came in sight of actual need and suffering, but for all that they could support a cruel policy. This is the curse of a bad policy. Men can put their personal feelings behind it, and so support issues whose cruelty they would shrink from, if they were directly responsible. A party policy is very much like a limited liability company where the liability, morally, is intangible and impersonal. But so we keep blundering on through tragedies and sorrows for the weakest, and so it will be until the strong and the weak are just, and the bond of brotherhood unites both.

I have seen signs of plenty and gladness in that market for many years since that time. If the old scene could be reproduced for a moment, the present generation in our industrial hives would rush away affrighted. Instead of that sad old market-place there is now the covered market, with its loaded stalls of what were once luxuries to the poor, and joyous thronging crowds, with chink of money in their pockets, buying those luxuries, or carrying them off. We hear now of the "submerged tenth," and it is written of as if it were a monstrous, abnormal condition, sprung upon us in this generation. There may be terrible social conditions in the purlieus of our large towns and cities, brought about largely by a mad gregariousness, and all the corrupt evils of gin palaces, but in the time of which I am writing, there was no over-crowding, and facilities for drunkenness were much less than now. The

MY NATIVE TOWN

towns were surrounded by fields and country lanes, and yet the social condition of industrial England was unspeakably worse than it is to-day. Many evils suffered now are self-inflicted; in those times they were largely inflicted by deliberate policy, as in making food dear and work scarce, and by keeping the people in designed ignorance.

The crime of keeping food out of the country was even less than keeping them in ignorance. I remember hearing a clergyman oppose educating the people on the grounds that they would write nasty things on the walls. They might write them on their lives. There have been dreadful things written on palace walls, but I never heard a clergyman propose they should be pulled down lest "Mene, Mene, Tekel, Upharsin," should be written upon them.

CHAPTER VI

A NEW SITUATION

AFTER working as a "mould-runner" for twelve months, and when eight years of age, I was sent to work at another pot-works as a handle-maker. This occupation was much lighter every way but in the matter of long hours. I had mainly to make tea-cup handles and porter-mug handles. These were made by two half moulds made to fit into one another by notches on one side and holes on the other. The piece of clay to form the handle was placed in the bottom half of the mould, then the top half was put on and pressed down by the boy's stomach, with a sort of wriggle. The clay for making handles after being "wedged," was put in an iron box, round in shape. At the bottom of the box was a metal die through which the soft clay was forced by a large iron plate at the top of the box, and which was worked down to the bottom by a screw, with a long handle to work it down. The clay came out like a tape worm, through the die, varying in thickness according to the size of the die,

A NEW SITUATION

as required by the different sizes of handles to be made. The "bank" I now began to work at was to open to me a new world, strange and sad and terrible in its revelations. So striking were those revelations that after sixty years I could go over the old ground and point out the places where the incidents occurred I am now going to relate. I shall not indicate where this bank was, as some persons yet living might be pained by identification, even in a remote degree, with such memories. No one is now living who was in any way responsible for the things of which I write, but I vouch that every incident is strictly authentic.

I very soon found out that though I was required to be at the bank six days a week, that on Monday morning I was not required to be there before breakfast time. I found, too, that the place in which I worked bore a holiday aspect on Monday and Tuesday. This was the more noticeable from the size of the place I worked in. It was a long, narrow cellar, the basement of a five-storey building with a handsome frontage. At the lower end of the basement storey was the throwing-room, in which two throwers worked, and at the back of this was the "stove," in which the ware was dried. No daylight ever directly penetrated this place, being built below the surrounding earth, and only lit by the stove fire.

On the line of the throwers' room there

ran in front of the high road the turners' room, from thirty to forty yards in length, filled with lathes, and at the back of it another dismal dungeon, called a cellar, for the green ware brought from the throwers' stove or drying-room. Beyond the turners' room, still fronting the road, there were the handlers' rooms, connected by a dark, narrow passage, called "The Purgatory," which ran underneath a grand entrance to the bank. The first handlers' shop was partly occupied by six young women who made "stilts," or pot triangles, to put between pieces of flat ware in firing, so as to prevent cohesion. There was another handlers' shop in which a man and two boys worked; and "the top hopper," a small dark den, with little light and no ventilation, sometimes used by stilt makers and sometimes by handle-makers. All these latter shops were much below the high road, and were damp, dismal, stuffy holes, with little light even at midsummer. They always had a close, mouldy smell, as the only entrance to them was a deep, narrow staircase, some twenty steps deep. A similar entrance, some fifty or sixty yards away, led down to the turners' room.

When all the different workers were following their work, there was a busy hum from end to end of this long cellar. In the throwing-room were the two throwers, and four young women to turn the thrower's wheel, and to "ball" for them. In the turners' room, there were about eight or ten lathes, with a turner and a lathe-treader for each lathe. These lathe-treaders were young women. The stilt-makers and the handlers in the rooms beyond made up a busy community of workers when work was going on. But on Mondays and Tuesdays one or both throwers would be away drinking at a house properly called "The Foaming Quart," Sometimes half the turners would be away drinking too, and always one or both handlers. This course left the young women and boys very much to do as they pleased, and merriment and frolic were the order of those days. Sometimes the men would "drink on the premises," and the drink was got by the most stealthy and ingenious methods, so as to elude the observation of the "bailees" or overlookers. Once I remember a youth was sent to fetch some beer in a large slop-jar, and he was directed to bring the beer as if he had come from a well outside the works. He went boldly up the steps of the grand entrance in the centre of the building, but by some means tripped on the top step. Crash went the jar, and flooded the floor of the entrance. The noise soon brought officials from their offices near by, and the beer told its own story to the utter confusion of the lad, for he couldn't say he was fetching water. A rumpus followed in the cellars beneath, official threats were flung about, a cowed silence fell on all the men. No one was responsible. No one man knew anything about it. Somebody else had sent for it. But when the bailee had left, the sullen silence was broken by a torrent of curses hurled at the poor lad who had been so unfortunate. Never after this was the grand entrance tried again. The drink was got by the top gate of the works, and women and boys were used to get drink in vessels which would have deceived a detective. Drinking away at the beer-shop was bad enough, and this was the commonest course taken, but drinking on the works was far more horrible, being accompanied by jollification and devilry unnameable. Then the young women were persuaded to join in the indulgence. Drink was forced upon them in many instances, if new to the business. Before night came some of these women were drunk, and didn't know where they were. Then the most lustful and villainous of the men—young men, generally—would scheme to stay all night. The boys were sent home. The decent and sober women fled before their usual time. The night was a revel of drink, lust and beastliness. Whoever came early next morning saw a veritable pandemonium.

Men were seen still stupefied with drink, and young women blear-eyed, dazed, with a stupid shyness dawning upon them, with woe-begone faces, and with tumbled and torn garments. The faces of all carried signs of besotment and weariness. No food was wanted, and little work was done. Some of the men stole away to the beer-house to get revived, and the many self-accusing women were languid and silent, and ashamed, till the closing hour released them from the scene they evidently loathed.

I know this is a grim picture, but I know it is true in every detail given, while many repulsive details, moral and physical, are suppressed. I am not sure whether the employers knew of these proceedings. One of them was rarely seen at the works. The other used to come about ten o'clock in the morning in a carriage and pair, and stay half-an-hour or an hour. I never saw him in a workshop. He may have been in one. I only speak that I know.

The evils at this Pottery works were perhaps the result of the cold, aristocratic attitude of this employer towards his own business. He was a county magistrate, and in those days, "county people" looked disdainfully upon "Trade." There has been a change since then. How? It is not for me to inquire, but this, I imagine, is one of the cases where necessity becomes transformed into a virtue. Still, I don't think this the noblest form of social evolution. This old employer showed in many ways that his trade connection was rather irksome, so the business was left to others to manage, whose responsibility was leavened with freedom. But the employer did not disdain to accept the profit got out of seventy to eighty hours' labour per week for a child nine years of age, while the child got one-and-six or two shillings. Probably his carriage-horses would eat as much food at one meal as such sums would buy. But they were "carriage" horses, and I and others were only work children. Anyone can see the difference. Those were the times when not only in America but in England human nature was cheaper than beast nature.

I don't think the "bailees" knew of these orgies either. They nearly always left at six o'clock, and work was carried on for hours after that time every night, except Saturday night. The watchman, who went about the works with his bunch of keys to lock up every shop, should have known, and did know, but he was bribed. He shared in the drink, if not in the revelry, and so this foul form of corruption went on to my knowledge for two years at least, fresh victims and victimisers always coming forward by the changes of situations. Sometimes feasting and drinking on the works would go on together. It was easy to cook with a stove in each shop. A sheep's pluck and onions was a favourite dish. Sometimes ropes of sausages would be sent for. Sometimes the feasting would be accompanied with a broad practical joke. If any of the men kept fowls or rabbits, they stood a good chance of being swindled. A boy would be sent away to a man's house with a message that the husband wanted the black cock sent as he was going to "swop" it. No sooner was it got hold of at the works, than it was killed, plucked, and put in a pot of boiling water. When it was cooked, and bread provided, the owner would be sent for to join them in the "mess." Nothing loth, and not being given to ask questions when ravenous eating was to be done, he greedily devoured part of his own bird, and chuckled when he was told it had been "fetched" from some other man's house. He was a wiser man when he got home at night, but his own wife had to be "slated" for her foolery, as it was called. In spite of all the efforts to deceive the bailee in getting drink on the bank, sometimes he would drop on a lad with a lot of beer in some vessel. In such a case the beer was confiscated, and given to the "ovenmen," on account of their hot employment making them thirsty souls. On one occasion this had been done too frequently, as chance would have it, and the potters determined to be revenged upon the ovenmen. An order was therefore sent to the beer-house near the works for so many quarts of common beer, not ale this time. This beer was to be warmed and spiced, so that its fragrance should be most tempting. It was then arranged that a lad should bring it on the bank just when it was known the bailee would be about a certain place. The lad was seen, and he was marched off with his beer to the ovenmen. "Here, Evans," called out the bailee to the firemen, "those rascals have been sending for drink again. You and your men drink this." And they did drink it, but they didn't know it had been spiced with jalap as well as with nutmeg. Those poor ovenmen never wanted any more warm ale as cheap as that had been.

I have said there was generally little, if any, work done on Mondays and Tuesdays, and yet it was rare for any of the men to get on Saturday less than a full week's wage. From Wednesday to Saturday they worked themselves, and worked others, boys and women, like galley slaves. From four and five in the morning until nine and ten at night this fierce race for wages was run. There was no Factory Act then, nor for a quarter of a century afterwards. Women and children were then given up to the greed of employers, and to the drunken greed of many of their operative "masters," as they were called. Many a time, after fourteen and fifteen hours' work, I had to walk a mile and a half home with another weary little wretch, and we have nodded and budged against each other on the road, surprised to find our whereabouts. No wonder ghosts were seen in the dark, gasless "Hollow," with flashing lights of furnaces in the distance, and with noise of water from the flour mill in the valley. Oh, yes, I have seen ghosts and heard their wailings on such nights, when my senses were dazed with weariness. Boys don't see them now, even in the "Hollow," because the Factory Act sends them home at six o'clock, and because the road is lit up with gas lamps. These long hours were worked, too, on the poorest and most meagre fare. Bread and butter were made up in a handkerchief, with a sprinkling of tea and sugar. Sometimes there was a little potato pie, with a few pieces of fat bacon on it to represent beef. The dinner time was from one till two o'clock, and from then until nine or ten the weary workers got no more food. Weary for sleep, weak with hunger, and worn out with hard work, many wretched children, through summer and winter nights, had to make their way home at these late hours. Summer was no summer for them, except for warmth and light; while winter, dark and pitiless, always brought its full burden of horror and suffering.

Imagine a poor child getting home at nine or ten o'clock, having left between four and five in the morning—a child, too, under ten years of age. His mother takes him on her knee and salts his porridge with her tears. She then carries him to bed, and makes that bed shake with her sobs. She cannot help all this, and this is all she can do. This poor child never sees his parents after Monday night, and on Saturday and Sunday nights, except at this weary meal, for four days a week, and a few minutes each morning. I, and others, had to endure this, in addition to scant food and clothing, and harshness and brutality besides from some drunken man who earns in four days what he should have earned in six. But even where there was no brutality, as happily in many cases there was not, the summer was no summer to these children, except on Sundays. Its light and brightness did not visit the dusty and stuffy rooms in which they worked daily so many long hours. Winter was winter indeed, for again they never saw clear daylight except on Sundays. Those Sundays for children! Who can tell their value? Beside the light and freedom they brought, there was the ever-fresh joy of the Sunday school. I am thrilled many times even yet as I think of those simple joys in contrast with the hardships.

CHAPTER VII

NEW EXPERIENCES IN A NEW SITUATION

BESIDES the over-driven work to make up for the time lost by drinking, the boy handle-makers were expected to get a lot of handles made ready beforehand, so that when the drunken "master" came to work he could rattle away at handling to his heart's content. The boys were only boys, and, left to themselves, indulged in frolic and play, besides going home earlier on Monday and Tuesday nights. It followed that the usual "task" was not done; fewer handles were made; and, when the man, who had been idle altogether for two days, came to his work on Wednesday morning, and found that a sufficient number of handles were not ready to hand, he went into a mad rage with his poor little handle-maker. He saw a possible curtailment in his resources for drinking during the following week. There was at that time a vicious custom of paying beforehand for work not done. This work was called "an old horse," and those who worked at it were never in a good temper while it lasted. The handler, then, who had wasted the two first days of the week, found on Wednesday morning the "old horse" before him, and fewer handles prepared by which he expected to work it off. This meant first, in his ungovernable temper, a flogging, and then longer and harder hours during the week. A flogging was after this fashion: the rope which lined the iron box I have mentioned before, an inch in thickness, and clogged with clay, was used for this purpose. The man in his wild passion laid this with all his might upon the back of the poor little handle-maker. In spite of yells and screams and cries for mercy on the part of the boy, and in spite of the entreaties of those who looked on, the blows fell thick and fast. I have seen when the shirt was forced into the boy's flesh, and after being dried in during the day's work, it has had to be sponged with warm water so as to get it out of the bruises.

The man for whom I worked, and who committed this brutality, was really to be pitied. He was a young fellow, only about twenty-five or six years of age, and yet a veteran in drunkenness. He had been tempted by those older than himself in his daily employment, and had yielded. He had become a notorious drunkard. As a rule, from Saturday night until Tuesday night he was under the influence of drink. When he came to his work on the Wednesday morning he was sometimes hardly sober. He was sullen with passion and vexation for the time he had lost, but he had the certain habit that he always earned a week's wage in the four days left. But this meant slavery for himself and slavery also for the poor lad who worked for him. But such brutality was never rebuked either by employer or bailee. I don't know whether they knew of such things, but I now think they ought to have known. But the times then were marked by a general callousness, and we should not judge the men of that day as we should judge them now. Newspapers never mentioned such matters in the Potteries. I never heard them referred to in the pulpit, nor even on the Radical Temperance platform from which I heard hundreds of speeches from and after my early youth.

Drink thus accounted for everything, and yet most of the speakers were working-men who saw not what was always before their eyes.

No doubt there were kind-hearted men among them, but so far as my observation went, they took little notice of juvenile workers, and the workshops were too seldom visited by the officials. All was piece-work, and examination of workmanship was generally done in the "greenhouse," where the pots were placed on long, narrow boards on stillages. These two conditions may account for the absence of close oversight of the workshop. I remember, most painfully, one Tuesday night, when that day or the day previous had been given up to the usual idle playfulness, and the required number of handles had not been prepared, having an overpowering dread of the flogging which would come next morning, when the handler would come to his work. In my fear I durst not go home, as I knew I should be sent to work the next morning. With a sickening dread of punishment, and of the darkness and loneliness of the night, I went to Booth's field, so called, but no field then, only a wide vacant plot of land which was reserved for building purposes. At the lower (western) end of it there was a brickyard, without any sheds, with only two ovens, and neither of them was being fired. No one was to be seen anywhere about. The night was very dark, though not particularly cold. I walked about until I was completely tired out. Then I searched about for some place to lie down. At last I found some mats for covering the clay prepared for the brickmaker. I got some of these mats, lay down on the bare ground, and drew the mats over me. This formed the bed of a boy nine years of age. Some would perhaps say, "Serve him right, the idle young rascal." Whoever says this, or feels it, I only hope he may never be put to such terrible straits for so small a crime as being a foolish boy when left without guidance or control. As soon as I got under the mats the most torturing apprehensions seized me, natural and supernatural terrors rushed through my mind. There were no stars to be seen in the sky, so I got no solace or comfort from their friendly gaze. Every noise was intensified by fear. Every flashing light was transformed into some ominous presence approaching. Sinister sounds and sinister sights were beating incessantly on ear or eye. Then the sense of friendlessness came upon me with acuter agony than any other experience.

The image of life, as wretchedness, and hunger,

and suffering made it for me, came bitterly before my mind. I asked why I was ever placed in this hurly-burly of awkward things, what was above, and what was below? I knew other children so differently placed to myself, who could go to school every day, who never wanted food, who never wore shoes with the toes out, nor jackets with elbows out. They had bright homes in which they could laugh and sing and play. I hardly ever saw my home except on Sundays, for I only slept there during the nights. But in spite of these questionings and comparisons, the flesh was weak, and I slept. Was there any guardian angel watching over me? God knows. I know there was one who lay on a sleepless pillow wondering and fearing what had become of her boy. I slept, and the grim, hard, fierce world was swept out of my mind, and I was a denizen of that great unconscious world where nightly "the wicked cease from troubling, and the weary are at rest." I woke soon after midnight, shivering with cold, and at once got up and begun walking about again. I was perplexed as to what I was to do and where to go. The night was still black and the heavens starless. There came noises and flashes from distant furnaces, and as these were familiar sights and sounds they relieved the awful sense of loneliness which came over me. The agony of this night's experience for a timid boy—the inward creepings of fear, the strained and acute apprehensions, the nerves played upon by a thousand sensations, with the dull, sickening fact before me that I might be flogged next morning—never can be fully described. At last I thought of Peake's Tile Works. I knew ovens would be firing there, and that I might not only meet with a friendly fire but a friendly face. I was chilled by the loneliness as well as by the cold. The ovenmen, I knew, if somewhat rough, were kind-hearted men. Many outcasts and wanderers in those days, before casual wards came into existence, were sheltered at these ovens. I was received there with a kindly welcome and given a drink of buttermilk. I was told to sit down in a little shelter opposite an oven mouth, and after my little story was told, I was left alone.

The warmth soon lulled me to sleep, and there I was found sleeping the next morning and taken back to my work. But I got no flogging. The horror of this was more to me than the lonely or chilling night through which I had passed. Another method of making up a full week's wage in four days was, when certain kinds of work were to be done, to set a handle-maker to work in the cellar for green ware, to do such work as his "master" should have done. Sometimes there would be orders for small mugs called "cans." They had handles put on them. These handles were simply made out of narrow strips of clay forced through the die in the iron box. These were cut into short lengths on a long board, and then twisted by the thumb and fingers into something like the shape of the letter S. After drying a short time, the ends were cut inside into flat surfaces, and dipped into "slip" (liquid clay), and put on the sides of the cans. For all such work done in secret, the handlers got full journeyman's price.

As to the cellar in which this work was done, three sides of it were formed by walls built against the solid earth of rising ground. The other side was formed by the wall in the turners' room, and in this there was the doorway. No natural light entered except through this doorway, and that was only sufficient to make the "darkness visible." There was no drain in it, and the uses to which it was put produced a sickening stench. In this hole I have worked for days, handling "cans," and if the bailee came into the turners' room, a signal was given, and out went my farthing candle, by whose dim light I was working. Such was the fidelity in deception, the bond of honour, that though between thirty and forty people knew all about what was being done, no one ever told. No one was ever concerned about me or any other lad suffering from confinement in this dark and stinking hole. It was taken as a matter of course, and the ignorant callousness accepted the whole thing merely in its aspect as a piece of sharp practice.

In these later days of sanitation, that "hole," and all the "shops" on the same floor, have been closed "by order." I have said that long hours were often the result of the drunkenness at the beginning of the week. When this was deemed a necessity, we handle-makers were commanded to be at work sometimes by three o'clock in the morning, and all sorts of threats were put before us if we failed to be there. The watchman was told overnight of this, and asked to let us through the gate of the works at that time.

Poor Bill S. and I wended our way home one night between nine and ten o'clock. Bill had been so often punished that he was full of fear on this particular occasion. We parted with the understanding that he was to call for me about half-past two in the morning, as he had to pass our door. As I was so often woke up when drenched with uneasiness, I was not surprised when told Bill S. had called for me. I was told further that it could not be the time Bill said it was, but as we had neither clock nor watch in the house, and poor Bill's fears made him urgent, we started. When we got near the turnpike, we met some nightsoil men with their "tumbrils," and when we asked them the time, they laughingly told us it was only just turned half-past twelve. With weary steps we toiled on to B——, and stood opposite the Town Hall clock just as it struck one. What could we do? We had seen a little old cobbler near the works, going into his cottage, as we passed, evidently just before going to bed, and we durst not go back and ask him to let us in. We durst not go to the works, for the watchman always had with him a big dog, and to mount the gate with such a terror before us was out of the question. So we stood looking at the clock under the window of an inn opposite for a whole hour; then, at two o'clock, we decided to go to D——, to call up another lad who had to be at work at the same time as ourselves. We sheltered in his home for half an hour, and then went to the works, and found the watchman and "Turk," the dog, at the gate, ready to receive us.

Perhaps about this time the statesmen in London were going to their luxurious couches, thinking of the greatness and glory and freedom of England, and thanking God we were not as other nations. We lit our farthing candles, and soon our handle moulds were rattling like dancing dolls. And yet these little white slaves were flogged at times nearly as brutally, all things considered, as Legree flogged Uncle Tom. Nearly all England wept about thirteen years later for Uncle Tom, especially the "classes," but no fine lady or gentleman wept for the cruelly-used pottery children.

Poor Bill S.! Where in the universe he is now I know not. I know he became in later life a professor of phrenology. What other dignities, social or mental, he may have achieved I have not heard. He was a lumpy lad, clumsy in many ways, and not deft or apt in his work. For this he suffered in many ways. He had more bumps made on his head for these things than ever his later phrenological science could account for. I have seen portions of bad handles which he had made taken and made into pills, and the poor boy made to swallow them. Brutality was fun to poor Bill's "master." Still, his good nature was inexhaustible. His smiles would soon succeed the cruellest treatment, but his amiable passiveness made more revolting the cruelties from which he suffered. Such cruelties ought not to have been possible in a pot-works. I blame no one, I simply recite facts.

CHAPTER VIII

PAYING WAGES AT PUBLIC-HOUSES

AS I have mentioned wages, I must describe the paying of wages on a Saturday night. We usually left the works between five and six o'clock. The custom was to pay three or four men, with their helpers, in one lump sum, say a five-pound note, and some odd sovereigns. It would have been just as easy for the employers to get silver or half-sovereigns, so that each worker could get his or her pay direct. No such thoughtful providence, however, existed. The wages were fastened up in one lump until loosened at some public-house. Men and women and children had to go there for their wages. The publican took good care to be in no hurry in changing the money given him. Each one—man, woman and child—was expected to have a hot roll and cheese, to be paid for out of the wage to be received, however small the pittance. The roll and cheese were right enough, but the payment was arbitrary and unequal. Those rolls and cheese were devoured with rare gusto. Such shining crust, and such white flaky insides, were never seen in "cottage loaves." The eyes of the youngsters had a paradisaical vision before them, and the coy hesitation with which the crust was broken, the first dainty nibblings at the cheese, lest roll and cheese should get small too soon, were most amusing. It was something like the play of a cat with a mouse before she devours it. The boys would hold out the remainders of roll and cheese to show how much each one had left, and he was considered the hero of the hour who could seem to be eating all the time, and yet be the last to finish. The lad who finished, impelled by the strength of his hunger, was regarded with ironical compassion, and he regarded himself as a sort of victim, but couldn't tell who had victimised him.

The men, of course, soon ate their portion of food, and began the drinking, which, with short intervals, would not cease perhaps till the following Tuesday night. As the drinking went on they became talkative and effusive. Boys and women would be asked to drink and pressed to drink. In the case of the boys this sometimes meant semi-intoxication before the wages were received. Boys, I know, have been sent home drunk with the miserable pittance of two or three shillings in their pockets for working a week in the way I have described. Meantime the publican kept the change back. Apparently he was counting untold pound-piles of silver, and if asked for the change, replied he was getting on as fast as he could, and that other folks were before them. Not until he was assured of a fair return for his "change," or until he saw his adult customers were settled for a night's booze, did he bring out the change. This

WAGES AT PUBLIC-HOUSES

may be said for the publican's honesty, I never remember a dispute about the change being wrong. When all were paid, the women and boys were sent home, the night's booze properly set in, and towards ten o'clock, poor wretched women would appear and entreat their husbands to go home. When this failed, they pleaded for money, as they had not a penny with which to pay the week's bills or to provide for the morrow. In some cases they would meet with brutal resistance, followed by a look of despair in the face of many a poor woman. In others they met with boisterous fun and a ready yielding of a portion of money. Not all this wretched work could have been avoided, perhaps, if even the wages had been properly paid at the works, but much of it could, and all of it so far as the boys and women (who in many cases were mere girls) were concerned. Yet their employers in many cases were religious men, who next day would do their utmost to undo some of the evil callous obedience to custom had produced. Some of them were local preachers and class leaders. Religion was amazingly unethical in some things in those days. If silver had been got at the banks in sufficient quantity, all this peril and wretchedness, or most of it, could have been prevented. But the poor wretches were driven to the publichouse for their change. If they sent for change to a shop for a sovereign, they did not get twenty shillings for it. It was put in the scales and weighed, and something nearly always deducted for short weight as alleged. I remember going to a shop of an old gentleman who was a class leader.

I put down a sovereign, and he took it up and put it in the scales he had on the counter. After weighing it, with a beaming face he looked at me and said, "My boy, I can only allow you nineteen shillings and sixpence for this, as it is light." He was always a very amiable man, and of high reputation, but I have wondered if he only got nineteen shillings and sixpence for that sovereign from his banker. Advantage was taken of the ignorance of the people.

What would be said now if a man who earned a pound a week had two and a half per cent. deducted for being paid in silver. Such a sovereign paid forty times to a wage-earner would be fully redeemed. Did the Royal Mint ever get that sovereign presented to it for nothing after its fortieth change? Yet even in those days, when the total product of labour and capital was so unequally divided, we heard of the rapacity of the working classes, though they were robbed by good men in details outside their labour, robbed, of course, within certain constitutional usages which took away the odium and dishonour of personal guilt. We heard of their reckless and wicked attempts to get more than they ought to have. If a strict record could be written of the transactions of those days on a parchment of veracity, were that possible, the working classes would not receive the heaviest condemnation. Wrongs, with trumpet tongues, would speak out against those who wronged them, and if the final restitution of all things could be anticipated, some very awkward readjustments would have to be made, causing many social and financial inconveniences to many people now living. But these things sleep yet. Nations sometimes have volcanic, political and social disturbances. Let us hope that in our old country the forces of wrong and discontent will pass away in happier and more equal adjustments between all classes, and that the sweetening and endearing influence of brotherhood will spread security and confidence throughout all their ranks.

I have referred to the holiday feeling prevailing on Monday, especially in the workshops. In winter-time the girls would make a mess of toffy, boiled on one of the stove pots. In summer, and right into the autumn, visits would be made to the market-place, and carrots, turnips (to be eaten raw) and fruits would be bought. As we were near Cheshire, cheap and good vegetables and fruit could be bought. We didn't call them "fruit banquets" in those days, as those sterner times were not given to such luscious phrases. These Monday indulgences, owing to paucity of means, generally meant the lessening of even the plain fare which came later in the week. With the boys the Monday's dinner generally consisted of slices of currant dumpling, which had been left from Sunday's dinner, and which frugal mothers had an eye to when the family dumpling was made on the Sunday. These slices of currant dumpling were considered delicious compared with thick bread and thin butter spread on it and half dried in.

Now was the time for Wonnox to display his marvellous faculties for winning portions of the currant dumpling. But who was Wonnox? Well, he was a wedger of clay for the throwers. He was half-idiotic, with a broad back, sturdy limbs, a coarse face with two small holes in it in which rolled small, restless, ferrety eyes. His nose was a huge flat centre-piece, which might have been a ball of clay placed there and which someone had flattened. His mouth was a cavernous-looking place, with no feature about it but that of capaciousness.

It was what Bismarck in a later day has described as a "carpet bag mouth." Now there was one thing about Wonnox which never failed him—he was always hungry. He worked hard, earned little, and had a powerful constitution. Woe to the man or boy who got a wild blow in his anger. He never gave one unless provoked to anger. Now on Monday, Wonnox was particularly hungry, especially about dinner-time, when the fragrance of slices of currant dumpling warming on the stoves spread through the room. Wonnox then would "smell a rat." This was a regular performance of his. He would throw himself on his stomach, and snuffle and smell and bark like a rat dog. He would pretend to follow a rat, to chase and capture it. The excitement and the tumult were heightened by his pretending to lose the rat, and then when recaptured, with the noise of worrying the imaginary rat, pieces of dumpling were thrown down to him and devoured as no rat-dog ever could have devoured them. This was our regular Monday comedy which led on to a week always ending in weariness and wretchedness. Another Monday and Tuesday entertainment consisted in rough play when the men were drinking on the premises. One favourite form of this was to place a green ware vessel, sufficiently dried to hold water, over a door partially open, and send for someone as if the visit were eagerly desired. The 'cuter folks always gave the door a shove before they entered the shop, and down came the water on the floor. But those in a hurry, or the thoughtless, or the simple, went forward, and got the full contents of the vessel amid the uproarious jeers of those who were looking on.

In all these tricks and customs there were the fun and folly, the wild momentary abandonment which always attend recklessness. But this recklessness was born of overwork, abuse and degrading surroundings. No discipline ever interfered. Any revelry, any corruption and any cruelty might go on if no scandal arose, or if the week's full work were done.

Our employer was away in his country mansion, and while entertaining his guests, his workpeople, all unknown to him, were wallowing in drunkenness, or brutal enjoyments, or degrading indulgences for boys and girls to witness. But "the cash nexus" was the only "nexus" which connected him with his workpeople, and if this were right, what matter what else were wrong. Yet I remember what vile terms were used in relation to working men in those days, especially if they sought by a strike to better their condition, or expressed any desire for political enfranchisement. How like an unreal but ghastly comedy all this looks now.

CHAPTER IX

SPECIAL INCIDENTS

BUT these play-times were not invariable, sometimes an order would come requiring prompt delivery, and the "Bailee," by menace or persuasion, would make it well understood that the shuffling on Monday and Tuesday would have to be given up. Then these days would be as stressful in hard work as any Friday. Early and late all were hard at work, more and surprising wages were earned. Wearier looks were upon all by the week-end, and then, when the stress was over, the wilder and more excessive the revelry and drunkenness which followed. Nobody was the better off for the harder work, for the strain for the women and boys was more hurtful than the small gain in wages for them, and even though the men's wages rose to a great height, all above the average went in more drink and longer carousals. I have since thought that but for the reliefs at the beginning of the week for the women and boys all through the pot-works, the deadly stress of the last four days could not have been maintained. Of course, if there had been a more even distribution over the six days of the labour required, as was generally the case with the hollowware-pressers, it would have been better for all. And with proper oversight and management, a closer watchfulness on the part of officials, and more sympathetic intercourse between them and the workmen, these times of idleness and undue labour, these periods of revelry and profligacy, might have been prevented. It seems astonishing now in these competitive and economical days, that such wasteful methods of business should have been allowed. It seems astonishing, too, that so little attention should have been paid to the workpeople's habits in their shops. My present employer I never saw in any shop on the works. A later employer, I remember, very occasionally came through the shop with a tall silk hat on, and a swallow-tailed coat and shining boots. His habit was never to stop a moment, but to look up and forward, over the heads of the workpeople, with his hands under his coat tails, which tails were incessantly tossed, looking as if he had come on parade to show the awful or sublime contrast between his special humanity and that of the drudging humanity around him. Not one thrifty, economical, practical outlook did this man ever give, for we never heard that he had seen anything, and never heard that he recommended anything different from our ordinary procedure. But profits were large in those days, and those who gathered them got very exalted notions. This swallow-tailed coat "master," to whom I have just referred, some years before was a warehouseman, but as you saw him there in the dainty dress I have described, and with his haughty looks, you would have supposed he had been all his life accustomed to drawing-rooms and saloons.

Some of the pottery masters in those days were very amusing. They aped the manners of the country gentlemen in the neighbourhood, but only the manners. It was funny to see men who had been "working potters" themselves a few years before trying to look like "partridge breeders of a thousand years." The Pottery District lent itself to this influence, for there were many "country squires," and before, and for some years after, the Reform Bill, country squires were powerful social factors. I wish now to relate several special incidents.

A Farcical Funeral

Practical jokes, other than those I have mentioned, were sometimes carried out. One of the grimmest I remember was after this manner. We had a young "thrower," whose ware was always a matter of complaining by the "turners." A deft, artistic thrower could, in shaping his pieces on his potter's wheel, very much lighten the labour of a turner. Poor Joe H. was not deft, nor artistic in taste or faculty. He belonged to a higher social grade than most of the workers, but evidently his natural dulness had forced him out of his own rank, and unfortunately he had been put to an occupation requiring special facility in skilful manipulation and artistic instinct. The result was, that his ware was always leading the turners to vent their maledictions on his head. On one of the days of revelry, when drink had half bemuddled the men in that long range of shops, they decided to have a funeral. One of the usual boards, about coffin size, on which ware was carried, was selected for the purpose of representing the coffin, and on the board was a choice selection of the bad ware made by Joe H. He had an old clay wedger called "Owd Jimmy." This poor wretch seemed a cross between a skeleton and a scarecrow. He was long and lean, with a back curved outward, which made him look of only ordinary height, though he would have been a tall man if he could have stood straight up. He had a cadaverous face, with sunken cheeks, and eyes which squinted most viciously. He had a repulsive appearance, and yet his voice gave assurance to all of an inner kindliness. Poor "Owd Jimmy" was the victim of a cruel trade, as clay-wedging for a thrower was in those days. The man, too, was ordinarily half-starved, for his wages could not keep himself and his family. "Owd Jimmy" was appointed as chief mourner in this mock funeral. Two men were selected to carry the board with the bad ware. The women and boys were to follow in a procession of two and two. Nearly all were willing to join in the fun, so that some thirty people were attending this farcical ceremony. "Owd Jimmy" followed immediately behind the board of bad ware with a long brush held in his hand, the brush head uppermost. The procession started from the higher end of the long turners' room and wended its way in slow and solemn march towards the throwing shop. All heads were bowed to hide the grinning faces and to make the show all the more solemn. Poor Joe H. sat astride his box behind his wheel, unconscious of what was coming. The board-bearers and pall-bearers marched into his shop, with "Owd Jimmy" behind, carrying a face the image of desolation and fear. The bearers took the board alongside Joe's box, and tumbled the board and its contents upon his head. In wild rage he picked up ball after ball of clay, which were lying ready for his ordinary use, and he hurled them with all his force at his persecutors, who struggled pell-mell to get out of the room. Just then, as luck would have it, a most unusual visitor appeared in the person of the "young master." Making his way to the front, he came in for the ball from Joe's hand, which, catching him in the stomach, stayed his progress and rendered him unable to speak for a few moments. Poor Joe, with horror, saw what he had done, and stopped his ball-throwing. Jumping from the box, he begged, most abjectly, the "young master's" pardon. This personage saw at once the meaning of this broad, practical farce, and as he was capable of humour himself, Joe H. was let off on condition he would make better ware in the future.

This "young master" knew more of the condition in that range of shops than the "old master." He was a frequent visitor in one of the shops where a fair stiltmaker worked. Many visits were paid to that shop. Poor girl, after the "young master" began to pay his attentions she came to her work with a veil on, and decked herself with other cheap fripperies, to "look like a lady." It was a piece of simple folly, but I never heard that any mischief came out of it.

Distinguished Visitors and how They were Misled

We had sometimes great folks to come and look through our works, especially the showroom, in which the chief productions were exhibited in most inviting array. Once, I remember, we had a duke and a duchess and friends. On such occasions we had to clean the windows, wash the benches, remove every particle of dust and dirt, and sand the steps and floors with bright new, clean sand from the biscuit ovens. What happy lives we must have led, to work in such clean and beautiful-looking places, and how radiant and smiling we all were, with washed faces and hands. I have no doubt our visitors would go away to talk of the conditions of our employment in their drawing and dining-rooms, in their country mansions, and in "London town." If ever the condition of the pottery workers was mentioned as demanding some attention, how these people could confront Lord Ashley and others with their memories of our bright faces and those beautiful white sanded floors. They did not know that the day after their visit that sand was trodden into smudge and clay, thick and damp, to be taken off occasionally with spade and mattock, and no more white sand allowed until their next visit. They were not allowed to see the two shops in our long range, ending in the "top hopper." They did not see those women and boys leaving their work between nine and ten o'clock at night, after straining their eyes before farthing candles for four or five hours, and making a day's labour of fourteen or fifteen hours. These great folks lived in an illusion as to our condition, while we lived in the ghastly fact. No deception was intended, and yet they were deceived. Their pleasure only was sought, but it veiled the real nature of our suffering, for some of those dark, damp, undrained rooms were unfit for human habitation, and to-day no factory inspector would allow their occupation.

There were other forms of poison besides lead poisoning in those days. I don't think lead was such a deadly factor in those days as now, except among "the dippers," who were always using it. The same processes were not carried on then as now, such as have been required by modern developments. Earthenware then was a very different thing from what it is to-day, with its dirty, brownish-looking glaze, whereas to-day it has to look as brilliant and white as china ware. Still there was heavy sickness and mortality in those days. If I were to ask the question, "Where are the friends of my youth?" with comparatively few exceptions, I should have to say, "They have long been lying in their graves." What holocausts have been offered to our great but badly-managed industry?

CHAPTER X

HAPPY DAYS AND SAD CHANGES

IT came about that, after one of the box-rope floggings by the drunken "handler" for whom I worked, I was sent to work at the lower bank, where chinaware was manufactured. Here I found circumstances as different as could be imagined. There was no trace of the drunken rowdyism which prevailed at the higher works. The atmosphere was a perfect contrast to the one I had left. Throwers, turners and handlers worked quietly every day, not doing as much on Monday as on other days, for Saint Monday always received some regard. But there was no drinking followed, either at the beer-shop or on the premises. "The Foaming Quart" might have been a thousand miles away. "Old Rupert," the handler I worked for, was kind and considerate. He never stormed, never swore, and certainly never flogged. On some fine spring days he would set himself and myself "a task" to do so much work, and when done to go bird-nesting. The work was done early in the afternoon, and off we went to the Highlane, and roamed through the fields and woods. Many a charming ramble have we had, for Old Rupert knew the name and habits of every bird we saw. He very rarely took an egg out of a nest, but he liked to see them, and visited many nests until their young ones had flown away. I cannot tell the sense of sweet release from my previous slavery and terror that came over me in Old Rupert's service. He was poor, he was ignorant, and sometimes he got too much drink on the Saturday, largely tempted to do this no doubt by having to go to the public-house and wait for his wages. But his cottage away up out of the town at Highlane, with fields and woods for miles around, was the centre of a very simple and enjoyable life. Sunday, with no church or chapel near him, was, I am afraid, simply a day of rest and recreation. To me he was simply an amiable and lovable pagan. He never breathed a word about religion, and yet there was a winning gentleness in all his life. I know this—his goodness to me was better than the religion of some I knew. The old china bank to which I had removed was uplifting to me in another way. There were several men employed there who were really artists. They modelled specially beautiful figures in Parian. Occasionally they came across me, and sometimes I was in the places where they worked, though at times, when they were engaged on very special work, which "the master" did not wish to be known about until it arrived in "the showroom," they were locked up. But when I met these men their gentleness and refinement brought a new strange influence upon me. In my two years of

HAPPY DAYS AND SAD CHANGES

working life I had met with nothing but coarseness, even though it might, at times, be free from brutality. But now the speech of these men, and their looks and their ways, gave me a dim insight into another order of life. They came to their work as well dressed as "the master" himself. It was common in those days for "Bailees" and painters and gilders, as well as these modellers, to go to work in tall hats and swallow-tailed coats. But there was something about these men felt to be more distinctive than their dress. I did not know what it was then. I know now it was their culture and its simple refinement. To be spoken to in kindness, and with apparent interest and solicitude to please—this to a boy who had been mainly kicked and cuffed and sworn at for two years before he was ten years old was a new world, another atmosphere, and also charming and uplifting. Old Rupert was kind, but this new kindness of these artists breathed with a grace which fell about me like sweet, soft sunshine. All this was a strange, sweet contrast to what I had met so far in my working life, but I little knew then how it was to stand out in even more vivid contrast to the experience so soon to be mine. Unfortunately for me this bright interlude suddenly closed. One morning in the late autumn of 1842, instead of going to work with Old Rupert, right in the middle of the week, I was taken to the workhouse at Chell. This was a surprise to me, as I didn't know what it meant. I knew for weeks we had had scant food. I knew when Old Rupert saw my little bundle of food, which was to last till eight o'clock at night, he would eat less of what he had brought for himself and give me the remainder.

But I had to go, "not knowing whither I went." I was awed and wistful about the changes I saw going on, but where my parents went I must go. My elder brothers could keep themselves, and my youngest brother was taken care of by two sisters. I, and a younger brother and a baby sister, with my father and mother, had "to go to Chell." I had heard that phrase before. It was often used in those days in bitterness and contempt and loathing. I have often wondered if the word carries to other ears, and in these later days, all the inward repulsiveness of the words "Poorhouse," and "Bastile." Chell, Chell, Chell, was ever in those days a cruel word, with a metallic harshness in its utterance. The district, so called, was pleasant and healthy, with green fields stretching far away, and yet there was a building upon it which cast a blighting shadow, and this by no means from the structure itself, but from the poverty, the suffering, and the harshness it symbolised, and now I was going to Chell, "dumb-driven," not having said good-bye even to my dear friend Old Rupert. I remember I had earned tenpence for the work I had done, and I knew Old Rupert would see my parents or I had this tenpence whenever we came out of the workhouse.

But this I never received, and for this reason.

Before I left the china bank there had been talk of a large teapot, as tall as myself, I was told, which was being made for the showroom. This teapot I had never seen, and I suppose it must have been put in the "greenhouse" to dry the week I went to Chell. Somehow it got damaged. It was supposed wilfully, and all who had to use the greenhouse were fined for the damage done, so went my last poor earnings in the first era of my working life. While somebody else was using my poor tenpence, "the Parish" had taken me up in its arms. It is always said, "that life has its compensations." But I found "parish" compensations to be more bitter than what I had lost. I know I ought to have been grateful for my country's institutions. But ingratitude is a stubborn factor in all "ill-regulated minds."

CHAPTER XI

PARENTAGE

AS I shall now have need to refer to my father, to explain how it came about that I had to go to Chell, I may as well say a word or two about my parentage, and even touch part of my ancestry.

My father was a " painter and gilder." This sixty to seventy years ago was somewhat of an artistic pursuit.

The tide of " cheap and nasty," which Carlyle was then beginning to denounce, had not as yet touched the decoration of china ware. My father was led into this business because it was only when growing up into a young man that he found he would have to seek employment outside his father's business. His father was a general dealer in china and earthenware, buying the productions of manufacturers and selling them in warehouses in Liverpool and Birmingham. He frequently went to London too, and many years after I came into possession of his coachbox covered with brown hairskin, with his initials, " C. S.," in brass-headed nails on the top of a semi-circular lid.

An incident which occurred when I had gone to

Hanley, to be received as a local preacher on trial, in the yard vestry of Bethesda Chapel, gave me an insight into my grandfather's position which I had never known before. When my name was read out to the meeting, a Mr Mort, a gentleman well-known in Hanley, came and sat by my side and inquired if I had any relationship to the "late C—— S——, of Brownhills." I told him I was his grandson. My grandfather had died nearly four years before this time, in the eighty-eighth year of his age. Mr Mort then expressed his great joy at meeting the grandson of one whom he had known and esteemed. "I knew your grandfather," he went on to say, "when he commanded more ready money than any man I knew in the Potteries." This was a revelation to me in view of what I had gone through in my early life.

I was led to inquire into this matter, and then my father told me that his father's business had been ruined by the profligacy, neglect and deception of one of his sons. This son had remarkable faculty for business, but being away from home, and in a great town, had been tempted and yielded, and so brought ruin upon his old father. This of course is an old story, but it is a link in my own.

I remember some things left to the old man from the wreckage of his fortune, and which used to excite my curiosity and make me feel that my grandfather must have belonged to another order of life from my own. I remember a great beaver hat, a large overcoat, with deep fur collar and cuffs, his knee-breeches and silk stockings, his frilled shirt, worn now on rare occasions, and his low shoes with their silver buckles worn frequently. I remember seeing the old man, in the few last years of his life, sitting in the sunshine at Brownhills, on the roadside, just below the house which was once his own, and which was then quite in the country.

Though he had a fair distance to walk there from where he then lived, Brownhills, in his last days, always seemed his favourite resort. Whether it had an inner charm which he saw, in spite of outward changes, I don't know, but he always seemed to look upon the passers-by with a strange, far-away look. He knew but few in his later years, but if his old friend and neighbour, John Wood of Brownhills, came to talk with him, a new brightness seemed to come into his eyes, and a new animation into his life. It was interesting to see the antique courtesies of the two old men, and how they both seemed to revive in each other's fellowship.

I remember his funeral, and his burial in Wolstanton Churchyard, and I wondered he had chosen to be buried in such an old graveyard with so many hoary gravestones, instead of in the spick and span churchyard of Tunstall.

I don't wonder now. I have since found that my wonder was the unripe fruit of my youth.

My mother was the daughter of James Mawdesley, once an exciseman, and afterwards manager of the china and glass works of Davenport's of Longport. After the peace following the victory of Waterloo,

Mr Davenport determined to celebrate this victory by a demonstration of his own workpeople. These walked in procession from Longport to Burslem, with a band of music which was connected with the works. I have been told that Mr Davenport and my maternal grandfather walked at the head of this procession, wearing glass hats which had been made at the works specially for this occasion. I have dealt with this incident to show the curious play between one generation and another.

My maternal grandfather was honoured by his employer, while my father was ruined by the same employer's son. This was done with such calculated deliberation and with such force of animus that, as I shall show, it gave me a residence in Chell, where I began early to have experience of the new Poor Law. I never knew then the amount of statesmanship its beneficent care of me involved. Had I known it, and if I could have detached myself from early sufferings so as to admire the general wisdom of the measure, I might not have suffered or complained so much. But philosophic patriotism does not readily mingle with the violence done to a boy who is forced from his home, who sees his parents turned out on the high road, who sees their silent tears and hears sobs on that highway which could not be suppressed.

CHAPTER XII

A STRIKE AND ITS CONSEQUENCES

MY father, as I have stated, was "a painter and gilder." He worked at Davenport's. A new manager there introduced new methods of conducting the business. For one thing he introduced female labour in a department which had hitherto belonged almost exclusively to the men. This new competition was resisted, partly as an innovation and partly because of the serious reduction in wages it involved.

The men resented and resisted the change. They struck work with the winter before them, and with no organisation on which to depend for assistance. They had no resources whatever. Like too many strikes in those days, it was based on their resentment, with no means to sustain the strikers during the struggle. The sense of injustice made the strikers brave, self-sacrificing, and they were heroic in many senses, but heroism is a poor substitute for organisation, with the sinews of war laid by for the time of need. This has been a later discovery of trade-unionism, and is now carried out with a clear-headed statesmanship which rivals any political or commercial management in the country. This later organised trade-unionism has become a force which governments as well as employers have to reckon with. It can speak in the gate with an enemy, or it can enter a council chamber with the full consciousness that it represents both power and knowledge. This is all very different, and beneficently so, from the wild and frantic struggles of starving men.

I suppose my father must have been a sort of ringleader in this strike, for many years after I saw a letter from his brother-in-law, who was one of the managers of the works, to say that, if he did not give up his support of the strike, Mr D. had told him he would ruin him, and force him and his family into the workhouse. This bitter prophecy became bitterly true. Such intimidation in those days could be easily carried out by employers. They had means, too, of circumventing a man industrially; and he could be run down by their sleepless vengeance like a rat. It appeared that my father would not be "intimidated," nor would he desist in his effort to maintain the strike. So we were indeed driven into the workhouse. I have sometimes wondered whether a direct Nemesis was sent to balance this sorry, reckless piece of vengeance. It would be easy to unfold a harrowing tale of what followed this man's wild revenge in his family history. In this matter, to attempt to trace cause and effect would be inexpressible presumption, but, at the same time, coincidences arrest attention. I can well remember seeing one piece of furniture after another disappearing from our home. This explains why we had no clock to consult when poor Bill S. called for me and took me off to work between twelve and one o'clock. I can remember, too, how on bitter winter days I went to work with Old Rupert without food, and how the old man supplied me out of his little store. I can remember many Saturday nights coming home when there was not a morsel of food in the house, and the next day Sunday, and all the shops to be shut up.

A Warm Heart under a White Apron

One particular Saturday night, when the younger ones were crying for food, and hardly any fire in the grate, there came a knock at the door, and a young potter came in. He knew our family well, and though not related directly, he was so indirectly. He carried signs of being better off than most working potters, as he was, for he had some private means besides his weekly earnings. He was dressed in black, with the usual potter's white apron rolled round his body, just over his waistcoat pockets. It was usual to wear a white apron in those days, even during holidays, and I have heard of a young fellow, between eighty and ninety years ago, who was sent out as a Methodist preacher on trial, who went to his circuit with his white potter's apron rolled round his waistcoat. What makes me remember so vividly the position of this particular apron, was that after this young visitor had been in the house a short time, and had heard the story of our need, I saw him put his thumb and finger down between his apron and his waistcoat. When he brought them back I saw a silvery gleam between his finger and thumb, and in a very few minutes I saw bread and butter on our table. I always connected the apron with that change on our table, and the feast which followed. This young potter I gratefully remember, too, for another reason. His name was William Leigh. He was then, as in his after life, of studious habits, modest, and upright in all his ways, and whose life had much fragrance and sweetness in it. He found out, from seeing me reading at nights when he came to our house, that I was fond of reading, and up to the time of going to the workhouse he regularly supplied me with books, and these were as precious as the bread he gave us. It was he who first opened to me the great world of literature, and from that day I have known "the world of books is still the world."

My actual world was bare enough and narrow enough, but in the world of books I had "ample verge and room," could commune with those "who rule our spirits," and hold my mean environment in some disdain when compared with the wealth and imagination poured at my feet. But to come back to the impression of that white apron. For years after I always looked with a curious interest on a white apron when rolled round the body, and had a sort of undefined feeling that there was a sort of magic lying within its folds. It was some years before I distinctly realised that there was a waistcoat pocket hidden by the apron, and that in those days men generally carried their money in their waistcoat pockets. How that winter was got through God only knows. We were not the only sufferers. In that year, 1842, distress was general and deeply bitter. Mr Walpole, in his history, says that England touched in that year the lowest point in its condition. I saw it proved in that year by daily and powerful illustrations that " if it were not for the poor the poorer would perish." Semi-starvation was the normal condition of thousands, pinched faces and shivering bodies were seen everywhere during that cruel winter, carts were followed for miles for any coal they might lose on their journeys, and a jolt was a godsend to the eager follower at the cart tail. The glistening lumps as they fell made eyes glisten, as it meant fire in the black shining treasure. Shord-rucks were searched by shivering women and children for cinders, as hens scratch and search for food. Fingers bled as they picked in among the broken pitchers and shords, and the bleeding was only staunched by dirt and frost. Those who got a miserable pittance of out-door relief got bread which might have been made of sawdust, blotched with lumps of plaster of Paris. It is a pity one of those loaves could not have been preserved for inspection and comparison in these later days. Those were the good old days when the Corn Laws made rent high and living low, and made semi-famine the ordinary condition of the country for the toiling masses. Toil, however, grinding as it was, was rendered fitful and uncertain by that ubiquitous Protection, which protected nothing but the wealth of the landlords, and really not even that. The home in which I lived was getting less homelike every week. Everything which could be turned to money or goods had to go. I remember two beautiful tiles which had been painted, so I was told, years before by a friend of my father's, a skilful flower-painter. Many a time did I look at those beautiful flowers on the tiles as they stood on the mantelpiece. They were china tiles, with a rich shining white glaze. They had fruit and flowers painted on them, and one of the roses charmed me then in sight, and has charmed me more than sixty years in thought. Especially when I see lovely roses do I think of that rose on the tile. I have never seen one quite so lovely as that which shone forth amid my early sorrows.

One morning, however, in that winter time, I remember, as we were shoeless and clogless, I was sent with those tiles to a clogger to ask if he would give two pairs of clogs to two barefooted boys for those tiles. The clogger looked in wonder and pity upon the little applicants. It was plain, even to me, that he had no hesitation to make the bargain on the ground of value. He went out of the shop, however, to consult someone, and returned without the tiles, and put us the clogs on our feet. So went on the rack of home until ruin came, and all had to go. Thus far my father's employer's prophecy had come true. No one would employ him, and so the other part of the prophecy hastened on to its fulfilment. This accounts for the incident I have referred to before, that one morning, instead of going to the works to join Old Rupert, I was taken to Chell Workhouse. Early in the morning we left a home without a morsel of food. We called on a relative who had kindly provided breakfast for us, and yet it was a wretched meal for my parents. I remember the choking sobs, though I did not understand them as I did afterwards. I remember, too, how the food seemed to choke as much as the sobs, and the vain entreaties to " eat a little more." We went by the field road to Chell, so as to escape as much observation as possible. One child had to be carried as she was too young to walk. The morning was dull and cheerless. I had been through those fields in sunshine, and when the singing of birds made the whole scene very pleasant. Now, when the silence was broken, it was only by deep agonising sobs. If we could have seen what was driving us so reluctantly up that hill to the workhouse (" Bastile," as it was bitterly called then), we should have seen two stern and terrible figures— Tyranny and Starvation. No other powers could have so relentlessly hounded us along. None of us wanted to go, but we must go, and so we came to our big home for the time. The very vastness of it chilled us. Our reception was more chilling still. Everybody we saw and spoke to looked metallic, as if worked from within by a hidden machinery. Their voices were metallic, and sounded harsh and imperative. The younger ones huddled more closely to their parents, as if from fear of these stern officials. Doors were unlocked by keys belonging to bunches, and the sound of keys and locks and bars, and doors banging, froze the blood within us. It was all so unusual and strange, and so unhomelike. We finally landed in a cellar, clean and bare, and as grim as I have since seen in prison cells. We were told this was the place where we should have to be washed and put on our workhouse attire. Nobody asked us if we were tired, or if we had had any breakfast. We might have committed some unnameable crime, or carried some dreaded infection. "No softening gleam" fell upon us from any quarter. We were a part of Malthus's "superfluous population," and our existence only tended to increase the poverty from which we suffered. "Benevolence," he said, "in a being so shortsighted as man, would lead to the grossest error, and soon transform the fair and cultivated soil of civilised society into a dreary scene of want and confusion."

This truly was "a nice derangement of epitaphs" to come from the pen of a clergyman in a Christian country. I have wondered if the pen with which he wrote was "a steel" pen. In this spirit Carlyle's "Poor Law Bastiles" were not made "pleasant places." The place was as innocent-looking as to hospitality as if it had been built in a flinty rock, and never had a human being in it. We youngsters were roughly disrobed, roughly and coldly washed, and roughly attired in rough clothes, our under garments being all covered up by a rough linen pinaforte. Then we parted amid bitter cries, the young ones being taken one way and the parents (separated too) taken as well to different regions in that merciful establishment which the statesmanship of England had provided for those who were driven there by its gross selfishness and unspeakable crassness.

Talleyrand has said that it was astonishing what pleasant lives the French noblemen lived before the Revolution. It may be said equally, that many well-to-do people lived pleasant lives in England before the Corn Laws were repealed, while little children, through long hours of labour and scant food, were passing through a very Tophet of agony, and their cries were only heard by such folks as Mrs Barrett Browning, Carlyle, and Lord Ashley.

And even "Young England" to-day, among the working classes, hears not nor heeds the ground surges of the first half of the last century.

CHAPTER XIII

A GLIMPSE OF WORKHOUSE LIFE SIXTY YEARS AGO

I WAS now making an epochal entrance into a new life, conducted by "the august Mother of Free Nations," and by the genius of the country that was then said to be "great, glorious, and free." I did not then realise the high guidance that was given to a little hungry waif like myself. Even if I had been told of this high guidance, I am afraid it would not have helped me to dine that day with any more pleasure. I was ushered or shoved into a large room which I found was both dining and schoolroom. There were many guests assembled, and on the principle, "The more the merrier," we ought to have dined merrily. But I saw no merriment, not even in that company of boys, at whose age Heaven usually endows them with almost irrepressible fun. I saw hungry-looking lads, with furtive glances, searching everything and everybody, and speaking in subdued whispers. I saw a stern, military, cadaverous-looking man, who was said to be the schoolmaster. I noticed his chilling glances, carrying menace in every look. When dinner was ready this stony-looking individual bent his head a few seconds and mumbled something. I suppose it was grace he was saying before meat, but as far as I could see there was no grace in anything he did. I noticed he did not join us in our repast, and I know now he was a wise man for not doing so. He had asked God's blessing on what we were to eat; but he would have cursed it had he had to eat it himself. It was a fine piece of mockery, though I did not know it then, or I should have admired his acting. I was hungry, but that bread! that greasy water! those few lumps of something which would have made a tiger's teeth ache to break the fibres of! the strangeness, the repulsiveness, and the loneliness, made my heart turn over, and I turned over what I could not eat to those near me, who devoured voraciously all I could spare. It was the first great dinner I ever attended, and I didn't like it. I have been at other big dinners where there were many courses, and flowers, and gleaming silver, glass, and other amenities. But this big dinner was simply coarse, and looked only coarse even for a poor lad who had not been too daintily fed. In the afternoon we had our school work to do, and as I could read well I had no trouble with such lessons as were given. But if some of the other lads had had heads made of leather stuffed with hay they could not have got more knocks. It was a brutal place for the "dull boy." However hard he worked, and however patiently he strove, he got nothing but blows. If the devil had kept a school to teach boys how not to learn, he could not have succeeded better than that schoolmaster who asked God's blessing on the dinner he didn't share. Tea and supper by a wise economy were joined together. The New Poor Law was to be economical if anything, even to the least quantity of food a growing boy's stomach could do with. But supper time came. What would it bring? That was the question for me. It brought a hunch of bread and a jug of skilly. I had heard of workhouse skilly but had never before seen it. I had had poor food before this, but never any so offensively poor as this. By what rare culinary-making nausea and bottomless fatuousness it could be made so sickening I never could make out. Simple meal and water, however small the amount of meal, honestly boiled, would be palatable. But this decoction of meal and water and mustiness and fustiness was most revolting to any healthy taste. It might have been boiled in old clothes, which had been worn upon sweating bodies for three-score years and ten. That workhouse skilly was the vilest compound I ever tasted, unutterably insipid, and it might never have been made in a country where either sugar or salt was known.

Skilly in those days was the synonym for Bastile repulsiveness, and I can well understand how that came to pass, having tasted such a malignant mockery of food. My supper that first night was as disappointing as my first dinner had been. But here I was, caged as in iron bars, with no power to say what I liked, even to a pinch of salt. Oh, "august Mother of Free Nations!" too august to look down at thy poorest and weakest, bound in a tyranny which closed the lips from even saying, "A little salt, please."

Soon after supper, prayers were read by that saintly-looking schoolmaster—saintly, that is, if flintiness and harshness can make a saint good enough to read prayers in such a place. Our schoolmaster was distinctly two personages. In matters of school work, he was always militant and menacing. His face to all the appeals rising from the faces of those poor children day by day was as chilling as the grey of a winter's sky. No gleam of sunshine ever seemed to fall on the face of any child. Yet when he read prayers he tried to be awe-inspiring by speaking in his deepest tones, but the tones and the face never suggested the thought of a Father above who watched over us. The feeling in us was, while the prayer was going on, that He was rather an infinite schoolmaster who was mercifully distant and invisible.

We had been under the vicarious care of the Guardians during the day. We were now commended to the care of our Heavenly Guardian for the night. If we had to interpret the one by the other we should have gone uneasily to our beds. But some of us had the faith of children who had prayed at their mothers' knees, and we never thought of such a comparison. We thought only of One who was to us, "Gentle Jesus, meek and mild." We believed He was looking upon us in that cold loneliness, away from our fathers and mothers, and we thought of Him as we saw Him in His glorified form in pictures blessing little children.

WORKHOUSE SIXTY YEARS AGO

Our bedroom was a long, narrow room, with the beds in rows on each side of the room. Down the middle of the room was a long, narrow passage. The bed clothing was scant enough, and the beds hard enough for athletic discipline. At the end of the room, near the staircase, was a wide, shallow tub. There were boys there as cruel as neglect and badness could make them. They soon found out the timid ones, and would "walk the midnight air" to frighten all they could by ghostly appearances. A poor lad, seeking the tub at night, would sometimes shriek through some brutal attempt to frighten him. By sheer weariness some would soon drop off to sleep, while others, alive with fears, would have to listen to the most harrowing stories of ghosts, boggarts and murders. Every new boy had to sing a song or tell a tale —the other boys wanted a taste of his quality—the first night, and pitied was that poor boy to be who could neither sing nor tell a tale. He was bullied, was pulled out of bed, and scarified by pitiless mockery such as that of "a schoolboy ere he's learned to pity." There were, of course, demons among these youngsters, made so partly by the cruel treatment they themselves daily received. These demons, by the grace of the Guardians, governor and schoolmaster, were permitted each night to hold their revels, and so long as they kept within their bedroom they might riot in their cruelty. That bedroom brought strange contrasts of company together. Misfortune brought boys there who shrank to the very narrow of their souls from the brutalities, obscenities and coarseness allowed. Other boys were there who were verily "children of the devil"; yet these two sorts of boys were forced into association and community. If "guardian angels" looked over those beds they must have seen little hearts palpitating with horror and fear, and that helpless wonder of a child which finds no reason anywhere for things as they are. Feverishly and restlessly I spent that first night. Hunger and terror were about my bed. A lively imagination made real and present some of the characters in the tales which had been told by the boys who were now asleep. I saw the ghosts they had spoken of. I saw the murderers, red-handed, rushing through the room. I heard their footsteps, and only found out too late that the footsteps were those of the poor little fellows who were visiting the tub at the end of the room. Sanitation was an angel undreamed of in the workhouses in those days, as well as in England generally. That tub, too, had to be carried down the stairs every morning before breakfast by two small boys in turn.

It can easily be imagined how its contents were spilled on the staircase, but that was nothing. If fever came and took off a lot of the inmates, that was a double gain—the parish was relieved and Heaven was enriched, for who can suppose that such workhouse boys, even the "demons," went anywhere else. Such was the sleeping-room, the order, and the sanitary arrangements provided for these boys by the statesmanship of England, aided by the perfect wisdom and disinterestedness of "the Guardians of the Poor." I wonder who invented that phrase for those times. If Voltaire, with his supreme cynicism, had been invited to coin a descriptive phrase for these men, he could not have surpassed this in mockery, in relation to the men who held these positions in those days. I knew some of these men in after years. They were gentlemen farmers and large employers, who had a remorseless faculty for "keeping down the rates" just when the Protection policy of Parliament was as remorselessly forcing them up by robbing the people of their industry and cheap food. It was a grim battle, but I think "the Guardians of the Poor" won. At what price, you ask? Never mind the price. The pockets of the principal ratepayers were saved, and pockets during the reign of the Corn Laws were considered by "Queen, Lords and Commons" to he more sacred than stomachs any day. The Queen's name here is only used as part of a constitutional formula. We know she had an overflowing personal solicitude for all her people, but especially for poor children.

Even those, too, represented by "Lords and Commons" were better than the Corn Laws behind which they stood. Men can do things by "policy" and Acts of Parliament in their impersonal generality which they would not do individually, and many of them, even in those cruel days, nobly strove to soften the blow of their own "laws."

Sunday Dinner

This first day's experience of the Bastile was like most others, and the night's too. On the Sunday, I remember, we were taken to church in the morning. After the church the clergyman came to our "dining-room," but, like the schoolmaster, not to dine with us. He was to say "grace before meat" in place of the schoolmaster as it was a most sacred day. He also gave us a preliminary homily as long as the sermon he had given in church. We stood up while this was given. We were told on that and other Sundays, as I well remember, of the great mercies we enjoyed, of the good food provided, of the comfortable clothing we had, and how we were cared for by those about us. All this was said while before us on the table lay a small hunk of bread, a small plate with a small slice of thin, very thin cheese, and some jugs of water. This was our Sunday dinner, and for such a dinner "that good man, the clergyman," was brought to say grace. It was a dinner we liked, nevertheless, because of the bit of cheese with its appetising taste, and its power, as was said in those days, "to eat a lot of bread." And because we liked it we disliked the parson for keeping us so long from enjoying it. However, the homily and the grace came to an end at last and the parson departed, but not to a dinner, however sumptuous, that he relished more than we did that bit of cheese. This was the one bit of food that reminded us of home. It was tasty in itself and cheering in its association, so there went up to Heaven that day from the hearts of those poor lads a thanksgiving, "uttered or unexpressed," more acceptable to the Divine Father than went up from many a table "groaning with luxuries."

Sunday afternoon brought an hour of unspeakable joy. The children who had mothers were permitted to go to the women's room. It can easily be imagined what happened then. Bedlam was let loose for an hour. Wild joy, frantic exclamations, every conceivable form of speech possible to such people under such circumstances were employed. Love went mad in many cases. But all did not give way to the wild revelry of passion. Some mothers and children hung together in quiet, intense endearments. These were conveyed more by soft pressures of hands, embraces, and lips, than by words. Even among the poor many stand worlds apart. This was the one sweet merciful relief in the harsh discipline of the workhouse.

It was a reminder of home and of the humanities outside. It was an oasis in the desert of our common life. The Sunday afternoon shone through all the week. Even the troubles which burdened the children's hearts got release on the Sunday. Many stories of young griefs were told in the mother's ear, but forgotten as soon as told. There was, however, one dreadful moment came, when the bell was rung in the room by a porter to tell us our time was gone. It would have made no difference if that bell had been a silver one, its tones would have been as harsh as metal could make them, and the man who rang it would have been regarded as the incarnation of cruelty. We never thought of discipline, order and authority. The man who rang the bell was alone the author of all this dismay, and hurry-scurry, and sudden tears, and even yells, seen and heard in the women's room. We knew that he would let us have no supper that night if we did not leave the room at once. Woe to any stubborn or nervous loiterer. For that child there were menacing words, harsh looks and a supperless night. "There must be discipline, you know"; yes, there must, as there must be many things under which "the whole creation," gentle and simple, must groan and travail in pain. But true discipline should never take the form of cruelty.

CHAPTER XIV

OTHER WORKHOUSE GLIMPSES—A CASE OF DISCIPLINE

THERE was one "case of discipline" while I was at the Bastile to which I must refer. It was a conspicuous case, and therefore had "to be made an example of." So ran the official cant. Discipline was administered with unfailing regularity every day. Hardly a boy escaped some form of it, and it was usually a merciless form. It seemed to be a standing regulation that this treatment was as necessary for the soul as skilly was for the body. No distinction was made, the same cuts and slashes and cuffs were aimed at the mobile and sensitive boy as were aimed at the sluggish and dull boy. The one boy would writhe and sob, and the other maintained a stolid silence. The case I am now going to refer to was that of a boy of lively temperament and unflagging energy. His activity was always bringing him into trouble. The theory formed by the officials seemed to be that his activity was essentially vicious, and so, instead of trying to guide it into wise and useful developments, it must be sternly repressed. Such a policy goaded the lad. He became defiant and reckless. Punish him they might, but he could not be repressed. One day, after being unusually provoked and punished, he scaled the workhouse wall, and bolted. Soon a hue and cry was raised, searchers were sent out, and after a few hours the lad was captured and brought back. This incident made an awful flutter in our little dove-cote. All were sorry for the lad, for he had made no enemies among us. All sorts of punishment were imagined as likely to be inflicted, but the boys who had been longest in the workhouse said he would be flogged in the presence of the other boys with a pickled birch rod—that is a rod which has been kept soaking in salt water. After the usual skilly supper that night we were all told to remain in the room. None were to go out on any account. The long table was cleared, and a smaller square table was brought in and placed in the middle of the room. The knowing ones whispered that the flogging would take place on this table, and this news made us all curious, eager, yet fearful. Several persons came in whom we did not usually see. Then the governor came in. To us poor lads he was the incarnation of every dread power which a mortal could possess. He was to us the Bastile in its most repulsive embodiment. Personally, he may have been an aimiable man, I don't know. He never gave one look or touch which led me to feel he was a man. He was only "the governor," and as such, in those days, when the New Poor Laws meant making a workhouse a dread and a horror to be avoided, he was perhaps only acting the part he felt to be due to his office. His functions, and any outward compassion, were as wide asunder as the poles. He may have had compassion. He may have been inwardly tortured by the necessity for outward callousness. May Heaven forgive me if I do him any wrong, but word or act of kindliness from him I never heard or saw towards myself or anyone else. Now, however, the governor was in the room, and his presence seemed to fill it with an awful shadow. We were duly informed by him what was to take place, the bad qualities of the runaway were ponderously and slowly described, and we were exhorted in menacing tones to take warning by his "awful example." This homily was enough of itself to make us shiver, and shiver most of us did with fear of those present and fear of the sight we were about to witness. When the solemn harangue was finished, the poor boy was pushed into the room like a sheep for the slaughter. He had a wild, eager look. His eyes flashed, and searched the room and all present with rapid glances. His body was stripped down to his waist, and in the yellow and sickly candlelight of the room his heart could be seen beating rapidly against his poor thin ribs. To punish such a boy as that, half nourished, and trembling with fear, was a monstrous cruelty. However, discipline was sacred, and could do no wrong in a Bastile sixty years ago. The boy was lifted upon the table, and four of the biggest boys were called out to hold each a leg or an arm. The boy was laid flat on the table, his breeches well pushed down, so as to give as much play as possible for the birch rod. The lad struggled and screamed. Swish went the pickled birch on his back, administered by the schoolmaster, who was too flinty to show any emotion. Thin red stripes were seen across the poor lad's back after the first stroke. They then increased in number and thickness as blow after blow fell on his back. Then there were seen tiny red tricklings following the course of the stripes, and ultimately his back was a red inflamed surface, contrasting strongly with the skin on his sides. How long the flogging went on I cannot say, but screaming became less and less piercing, and at last the boy was taken out, giving vent only to heavy sobs at intervals. If he was conscious, I should think only partially so. The common rumour was that he would have his back washed with salt water. Of this I don't know. I do know there had been cruelty enough. A living horror, hateful in every aspect, had been put before the eyes of the boys present. To see a poor lad with red rivulets running down his back and sides, as I see it all again even yet, among strangers, with the governor's awful presence, with the schoolmaster's fiercely gleaming eyes, away from father, mother and home ;—all this when our late gracious Queen was a young queen. The spirit of the New Poor Law and of the Corn Laws was present in that torture-room that night. Lord Brougham, not many years before this, had said that "charity is an interference with a healing process of nature, which acts by increasing the rate of mortality, and thereby raising wages." Political Economy was then on the side of harshness. This was the time of Ricardo's "iron law." Flog on then, my governor and schoolmaster. No "Guardians" will protest against your cruelty to that writhing waif, and there is "no chiel among ye takin' notes," as in a later day, to bring down the judgment of the public conscience upon your heads. So far from this, perhaps the said "Guardians of the Poor," will "note with satisfaction," at their next meeting, that "you have quite properly maintained the discipline of the house." House? That should be the shrine of a home. Was there a more ghastly mockery than that to be seen that night on that table with its bleeding waif? Such was the Bastile sixty years ago. Such was one scene in Chell, and if you drop the "C" in the word it only remains more truly descriptive of the place where such "discipline" could take place. How that poor little wretch got on that night I never knew. He did not come to his usual bed in our room. Perhaps he was thrust into some "black hole," or lonely room, to add to his sufferings. His "guardian angel" and himself would have a sorry night that night. Probably the governor and schoolmaster, and those other "Guardians," would all sleep in peace. The former "had done their duty," and the latter slept in the assurance they would do so.

What tragedies and mockeries get mixed up under our stars. Governor, schoolmaster, the Guardians and the poor waif have probably slept for many years. Let us hope that sleeping so long with the clods of the valley, and in combination with divine influence, they will come forth to a sweeter life. We went that night to our beds scared, and wild with fear and excitement. The long, dark room became a veritable purgatory, with red flames of memory mingling with the red blood we had seen flowing down the boy's back. There was little sleep in our room for some boys, all their pulses were alive with fear and terror. The night bore on slowly and wearily. The broken whispers told of restlessness and sleeplessness. But the morning came, and the skilly, and the room where we had witnessed the bleeding back of the boy. The boy didn't come, however. Where he was none of us knew. I never saw him again, for in a few days came the joyful news that my father had got a situation. I left the place with a delight no words could express, and I have only once since permitted myself to see the place where I first felt the degradation of existence, and saw the infamies which were associated with such guardianship. The New Poor Law was wise enough, economically considered, but there could have been the economy without the brutality and harshness and humiliation pressed into the souls of old and young. Any system which makes young boys ashamed of their existence must be somewhat devilish in its evil ingenuity, and that was what Bastile " discipline " did for me.

CHAPTER XV

BEGINNING OF LIFE AGAIN AT TEN YEARS OF AGE

IT was somewhat unique for a boy of ten to be started on three stages of life before he touched his eleventh year. I had begun as old Betty's scholar at about three.

I had then begun to work at seven, and after working a little short of three years my career was suddenly arrested. I had tried in my poor way to earn my living, though such a young sojourner in the world, but having failed to do this my country came to my rescue to save me from starvation. Suddenly I might have become a gentleman's son, with no need for work, and "only to go to school." So I went to school instead of to my work as a handle-maker, and to a workhouse where I had no work to do. If I had been a philosopher at that time, I might have been puzzled at these contradictions and caprices, but I was only a boy and took what came before me as a horse takes a road, not asking why it is paved or unpaved, muddy and soft, or clean and hard.

But now the one dominant feeling I had was one of exultant joy. All the world was changed that day when I left Chell Workhouse. It was a grey day when I went there, with a chilling air. It was now four or five weeks nearer mid-winter, yet I have no remembrance of greyness or chilliness. All seemed sunshine and gladness. As I came down the hill from Chell to Pittshill, and then on to Tunstall Church, everything seemed to welcome me. We had stealthily gone to Chell by field-paths as far as possible, but we came back by the high road. Everybody seemed to smile upon us and say they were glad to see us. Tunstall itself, my native town, seemed to put its arms round me as a mother who had lost her child for a time and had recovered him. Of course, all this was illusion on my part, but illusions are sweet when they are born of a real experience. If the people I met and the places I passed were not glad to see me, as I supposed, I was glad to see them, and that was joy enough for me sixty years ago. Few realities I have met with since have given me as much joy as those illusions did. The world was now to me a great, glad place, full of freedom and hope, and yet if the experience of the next ten years could have been foreseen it would have been found what bitter mockeries my hopes were. But I was free now. I had escaped the loathsome terror of the workhouse, where my whole career might have been poisoned at its source. My father had had a situation offered him as a painter and gilder by a toy manufacturer, a friend of his. His late employer's vengeance had been gratified and his prophecy fulfilled. The year that man drove my father to the workhouse, I have since learned, he bought an estate for about £200,000. Yet trade was so bad he had to reduce the wages of his painters and gilders.

I will not say how Nemesis has worked since, but that estate belongs to no descendant of his to-day. Fortunately for me and others, his influence did not rule at the toy manufactory, or we might have been forced to longer residence in the Bastile, with what issues God only knows. That employer has been dead for many years, and the grand mansion he then resided in has been pulled down, but the issues and memories of his vindictiveness cannot be so easily removed. I have long since forgiven him and pitied him as the creature of his time. The times then were hard and cruel for the poor. The rich were hampered with the notion they must not be resisted, and so even justice, in resistance to the rich, was counted as insolence in the poor. In such a time a man might make a mistake, even tragic in its consequences. That man made a mistake, and one which, could he have foreseen the cruel wrongs and memories it gave birth to, in his life and after his death, I am sure he would have shrunk from. When I left the workhouse I became a toy-maker, just as my father had become a toy-painter and gilder. My new work introduced me to a few curious circumstances. My new employer was a man who had been seriously reduced only a few years before he took this toy factory. I remembered seeing him, before his trouble came, on his white horse. He was considered a good horseman, and was to be seen daily about the town. He had then an earthenware manufactory, and was, in what was then considered, a large way of business. George H. was a man everyone liked, gentle and simple. He had a breezy heartiness, and a "hail-fellow-well-met" air always about him. He was a conspicuous figure among "the gentlemen" who used to attend the bowling green of "the Highgate Inn." That green was sacredly reserved for "the gentry."

George H. was an old friend of my grandfather's, and so befriended his son in his need. He was now outside the circle of boycotting manufacturers. He was a short, stout man, with a notable head and face. His head and face had a sort of rude majesty about them. They compelled attention, and they had that cheery, hearty something of which John Bull is always typical. Poor fellow, as I saw him afterwards, in a little, stuffy room, moulding little toper publicans and other figures, and thought of his carollings on his white horse, I could not but pity him. He was like a great lion in a small cage, but without the rage. He was silently enduring. He had no sour memories, and no bitter words do I remember ever falling from his lips, though I worked near him day by day. He was like a man who, in a way, glorifies misfortune by a quiet magnanimity.

He was said to have been deeply wronged by a principal servant, yet I heard no word fall from his lips about this man. One day, however, he gave me a fearful shock which I shall never forget. He and I worked back to back at benches on each side of a small room. One day I turned round and saw him lifting the top of his head off. I was thrilled with horror and unable to move. I had never seen a wig, nor heard of such a thing; and even when I saw him drop his wig on his head again I hardly knew whether to regard him as a man or a demon. He never saw or knew of my horror, and it was only when I told the incident that night at home that my mind was set at rest. This reference to "home" reminds me that I have forgotten to mention our recovered home on the night of the day we returned from the workhouse.

It would be difficult to describe the place provided for us on our return, yet Patti can never give to the words, "Home, sweet home," the thrill of emotion I felt that night. Its furniture was so scant I cannot describe it. For one thing, even in a wild dream, I could not have fallen out of bed. Our first meal there was a supper, poor enough, but no harsh bell rang us to it, and no schoolmaster's grace fell upon it to poison it, or make it almost repulsive. In fact, I have no recollection of any grace being said, nor was there any need. It shone on our faces and moved in our hearts. We were free in our own home. To see one's father and mother too at the same table, after an absence which, by its poignancy, seemed very long. Every element in that new life was a joy because it brought back the life of which we had been so suddenly and cruelly robbed.

I went to bed in a bare room, but it was not haunted. I heard no young voices pouring out hoary blasphemies against the schoolmaster and governor. I heard no stifled sobs of timid children, who were appalled by what they heard and the fear of all that was about them. Guardian angels might now have been in that room, shedding upon me the healing of their wings. Between me and the highest heaven there was "peace, perfect peace," and so I rested for the first time for weeks without a wakeful fear keeping my eyes open.

"Th' Hell Hole"

The neighbourhood in which this toy manufactory stood was then called "Th' Hell Hole" in the town of Burslem. This lurid designation was one of those popular descriptions which often amaze us by their truthfulness and their vivid perception. This description in its directness and grimness could not have been truer though given by a Shakespearian pen. In squalor, in wretchedness, in dilapidation of cottages, in half-starved and half-dressed women and children, in the number of idle and drunken men, it was as terribly dismal as its name would suggest. Drunkenness and semi-starvation, broken pavements, open drains, and loud-mouthed cursing and obscenity seemed its normal conditions. As the window of the room in which I worked overlooked the main thoroughfare, I was a forced daily observer of all this vile presentment. I don't know what form of Local Government prevailed in the town. I know there was no Local Board and no Corporation. There was a chief bailiff, but what he was chief of Heaven knows. There were gentlemen manufacturers going about daily in swallow-tailed coats and tall silk hats. There were doctors, and clergymen, and ministers, and yet I never heard a complaint about the doings and conditions of this "Hell Hole." Bullies and their victims lived there, and for unsanitariness and immorality I should think it could not have been surpassed in all England. Sixty years ago this was a slum in the town carrying the proud name of "the Mother of the Potteries."

Josiah Wedgwood, its great son, had left his native town many years before to prosecute his brilliant work in Etruria, a village a few miles away. Etruria, by its very name, would seem to indicate a place of classic beauty. I am afraid, from my remembrance of it in those early days, its architectural achievements and sanitary conditions were not quite a world removed from those of Burslem. Josiah Wedgwood found the trade of Burslem rude and crude, but started it on a noble career, yet the town of his birth he left very much as he found it. I am not saying this to his dispraise. He wrought marvels in the art of potting, but the time of social marvels was not yet. Within a mile east or west of this "Hell Hole" there were sweet fields and country lanes. To the north of it, within a quarter of a mile, there was the old windmill on a breezy upland overlooking the very market-place, and to the south of it, at a short distance, was Sneyd Green, then a pretty, old-fashioned village as yet undisturbed by the coal industry, which, since then, in its outward aspects, has blighted and scarred it. This "Hell Hole" was only a stupid creation of ignorance, folly and greed which crowded a narrow area with cheap houses, irrespective of the health, life or character of its denizens. It was a grim monument of what even some good and excellent people can do when their greed counsels their power and opportunity. It was a ghastly proof of the need of such work as that introduced by Edwin Chadwick, and which has now gained beneficent and magnificent incarnation in all the works of municipal government.

In the early days of "Th' Hell Hole," Burslem would be leavened largely by good Churchmen and Methodists. The latter were a large and powerful section of the community, yet, while often singing about the beauties and delights of the "New Jerusalem," they could allow a part of the town to be made a "devil's ground" for the ruin of bodies and souls. It would not do to allow even saints to build a city on green fields without restraints, if they owned them. Force may be no remedy for some things, but it has the action of grace in some departments of our human life. In sanitary affairs, at anyrate, it has made "the habitation of dragons" a way for the redeemed to walk there with joy and gladness.

A Toy Manufactory

The toy manufactory itself was a curiosity in structure and management. It was rusty and grim. As to form, it might have been brought in cart-loads from the broken-down cottages on the opposite side of the street. The workshops were neither square, nor round, nor oblong. They were a jumble of the oddest imaginable kind, and if there had been the ordinary number of workshops on an average-sized pot-works, placed as these were placed, it would have been impossible to have found the way in and the way out. As it was, though so small, it was rather difficult. The one cart-road went round a hovel nearly, and then dived under a twisted archway. Only about a dozen people were employed on this "bank," and if we all turned out together we were thronged in the narrow spaces outside the shops. To be "master" of such a place as this poor G. H. had had to come down from his white horse and from his much larger works at Tunstall. So the world has been jogging and jolting for centuries, jolting some upwards and jogging some downwards. I remember the figure of Napoleon Bonaparte was the leading article of our industry at this toy factory. When Napoleon was finished he stood up with arms folded across his breast, his right leg a little forward, looking defiance at his own English makers. He had a dark blue coat on, tightly buttoned, a buff waistcoat and white breeches. There were touches of gold on his coat and on his large black hat, with flat sides and point, with a high peak. These Napoleons must have been in large demand somewhere, for shoals of them were made at that time.

It is curious how a man who thirty years before had been a veritable ogre and demon to the English people should now have become so popular. If all the Napoleons made at this toy manufactory could have had life given them, then England, if not invaded, would have been crowded by military Frenchmen, and of the dreaded Napoleonic type.

I remember looking pensively at the figure many times, and wondering about all he had been a generation before, and of which I had heard so much.

It is difficult in these days to realise how the terror of Napoleon had saturated the minds of the lower classes in England. Yet, as I looked at the figure, it only then represented a name.

At this toy manufactory we did not make many figures so tragic and terrible in suggestion as Napoleon. George H. had designed a little toper publican with his left hand in his breeches pocket, and in his right hand a jug full of foaming beer. The face wore a flabby smile, which carried welcome to all.

We made cats, too, on box lids, representing cushions. We made dogs of all sizes, from "Dignity" to "Impudence." We made the gentlest of swains and the sweetest of maids, nearly always standing under the shade of a tree, whose foliage must have been blighted some spring day by an east wind, as it was so sparse in what seemed to be midsummer time.

It is astonishing what amiable squinting those swains and maids did in pretending not to look at each other. I have never seen squinting so amiable looking in real life. But that was where the art came in. The course of life in this little toy-works was always pleasant. There was nothing strenuous or harsh. "The master" was the president of a small republic of workers. All were equal in a sort of regulated inequality. We did different work, of different grades of importance and value, and yet no one seemed to think himself better than anyone else. We had no drunkenness and immorality such as I had seen elsewhere in the same town at a "bank," which would, if it could, have looked down on our "toy" place as the Pharisee looked on the publican. There have been worse employers than George H., even in his adversity, and his little place of business was a quiet refuge for a few toilers, and one free from the demoralising influences prevailing in much larger concerns.

I felt a distinct access of better influences while

I worked for George H., and though he never spoke of religion, while placing no obstacle in the way of its pursuit, it was easier to follow it there than at some works whose "masters" wore broad phylacteries on Sundays.

The Extreme of Poverty

Right opposite the shop I worked in was a house more tumble-down, if possible, than any of the rest. It was approached from the street by a shelving clay bank about two yards above the level of the street. This ascent was unpaved, and was roughly stepped by treading on the clay bank. In this squalid-looking house lived a squalid-looking man, with a squalid-looking wife and with several squalid-looking children. The man was called "Owd Rafe" (Ralph). He was an "odd man" on a pot bank, who did all sorts of rough, irregular work. He was considered half daft. This arose, however, more from an impediment in his speech rather than from any special mental weakness. This made the poor wretch's life all the more miserable because he knew he was not what he was taken to be. He was miserable enough, for what he earned only kept himself and his family from starvation. His difficulty in speaking was both painful and ludicrous. It was said that one morning he went home to his breakfast and asked his wife what there was for breakfast, and she answered, "Roasted potatoes." He went to his dinner, and in reply to his inquiry got the same answer. He went home at night, and asked what there was for his supper, and he got the same reply. The poor wretch, moved by a useless indignation, called out in a fit of dreadful stammering, "Roky taker (roasted potatoes) brekka (breakfast), roky taker dinner, roky taker sukka (supper), dam, bass, roky taker." This was one of the cries—pathetic, comic and tragic in its way—among thousands which arose in that day as the result of the starvation and rent-producing policy of Protection. Poor Ralph never lived to see the times of a wiser policy. He died and was put in a workhouse coffin, and on the day of his funeral, as the bearers were bringing the bier and coffin down the clay bank in front of his house, they either slipped through the wretched condition of the bank or through semi-drunkenness, with the result that poor Ralph's body came out of the miserable shell the workhouse had supplied. His poor "remains" had to be re-coffined, so that before his body got to the grave it had been committed "earth to earth" without the Church's ceremony. Let us hope that the angels which took Lazarus to Abraham's bosom took better care of Ralph's soul than the bearers of the parish coffin did of his body. These were grim days, but equally grim was the unconcern of the people themselves and "their betters." The former, perhaps, were so degraded or hardened, or maddened, as to look at these things with stolid defiance or indifference. But for "their betters,"

BEGINNING OF LIFE AGAIN 129

their callousness is unexplainable to me even yet. When I remember the men who stood at the head of affairs in the town at the time, I am amazed that such a house as Poor Ralph's should have been allowed to stand in such a place. But "Th' Hell Hole" itself might have been as far away as hell for any love or care I ever saw bestowed upon its dwellers while I worked there.

With what reverberations Carlyle's words, "mostly fools," come rolling through my memory as I think of many things which existed among the poor sixty years ago. We might be sixty centuries away from those times, and yet though no millennium is at hand, there is an immense change for the better in many ways and in many conditions. Adverse conditions now are largely self-imposed. In the times of which I write, they were imposed by reckless power, by heedless tyranny, and by fathomless fatuousness which was called statesmanship.

The ignorance of the people, the poverty of the people, and their helplessness, were the deliberate and direct issues of a certain policy which both Church and State sanctioned and upheld.

Of course, the people, as effective factors in these two institutions, were nowhere, legislators and bishops, the guardians of all privileges, thought the people should be kept in humble ignorance and humble poverty. Humbleness was so highly praised in the Scriptures, and also in some churches. If the poor stood and reverently watched the rich going to church on Sunday morning, that was as

I

it should be. A few of them, of course, were encouraged to go into the churches, to make up the proper contrast between the rich and the poor, so that whatever grace there was in their "meeting together" might fall upon those who so condescended to meet.

While ignorance and poverty so abounded, the aforesaid legislators thought it well to comfort the poor by inducing them to drink more beer.

So beer-houses were multiplied. I remember how "tuppenny a'-penny" beer-houses sprang up all round my own home.

If a man could get a barrel of beer into his little coal cellar, he became a beer-seller. I didn't know what it meant at the time, but I frequently saw and heard the contrivances and purposes of certain men discussed, by which they might become beer-sellers. They wanted to eke out a living for themselves, but I am certain, in some cases, the poor fools never thought they were going to do this by lessening the living of their poor neighbours. But such was the transcendent and beneficent wisdom of our legislators—representatives, and lords spiritual and temporal—exhibited in a time of extreme ignorance and poverty within the last seventy years.

This was not the work of a degraded democracy, thinking only of its own lusts and passions.

It was done by the culture, the privilege, and the power of those who ought to have known better. Those beer-houses have spread disastrous issues through all these years, and it has required the full activity of all the better influences of later legislation, in education and progress, to resist the baneful legacy of the wisdom of the wise.

Mr Gladstone has said "the business of the last half century has been in the main a process of setting free the individual man, that he may work out his vocation without wanton hindrance, as his Maker will have him do."

This statement carries the fact that the individual man in the first half of the century was bound down by a "wanton hindrance," against the purpose of the great Maker of men. This wanton hindrance was seen in keeping the people ignorant, in keeping them poor, in maintaining harsh laws against all self-help, as in the conditions and price of their labour, and as in making their food dear when their labour was kept at the lowest value. Yet, in spite of this disastrous and degrading achievement of aristocracy in the latter part of the eighteenth and the early part of the nineteenth century, I have seen the question recently asked, "Why are we disappointed with democracy?" Following this question was the statement that "we used to believe that, when once the great mass of our fellow citizens had obtained control over the machine of State, they would use it energetically and persistently in the creation of better moral and material surroundings for those who cannot help themselves." Then we are told that this among other great expectations "has been ludicrously falsified."

When I read these words, I wondered whether

I had lived for nearly seventy years in a land of contrasted illusions. I asked myself whether it was true that I was allowed to be worked for fourteen hours a day when a little over seven years of age? Whether it was true that I had no education beyond what I received in old Betty Wedgwood's cottage along with George Smith of Coalville and others? Whether it is true that I now see Board schools almost equalling the colleges of some of the older universities? Whether it is true that even poor children now receive a better education than what I heard "Tom Hughes" once say he received when a boy at a much greater cost? I wonder whether it is true that children are not permitted now to begin to work until thirteen years of age, quite double the age of thousands of children when I was a child? I wonder if it is true that I ate the sparse and miserably adulterated bread of the Corn Law times; if the rags, and squalor, and severe labour and long hours of those days, as contrasted with the leisure, and plenty, and recreation of these days are all illusions? I wonder if these are real people in their thronging thousands, on holiday, that I see, who have shares in "stores," who have deposits in the savings banks, who have portmanteaus, boxes of all sizes and kinds, making up tons of luggage in connection with a trip, surpassing that of "their betters" seventy years ago? I wonder if the holidayless England I knew in my youth, when the bulk of the people in the Midlands had never seen the

BEGINNING OF LIFE AGAIN

sea, and the holidays of to-day, with their flowing wealth and freedom and joy, are grotesque, because contradictory, illusions, having no "local habitation" but in my disordered brain?

I know democracy has been disappointing in many great moral and intellectual issues, but to say that it has "ludicrously failed" to create "better moral and material surroundings" is to contradict history, and more, the living, burning and agonising experience of those who lived sixty to seventy years ago.

I hope democracy will not always be "indifferent to the cry of human suffering," "disregard justice when separated from self-interest," or "always delight in war."

But however it has failed, it is not likely to take England back to the conditions of life prevailing in the first sixty years of the new industry.

That new industry came like an ogre, devouring the domesticity and the child-life of England, and to its everlasting disgrace the aristocratic statesmanship of England lent itself to the dread carnival of greed and cruelty. Democracy will never match issues like these, or if it does, then it will be quite time for some "friendly comet" to come and surround us with its destructive embrace.

CHAPTER XVI

THE SUNDAY SCHOOL AND MY YOUNG LIFE

WHEN I left the workhouse, one of my brightest hopes was that I should soon be back at my old Sunday school. The inward joy I got from this no words can tell. Next to having a home of my own was the proud thought of being again in my Sunday school class. I had really loved my teacher, and as it was a grief to be parted from him, so now it was a joy to get back to him.

On the first Sunday morning I was up betimes to be ready for the Sunday school, and no schoolboy with "shining morning face" ever carried a brighter face or a cheerier heart than I did. But a cloud fell upon it, deep, dark, and chilling, and before that day was over I felt like "a lost soul," as if all the brightness and hope had gone out of my life, never to return. The despair of a child is an absolute despair for the moment. The child has no outlook beyond this moment. It is all feeling, pressed round by a grim ignorance which only feels.

But I must explain how this came about.

THE SUNDAY SCHOOL

When I went to the workhouse all my clothes were taken away, as I have already related, after having a cold bath on a cold day.

I was then supplied with stockings, clogs, moleskin breeches, roughly put together, and over these I wore a grey "brat" or pinafore, which served as waistcoat and jacket. My old clothes were bundled up and put away, with the idea that I should have them returned when I left the workhouse. But when I came to leave they were found to be in such a dilapidated condition that there would have been some difficulty in even hanging them about my body.

I was therefore told to keep my moleskin trousers and the "brat," and even another "brat" was given me so that I could have a change for Sunday.

When I went to my old Sunday school the following Sunday morning, I never thought about my clothes. I had an overriding eagerness to be there.

The Sunday school I attended was a three-storied one, and my class was in the top room, in the north-west corner, in a sort of recess. The other boys in the class were bigger and older than myself, but as I could read as well as any of them, I was promoted to this high position, thanks to old Betty's tuition. The teacher was Ralph Lawton, "a butty collier." He was a man whose strength of character lay in a simple and sincere piety. I never saw such instances of absolute devoutness and trust as in some converted colliers in those days. Many of them had been "brands plucked from the burning," as they were fond of telling in their love-feasts. I remember, even yet, most vividly, how, as I sat among the other scholars on the side benches placed in the chapel for scholars, Ralph Lawton's face shone as if transfigured as he sat in his pew under the gallery. I have seen him lift his eyes heavenwards while singing, as if he saw a beatific vision. There was one hymn and tune which always seemed to inspire him with a radiant rapture, which suffused his face and filled his eyes with an unspeakable serenity. The hymn was the one beginning with the words, "Would Jesus have the sinner die? Why hangs He then on yonder tree?" etc. The tune, unusual in those days, was tranquil and dwelling in its strains. He little thought that sixty years after the vision of his ecstasy would be like a "bright cloud" hanging over an old scholar's life, at once an inspiration and a joy.

When I went to my class on this fateful Sunday morning, Ralph Lawton received me with more than his usual tender interest. But the scholars in the class looked at me askance, and whispered to each other. I saw their eyes travelling, sometimes furtively, and sometimes boldly, over my clothes. They also kept apart from me. In a very few minutes I was given to understand that I was not to sit near them. Ralph Lawton did all he could to see nothing unusual as between the other scholars and myself. Still I went again to the school in the afternoon as I had not yet the consciousness that the workhouse clothes, and my having been to the workhouse, had made such a difference. But I found it out during the afternoon. No cry of leper, in the old days of Israel, could have put people more apart than I was apart from my old schoolfellows. In the afternoon they had become bolder. My clothes were mockingly pointed at, I was laughed at, jeered at, and I saw that I was clothed with contempt in their eyes.

"The golden gates of childhood" were thus rudely and suddenly closed. I knew now I was not as other children. I was tainted with a social leprosy. I was a sort of Cain, whose only crime was to have lived at a time when English statesmanship had so manipulated its help in time of need as to make it cast a social stigma even upon little children, to consign to social damnation those whom it had saved from starvation. Would Herod's policy have been more merciful? I felt that Sunday afternoon, when the school was dismissed, that, if not a fugitive, I was a "vagabond," I was "driven out" from the place I loved. Those that found me would not slay me, but would smite me with looks which were deeper than the wounds of swords.

In all this there was seen the deep repugnance which pauperism had created even among the children. Many of the boys in my class were almost as poor as I was, but they had not been in the Chell shadow, they had not been branded with a workhouse "brat." Cruel as all this was, it yet indicated a healthy influence in the midst of the barest poverty, and a self-respect which shunned the devil of parish beneficence.

Yet we sang in those days, "Britons never shall be slaves." Who was it who said if he knew the songs of a people he could tell their history? From this song could he have told the history of the poor in the Thirties and Forties? For weeks after this I was too shamefaced to venture out on a Sunday. It was winter time, so the near fields were not available.

But the passion for the Sunday school would give me no rest. Every week I got uneasier, until one Sunday afternoon I broke through all shame and fear. At the top of our street there was a little chapel belonging to the Methodist New Connexion, where the Sunday school was held in the body of the chapel. Taking my younger brother by the hand, who had also been to the workhouse, and who wore a parish "brat" like myself, we crept up the street, and stood against the wall of the little chapel, which fronted the market-place.

While standing there, a young man came to the door of the chapel, evidently on the lookout for scholars who might be loitering outside. When he saw my brother and myself, he came to us at once, and bending down, asked me, as the eldest, if we went to any Sunday school. I told him in hesitating words we had gone to —— Sunday school. He then inquired why we had left, and when I told him his already gentle face became softened in a way I cannot express, and the tones of his voice, I should say now, from what I felt then, had tears in them. Taking each one of us by the hand, "Come with me, my boys, and you shall be welcome in our school."

His name was George Kirkman. His name has been on a gravestone erected more than fifty years ago in Tunstall Churchyard, as a tribute of public respect, and describing the rare virtues of a young man who pre-eminently distinguished himself in all good works in the town.

His name is written upon the fleshy tables of my heart, in the light of a memory which may be eclipsed for a time, but shall shine out again "as the stars for ever and ever."

His name is written in "The Book of Life," for the Recording Angel never passes by deeds like his. I cannot tell all this "saintly" young man was to me, I shall have to speak of him later on in connection with another form of public service ; but in his hands I was as a plant carefully tended, nurtured and watered. He lent me books. He gave me counsel. He breathed his prayers for me.

He was teacher of the Bible class, as well as assistant superintendent, and as soon as he could he got me removed into his class among much older and bigger boys.

I don't know what became of the "brat," but as it made no difference to George Kirkham, I never cared what others thought about it. Unfortunately for me, and for many others in the town, I only had his care and love for about six years. To the surprise and consternation and grief of the whole town, one morning came the news, "George Kirkham is dead."

Tunstall was then a small town, with only some seven or eight thousand of a population, but that population poured into the streets on the day of George Kirkham's funeral. Our scholars and other public bodies joined the procession, and as we walked through the crowds on either side of the streets the common grief expressed itself in many tears and sobs.

Relatively to its population, Tunstall has never been more moved in its sorrow than when it mourned over the loss of one of its noblest and most promising sons.

After George Kirkham's death I felt a loneliness that chilled me. He had given me a dawning interest in a larger world than I had ever dreamed of. Like the blind man in the Gospel, I had begun to "see men as trees walking." I had not focussed many questions, but I had been made to feel there were many questions whose dimness spurred my interest in them. But now I felt my lack of guidance. No other adult human being had interest and ability enough to continue this guidance. I should in this perilous interval have lost all I had gained but for the Sunday school and the companionship of a few youths a little older than myself. Of this I shall have more to say later on, but for the time I was under a dark cloud.

CHAPTER XVII

JOSEPH CAPPER OF TUNSTALL

I MUST now refer to a most important event which occurred two or three months before I went to the workhouse, an event, too, whose influence in many ways affected all my later life. In August of 1842 the Pottery towns were seething with tumult. This expressed itself in riots in nearly every town, and in a dismay which was one of my earliest, most vivid, and most dread experiences.

I wish, however, before giving my impressions and recollections of this time, to refer to a man who lived a few doors above my own house, in the street where I was born. He had known me all my life, and was in the habit of patting me on the head, stroking my hair, and always telling me to be a good boy. To me he looked a much older man than I knew afterwards he really was. He was a stout man, with a round, placid face, a sort of saintly-looking John Bull, rather than of the Boniface type. On Sundays he wore a white cravat, such as was worn by the early Methodist preachers, and some Quakers.

His name was Joseph Capper, and no man in Tunstall was better known or more highly esteemed. Joseph Capper, by a most innocent circumstance, was brought into prominence, by these riots, only next to that of Thomas Cooper, whose trial and imprisonment in Stafford Gaol, and whose writing of his book, *The Purgatory of Suicides,* in that gaol have made his name famous in connection with those riots. Both Cooper and Capper were strongly and capriciously involved in them. Both were Chartists, but not of the " physical force " order of Chartists, though they attended the same meetings and spoke on the same platforms. Both were thinking only of a national movement, the advocacy of " the Charter," when they became entangled with a local movement which brought disaster upon themselves, and hindered the greater cause they had at heart.

In June 1842 there had been a dispute between a local iron and coal master on account of a proposed reduction of wages. This led to a strike, and the strike led to disorderly methods of begging in support of the strikers, and to attempts to stop other miners from working. For two months the whole Pottery towns were seething with agitation, with fear and apprehension. The potters, who always shunned violent methods, as a body shrank from this menacing unrest. The few who were drawn into it were driven probably by desperation. The cry of hunger was then heard in the streets, and in moanings in the homes of many of the people.

JOSEPH CAPPER OF TUNSTALL

When Cooper came to Hanley, probably knowing the extreme tension of feeling in the neighbourhood, he took for his text the Sixth Commandment, "Thou shalt do no murder."

There is another singular coincidence. Cooper went to Hanley to support the "Teetotal Chartists," a mild body of men bent upon seeking the redress of their grievances, and the passing of better laws by all just and reasonable methods. Yet in a few days the so-called Chartists were burning down houses and ransacking wine cellars, and turning their movement for liberty into an orgie of drunkenness.

I have described these events so far, but not how such a man as Joseph Capper became involved in events so alien in their methods to his principles and aims. His character will bear the fiercest light which can be thrown upon it. It is significant that Mr Ward in his *History of Stoke-upon-Trent*, while strongly marking his condemnation of Cooper and Ellis, has no word of reproof for Joseph Capper.

Joseph Capper was born near Nantwich, in the year 1788. In early life he came to Tunstall, and was destined to make it famous in a famous crisis in his country's history. He had had but little schooling, but he had learned to read his Bible, the sole lesson book of so many poor people in that day. It has been said that he was almost a man of one book. But this one book happened to be the greatest, even as literature, in our language. Capper seemed to have loved its storied pages, its sacred counsels, and its revelation of Divine love. Whatever he was, as man and citizen, as patriot and Christian, he was made so by the teachings of his Bible. His ordinary speech got its quaintness and unction and force from its pages. His imagination was stirred and illuminated by its imagery. Neither the schools nor society had tinctured his strong nature. He was a Bible-made man in every function and activity of his life. He was made, as the humbler Puritans were made, without any knowledge, perhaps, of their literature, excepting probably the *Pilgrim's Progress*. He was as stern as the Puritans were in their love of righteousness and their hatred of tyranny. With less of gloom in the tenets he held, he had broader conceptions of liberty. Perhaps this was because of the Methodist leaven which entered early into his life, for we are told he was one of the first converts in the great Primitive Methodist camp meeting held on Mow Cop in 1807. He afterwards became a local preacher in the same denomination. Primitive Methodism at first was a demand for wider liberty in evangelical methods in preaching out of doors. While it cherished all the fervour of the early Methodists, it resented the restrictions of what were believed to be the hardening and narrowing respectability of the parent body of Methodists. Joseph Capper found in the Primitive Methodist society an atmosphere in which he could breathe more freely and a sphere of labour he loved. He travelled many miles on Sundays, preaching the Gospel of Jesus

Christ. He was one of the noble band of men in all the Methodist bodies who made heroic self-sacrifices in carrying the Gospel to outlying districts, where, but for their labours, it would hardly ever have been heard, and certainly not heard with the fervour and simplicity with which they preached it. This habit of life was the reason why, in later days, finding the clergy among his bitterest political opponents, he so strongly girded at them and told them to preach for nothing, as he did.

Joseph Capper was a blacksmith by trade, and his shop was one of the most prominent places in the town in those days. It stood just past the lower corner of the market-place, and in the upper part of High Street. He was strenuously industrious, a capital workman, and just in his transactions. He was employed even by Mr Kynnersley of Kidsgrove, one of the largest Tory employers in the district.

In 1832, when the new church at Tunstall was built, he was engaged to furnish the ironwork for the steeple, though for this particular work he was not fully paid until 1843. Near his shop, higher up in High Street, and on the opposite side of the street, stood the "Lamb Inn." This was one of the favourite resorts of the local aristocracy, for attendance at the "Lamb" was a patent of the highest respectability. Many sneers and much badinage did the patient blacksmith get from these gentlemen. Their jeering, however, fell harmlessly upon this sturdy soul. Besides his Sunday preachings he preached on week evenings, and attended other meetings, all of them devoted to uplifting his fellow-men in the way he deemed best. By his diligence in business he was comfortable in his worldly affairs. Mr Ward relates that in 1816 Tunstall began to develop most rapidly, even amazingly so, and that the principal inhabitants held some meetings to concert measures how best to promote general good order and tranquillity, and stop the increase of drunkenness. It may be safely assumed that in this work Joseph Capper would be an ardent supporter. When a building society in the town in the same year was started by some working potters, Capper joined them. In this he showed his social insight and thrift. A row of houses was built by this society, and Capper became the owner of two of them. The street thus formed was called Piccadilly. I don't know why such an aristocratic name was given to a place made for working men, except that in those days the working classes had "a sneaking liking" for the names and ways of their betters. In one of those houses, sixteen years later, I was born, and Joseph Capper was the most familiar figure to me in our street. His stalwart figure, his broad, beaming face and his ever kindly smile and word for children made him attractive and beloved.

Capper and the Reform Agitation of 1831-32

Joseph Capper was a considerable figure in this agitation. It was an epoch movement in the history of the country. Capper was not only now qualified to vote on any reasonable franchise, but he thought he saw a new time of liberty and justice arising for his poorer countrymen. He was no mere middle-class seeker for his own order. His larger soul sought a wider freedom for all. In the election of 1832, under the New Reform Act, there was a Radical candidate, Mr George Myles Mason, and Joseph Capper made three speeches in one day on his behalf in Hanley, Burslem and Tunstall. How he spoke on those occasions the following brief record will show. "Mr Capper of Tunstall then came forward, and said he hoped the gentlemen electors of Burslem had made up their minds to give their vote and support to Mr Mason, a man whom he highly recommended as deserving their warmest support." He then went into a long history of the origin and conduct of the aristocracy and clergy of the country, whom, he said, "were all sprung from the same class as themselves—a class which, since they had got into different stations, they had endeavoured to oppress. He was bitter against the persons who ground them with tithes and rates. He said the parsons should do as he did, preach for nothing, he being a Primitive

Methodist." This account is all too brief, but it shows the fundamental and vital lines along which the mind of the blacksmith travelled. Probably he had never heard of the "mad priest," John Ball, who, as Green says, first made England listen "to the declaration of the rights of man." "Good people," said Ball, "if we all came of the same father and mother—Adam and Eve—how can they say or prove that they are better than we, if it be not that they make us gain for them by our toil what they spend in their pride?" Green says, "The popular rhyme which condensed the levelling doctrine of John Ball, 'when Adam delved and Eve span, who was then the gentleman?' was fatal to the whole spirit of the Middle Ages." Joseph Capper, by native insight, grasped this doctrine, and preached it in vindication of wider liberty for the poorest of his countrymen. This was the style of speaking adopted by Capper through the Reform Bill agitation. That agitation was no time for prim arguments, or well-cut conventionalities, or delicate phrases. It was a struggle with ancient oppressions, supported by every form of corruption and menace which wealth and position could employ. There were times when gentle ladies as well as haughty gentlemen touched pitch, "and this pitch, as ancient writers do report, doth defile." The highest stooped to defilement in that mighty struggle, and therefore we must not expect this sturdy blacksmith to mince his words. His tongue was like the sledge-hammer he used in his shop.

There was now before him the glowing opinion of his countrymen, heated seven times hotter than its wont, and the blacksmith struck with all his might to shape it to the form of freedom and justice. Because he so struck, he was a power at every meeting. His influence was felt far and wide, and he was the acknowledged leader of the hopes and aspirations of the masses. But powerful as he was, he could not do what was impossible. While he could carry the multitude, he could not break down the innate conservatism of the middle classes. So Mr Mason, the Radical candidate, was defeated, the two Tory candidates heading the poll.

Deep and loud was the disappointment of the working classes. In their wild frenzy they committed regrettable acts of outrage. They felt that the energy they had spent in getting the Reform Bill passed had led to their betrayal. They felt that they had put power into the hands of those who despised them, and they came to regard the Reform Act as a boon simply for the middle classes. Capper did not entertain this view, but vented his wrath against those he believed to be the real enemies of his country. The aristocracy and the clergy came in regularly for his satire, his wit, and his hostility. While making his audiences laugh at his opponents, he would send them away with deepened aversion for those they believed to be the real foes of progress. No man had a sunnier face, a readier wit, a pleasanter humour; but all these were employed to convince his hearers, and through their amusement there ran a deep fiery current of conviction.

In the reactionary disappointment following the Reform Act Chartism arose. "The six heads of the Charter" made very clear the demands of the unenfranchised people. The "heads" were all political, not social, as the Labour Party now demands. The principles of the Charter Capper warmly espoused. Unfortunately, the supporters of the Charter were divided into physical force men, and those who believed in the force of their principles. It was easy, therefore, in a tumult and riot, such as soon followed, to confound a man like Capper with those who openly and wickedly broke the law. This confusion was greedily sought by his enemies, and relentlessly used against him. He was the leading spirit of many Chartist meetings. His vigour was perennial, and, in spite of advancing years, he gave himself to the cause which carried the promise of political redemption. At a meeting held in Tunstall market-place, on the 24th June 1842, Capper, with other local leaders, and especially Ellis, who figured so disastrously at the Assizes following the riots, was, as usual, the most prominent speaker. He had brought with him a stool from his shop, and on this stool he announced as his text, "To your tents, O Israel."

This old Biblical rallying cry was followed by earnest and impressive words. He said they must have the Charter, although, he supposed, they would bring the red-coated gentry to stop them, but there was sufficient strength among the people to defeat their base tyrants and the soldiers too. He recommended the working men to arm themselves, as a great struggle would certainly take place shortly, when the people would have to fight for their political rights. The day, he went on to say, was close at hand when the people must make laws themselves, for their tyrants were deaf to all their petitions.

It is easy to see how these words could be misconstrued; but Capper never provided arms in the sense of his accusers, and, on the night when he was arrested in his own house, there was no weapon available but the stout fist of his stalwart son. This arrest took place on the Sunday evening following the riots of August the 15th and 16th. Capper had attended Cooper's great meeting on the 15th at the Crown Bank, Hanley. He had urged the people resolutely but peaceably to seek their rights, and then he had gone back to his shop. But while he was working, those whom Cooper and he had addressed were rioting and destroying property. During that terrible week the old man was let alone, and he never suspected what was coming against him. From the platform at Hanley he had returned to his anvil at Tunstall. No word of his had been meant to awaken a guilty passion. Through the week he had toiled hard, deeply and quietly grieving, no doubt, for the terrible things which had been done, that had come of the passion and madness produced by galling wrongs and sufferings, which had become unendurable, or by the villainy which revels in mischief for its own sake. But Joseph Capper was neither a madman nor a villain. Even the men who were the most opposed to his political principles, men like Dr Davenport or Mr Kynnersley, would have discarded such epithets as applied to Joseph Capper. The Sabbath following the riot week, no doubt, came to this man with a deeper pensiveness on account of the sad events which had occurred, but, for himself, no reproach darkened his conscience, no sense of guilty responsibility shadowed for a moment the clear light of that holy day.

On Sunday evening, August 21st, he had been to chapel, and probably no one there had prayed with deeper fervour for the healing of the sorrows and troubles of the time. Then, after service, he wended his way home, and, in the soft evening light, engaged in reading his Bible to his wife and son and daughter, who were joining him as usual in "family worship." That Sunday evening's devotion rivalled, in its peaceable and holy elements, "The Cottar's Saturday night." But this touching scene was soon transformed into one of confusion and terror. Four men burst into his house most unceremoniously. "Well, gentlemen," said the old man, "what is your will?" Two of them rudely seized him, and said, "You are the man we want, Joseph Capper." His son, a man I well remember, lithe of limb and with more than ordinary muscular force, with one swinging blow laid poor Frith, a local tailor and draper, on the floor. It was a rash act; but for such a father such a son may be excused under such sudden exasperation. Frith lay beneath the terrible fist of the son, and but for the father's quiet word he would probably have soon had companions in his humiliation.

This man was one of the principal witnesses afterwards against the old man. Poor Frith; I have often wondered how he would look with his buckram manners as he lay there on the floor. The suppleness of his tailor's body was hidden beneath a perky and affected mannerism. He strutted in a way that was an outward and visible sign of his inward attempt to be like " his betters." Like many others, he only understood what it was to be respectable, and anyone who attacked respectability, as it existed before his eyes, was his enemy. He had heard old Capper speak at the meeting in June of arming for a great struggle, and as this could mean nothing to his mind but physical violence, he swore with all the strength of which his nature was capable.

The old man quietly surrendered to his captors. That August evening, in its quiet beauty, presented a perfect contrast to the tumult and excitement which prevailed as old Capper was led through the market-place, past his own workshop, his old wife and son and daughter following, accompanied by a sympathetic crowd. Poor Frith strutted along with more than the pomp of a judge. Capper was taken to Newcastle-under-Lyme for safety, and next morning he was committed for trial on charges of sedition, conspiracy, and rioting, Frith being the principal witness, and Frith knowing, whatever else he knew, that Capper was as innocent of rioting as he himself was. Capper's son was charged too, the same morning, with assaulting Frith, but the magistrates only gave this pompous patriot the meagre consolation of binding his assailant over to keep the peace.

I must leave old Capper now until the sequence of events brings him again to the front in the issues following the riots.

CHAPTER XVIII

THE POTTERY RIOTS OF 1842

THESE began at Hanley on the 15th of August 1842. A strike of colliers had occurred some weeks before. This event had deepened and intensified the general discontent and poverty of the whole district. People in large numbers were living on the verge of starvation. Some praiseworthy efforts were made to relieve this distress, but these were fitful and narrow in their scope. The only sure source of relief offered was one repulsive to the bulk of the sufferers—"The Bastile." To this many were driven by dire necessity. I cannot but think of the contrast afforded between the time I am now referring to and the condition of things to-day. I am now writing in a district where a strike or a lock-out has existed for twenty weeks. During this time thousands of pounds have been contributed to the relief of the suffering, so much so that very few cases of deep need exist. Fifty years ago I could have found more acute suffering in a population of 7000 inhabitants than I can see to-day in moving among a population of 160,000.

So much for the difference caused by a beneficent and Christian Socialism.

At the time of which I write there was no such Socialism. The time of figs was not yet. There was rather a determination "to put down" the masses. The people, nevertheless, were willing to work. They were even anxious to work, as some years previously trade in the Potteries had been in a fairly flourishing condition, so far as the constancy of it had been concerned. With plenty of trade, however, the long hours of labour had tended to lengthen. Wages remained scanty, and as there was no effective trade-unionism the workers did not share in the improved profits, but simply got more abundant toil. When slackness came again, as it did about 1839, with this slackness came attempts even to reduce wages, increasing poverty and increasing exasperation of the people went hand in hand. This state of things produced a general condition of mind favourable to any change. Hopeless poverty is a fruitful soil for revolution. Chartism, just then rising into notoriety in the country, professed to be able to show the sure way to beneficent changes. The people had no power. The people must have power, and hence the "People's Charter," which gave assurance that all this, if loyally and generally supported, would make this a glorious fact. The tyrants who had so long oppressed them would be laid in the dust. The Reform Act of 1832, which had betrayed them, would be superseded, and their newly-made oppressors — the middle classes—would be cast down as well as their ancient foes, the aristocracy and the clergy. Such were the pleas pressed upon desperate men by fervid eloquence, and by enthusiasm which shrank from no self-sacrifice and no peril. We are all Chartists now, as it is said, " We are all Socialists now," and there can be no real wonder that principles which have conquered both Liberals and Tories in sixty years should have won the hearts of men who saw through these principles the pathway to increased constitutional power, and so the way to justice and prosperity.

There was another cause which helped on the general discontent. While the employers were becoming increasingly rampant in their exactions, pressing the utmost hours of labour at the lowest prices, there were increasing signs on every hand of their growing wealth. Men who, a few years before, had been themselves workmen or small manufacturers were now becoming large manufacturers, building big houses, and surrounding themselves with luxuries and elegancies, which were the sure signs of growing wealth. These signs were coincident with the pleading of manufacturers of the need for lower wages. The result was a deepening sullenness, a deepening defiance over the whole district. This was the common mood when " the six points of the Charter " were brought forth like so many radiant finger-posts, pointing the people to a Land of Promise near at hand.

These were the conditions prevailing when the

colliers' strike occurred in July 1842. The effect of this strike was to stop many of the pot-works for want of coal, and thus to aggravate the general distress and disaffection.

I have already told of the colliers coming to a colliery near Tunstall and breaking up everything breakable on the pit bank, when the poor constable was pitched into the pond near by, and shoved back with a rail when he came near the edge of the pond. That was an ominous sign of rougher work and wilder deeds soon to follow.

After Thomas Cooper's harangues at the Crown Bank, Hanley, on the 14th of August, and on the following morning, at the same place, his fervid denunciation of the people's oppressors acted like a fell inspiration in the hearts of his hearers. As soon as Cooper had done speaking someone cried out, "Follow me." This invitation was loudly cheered and eagerly followed. The maddened crowd swept first across the Crown Bank and nearly demolished a rate-collector's house. In increasing fury and numbers they went to Earl Granville's collieries, stopped the engines, and ducked some of the men they found at work. In their madness they were merciless even to men of their own order. Potters too were turned out of the different manufactories where they were employed. The police office was attacked and the prisoners released. They fell on the Court of Requests at Shelton, destroying books and papers and furniture, and violently attacking the clerk. When they arrived at Stoke they over-

THE POTTERY RIOTS OF 1842

powered the police and tried to burn down their office. In marching to Fenton they were met by some soldiers, and were prevented doing much mischief there. But in their journey to Longton their numbers increased, and when they arrived there they held an open-air meeting. As soon as this was over the mob broke into a wild havoc. Shops were broken open and their contents thrown out to the hungry crowd. Indiscriminate plunder was thus pursued among unoffending people. Then the rectory was marched upon, occupied by a well-known clergyman, the Rev. Dr Vale. The furniture was first destroyed, then the cellars were searched and the beer and wines in them quickly consumed, and thus further rendered reckless, the leaders set the house on fire and burnt it down. The military came upon this scene of destructive fury, and there was a fierce conflict between them and the rioters. The riot, however, was quelled here for the time and the ringleaders arrested.

But in Hanley another attack was being made upon the parsonage of the Rev. R. E. Aitkens. Here, unfortunately, more beer and wines were found, and the desperate men who drank them were ready for any villainy. This house was set on fire and its contents destroyed. From this house they went to Lawyer Parker's, and his house was soon wrapped in flames. The same fate befel the house of Mr Bailey Rose, the stipendiary magistrate. Thus ended this day of wild destruction. Mr Ward, in his account of this matter, says that when the rioters returned to Hanley in the evening, Thomas

Cooper commended them for their depredations, but reproved them for their drunkenness. This was intended, no doubt, as a sly sarcasm upon Cooper's temperance principles, but if Cooper is to be believed, it was an absolutely false statement. Such commendation would have been as wicked in its nature as it would have been perilous in its policy.

Cooper's career and character have now been made known for some years, and no one now believes that Cooper was capable of such malignity as Mr Ward alleges. He never engaged in an act of violence himself, he never wilfully suggested such to others. No doubt his passionate declamations were misunderstood, but while many of his hearers forged evil purposes in their hearts by the fire of his hatred of wrong, the fire in his own heart was kindled by as patriotic and noble a purpose as ever burned in the bosom of Hampden.

Cooper was unfortunate in his time rather than in his method of advocacy. He was equally ardent in his later days, but in 1843 the "schoolmaster" had not been abroad. The ignorance of those days—the direct product of such government as the people had had for generations—was responsible for the mischief which followed, and not Cooper's smiting the wrongs under which the people suffered.

This day's work at Hanley and elsewhere on the 15th of August was a grim preparation for the following morning at Burslem. Crowds of men, with large sticks in their hands, and some, it is said, with blackened faces, marched upon

THE POTTERY RIOTS OF 1842

Burslem. Perhaps the blackened faces were those of unwashed colliers, whose desperation had made them regardless of their toilet that morning, and for many mornings before. The mob, thousands strong, marched along singing the Chartists' hymn of the day—

> "The lion of freedom's let loose from his den,
> And we'll rally round him again and again."

The rough rhyme suited the rough singers on their desperate march. Arriving at the Swan Square in Burslem, they found another mob breaking into the George Inn. This place was forced, the cellars invaded, and drink again consumed to give a fiercer fury to those who had shared in it. These two mobs having united, were attacked by a number of soldiers, but only using the flat sides of their swords. This looked like a friendly warning on the part of the military—like the gleaming of teeth which could bite in case of need. There was also a troop of Dragoons from Newcastle, under the command of Major French, and these men were being drilled in "the Legs of Man" yard. Two hundred special constables were hiding, who, from all accounts, would have preferred to hide until the fray was over. Contemporary reports represent these poor specials as presenting anything but a valorous appearance, even though they were being primed with the best beer. Gathering contingents of desperate and curious men came from many quarters. Seeing this, Major Powys, who was a magistrate as well as a soldier, asked those who were quietly disposed to go home. He did this in Chapel Bank, and then in the market square. Finding this comparatively useless, he proceeded to read the Riot Act. This only produced a more menacing disposition to defy. He again appealed to the crowd to go home, but they stood before him in resolute defiance. Then came from his lips the ringing command, "Clear the streets!" Amid the rattling of swords drawn from their scabbards came the cry, "Charge!" The soldiers then drove in upon the mob, but again only used the flat sides of the swords. Confusion and noise prevailed everywhere, but the crowd driven away in one direction returned in another. Burslem market-place had many outlets, and these enabled the people to baffle somewhat the attacks of the soldiers. Some of these got separated in the roads, and were maltreated. This small success of the crowd fired them with greater daring, and sticks and stones were used with reckless courage. But above the uproar of this conflict in the market-place there came the piercing sounds from a band marching along Moorland Road. Soon there was a cry, "They are coming from Leek," and a wild shout of "Hooray." This movement led the soldiers to leave the market-place, and gallop towards the "Big House" at the Moorland Road entrance to the town. This new mob came on, composed of weavers from Leek, Congleton and Macclesfield. The poor wretches, from all accounts, did not present a very formidable aspect. They were mostly half-dressed and half-starved. The only really vigorous men among them were a few agricultural labourers whom they had picked up on the way. Many of them carried thick sticks and thin arms. Others mustered all the stones they could carry in torn aprons and handkerchiefs. They were a motley crew, pale-faced, and cadaverous looking. Near where they entered the town the special constables stood, and it is questionable which had the paler faces, the new crowd or these defenders of law and order. Major Powys demanded when he went out to these men what they wanted. The reply came quick, "Our rights and liberties, the Charter, and more to eat." Perhaps if this last want had been supplied by the wisdom of English statesmen and the more generous treatment of the employers, their rights and liberties, and the Charter, too, would have been sought in quieter and more loyal ways. "More to eat!" they cried, and who can say that their demand was unreasonable? It was the cry of divinely given appetites trampled upon by a false and wicked human policy, and when these two things come into collision, law and order, respectabilities, shams and pretences, without an element of justice, must go down or fight for ascendency. Major Powys, soldier-like, gave voice to the gibbering respectabilities when he said, "assembling in a disorderly mob is not the way to get your rights and liberties. I entreat you to disperse and go quietly to your homes."

This advice was received with mocking and defiant yells. Major Powys did not tell these men how to get their rights and liberties. They had tried to get them by more orderly agitation for twelve years and failed. He told them to go quietly to their homes. But let it be remembered what many of those homes were. They were places robbed of nearly all the elements which make home. They were places where they saw the pinched faces of wives and children, and heard cries for food which they could not supply. To reason thus with these men was quite " proper " for a military magistrate, but it can be seen now that to take such advice would have been a miracle of self-restraint, and such miracles are not wrought by the grace of starvation.

> " Rude comparisons you draw,
>   Words refuse to sate your maw,
>   Your gaunt limbs the cobweb law
>   Cannot hold.
>
> You're not clogged with foolish pride,
> But can seize a right denied,
> Somehow God is on your side,
>   Hunger and cold."

That yell of defiance which rose from the crowd in response to Major Powys's words was not wholly of the devil's inspiration. Violence had been done to the rights and liberties of these men as wicked as the violence which was now provoked. "To destroy life and property" is as stupid as it is iniquitous, but let us recognise that it is equally stupid and iniquitous to provoke a destroying desperation. This had been done, cruelly and persistently done. Major Powys did not know that those he represented were primarily responsible for all the terrible possibilities which were before him in that awful hour. But the crowd knew this, and hence the loud mockery which followed his little preachment. This general yell was the signal for action. There went forth the cry, "We'll make the soldiers run and duck the specials behind." They were vain words, and they were followed by equally vain actions. Showers of stones were hurled at the soldiers, and the mob pressed forward, and those in front touched the horses' heads. It was now clearly seen that this seething mass of desperation must be resisted. Major Powys had shown remarkable restraint up to this ominous moment. Collision was now inevitable, and there went forth from his lips the fatal ringing cry to his soldiers, "Fire!" Immediately the guns were raised, and the crowd shrank back instinctively, but vainly, owing to its own mass. "Food for powder" was plentiful and near at hand. The musketry rattled; but the rattle was soon drowned by cries of defiance and terror and agony from that writhing mass of human beings. Numbers fell to the ground, either wounded or forced down by the general rush which followed the firing of the muskets. The confusion was complete. Maddened and still desperate, the crowd broke and fled in different directions. Standing against the gate-post of the "Big House" was a young fellow from Leek, and it was said he had a stick in one hand and a stone in the other. It was also said on the very day of this riot that he was not taking part in it, but was one of those men whose curiosity will take a man to the very verge of peril. However this may be, the blood of the soldiers was up, and this youth's brains were blown out against the gate-post. He fell dead on the footpath, and military valour had secured one fatal trophy, such as it was. So many shots as were fired, though they did not find fatal lodgment in many cases, nevertheless wounded many, who were carried away by friends, or hobbled away themselves. Some, it is said, went away to die of their wounds, but their injuries were prudently concealed in this time of suspicion and terror. It was a miserable, hideous and loathsome conflict, but, thank God, the last of its kind which has darkened the Potteries so far in this century, and probably no other century will witness in our country an event so charged with tyranny and injustice, and with folly and wickedness. As Lowell says in his " Ode to France,"—

> " The brute despair
> Leaped up with one hoarse yell and snapped its bands,
> Groped for its right with horny, callous hands,
> And stared around for God with bloodshot eyes.
> . . . .
> Brutes with the memories and desires of men,
> Whose chronicles were writ with iron pen
> In the crooked shoulder and the forehead low,
> Set wrong to balance wrong,
> And physicked woe with woe."

THE POTTERY RIOTS OF 1842

This charge, and the firing of the muskets which I heard a short distance away, was what led me to run off to the Burslem market-place. I was playing in a field on the side of the New Road, leading from Burslem to Tunstall. When I neared the town I met numbers of stragglers fleeing in terror from what they had seen and felt. Some of these had portions of their clothes torn off in the scramble to get out of the crowd, and were only half dressed. It was a grim sight, and yet it furnished plenty of food for laughter. This was not wanting on the part of cool and curious folks who had not been in the fray. In the streams of people I met some were limping through small wounds they had received, or through injury from the terrible crush in which they had been carried along. Nearly all were rushing down the New Road as if they were pursued by wild beasts. Just outside the town I came upon a man and woman who were excitedly relating the perils and sufferings through which they had passed. The man was a little cobbler whom I knew well as a Tunstall man. I don't know how it was, but in those days cobblers were nearly always in front, upholding the law as constables or breaking it as reformers or rioters. Thomas Cooper himself, said to be the arch-instigator of this outbreak, had been in this line of business. This poor little cobbler wore a tall hat, and the crown of it was cut clean off. The bridge of his nose, too, was neatly slit in two. The blood was trickling to the end of it and forming red drops there, which made the thing rather comical. As he had forgotten to take his pocket-handkerchief with him that morning before leaving home, he kept wiping off the red drops with the back of his hand. This gory hand was very prominent, and made him look as if he had been doing some terrible deed. When I came upon him he was telling a group of people how a horse soldier had made at him with a bloody purpose and cut off the crown of his hat with the first blow. Then intending, as the cobbler said, to cut his head off, the soldier made another slash at him with his sword, but he ducked and saved his head. The soldier, however, followed him out and slashed out again with his sword, but as the cobbler just then threw his head back, the point of the sword only went through the bridge of his nose. I well remember how vividly he described his dodging of this soldier who seemed to thirst for his blood, and how at last he shrunk into the crowd and so got free from his ferocious enemy. If all this was true there must have been a very hot episode in the midst of that wild crowd, and a very narrow escape from a second man being killed on that terrible day. The cobbler's narrative was mingled with groans of indignation against his military foe, and some strongly unpleasant things were said about him.

Near to the cobbler stood a woman who had been wounded in the leg. This wound had evidently been the result of a spent bullet as she was moving away with the crowd. Her dress was badly torn, and she looked as if she had been rolled down the shord-ruck on the New Road from Burslem. She, too, had her story to tell, but it was interrupted with so many hysterical outbursts and digressions that it would have puzzled a shorthand writer to have given a clear and connected account of it.

Not deterred by these visible terrors I pushed on to the Burslem market-place. The sight which presented itself was confusing and bewildering in the extreme. It was evident that masses of people had remained stolidly defiant or curious even after the fatal charge by the soldiers had been made. There were hundreds of people packed in the narrow street at the back of the shambles right down to the "Big House," where the man from Leek had been shot. The market-place presented a weird and dismal aspect. All the shops were closed, and the soldiers were busy driving the slowly-moving and sullen-faced crowds away. Windows were broken in the Town Hall, and many other signs of destructive work were to be seen. The more furious part of the mob had been driven out of the market-place, but streams of people were pouring into it again from the many side places of access. There were evidently gathering elements for another outbreak, and at last the word was given to the military to clear the market-place. The special constables were evidently not called upon to help in this work, but as the soldiers drove the people along the specials were placed opposite every avenue to the market-place to prevent a fresh rush of the people. When the word was given to make a clearance of the place, the soldiers' horses pranced and their swords gleamed as they pressed upon every section of the mob. I was at the back of the shambles when this movement began, but kept well up above the mass of the people, so that I could see what was going on without being entangled in the crowd. The horse soldiers came up this narrow street, pressing closely on the heels of the people, and using the flat sides of their swords upon those they could reach. Owing to the dense pressure of the crowd running was impossible, and numbers of people were tumbled in heaps through pressure or terror. The confusion and groans and shrieks were terrible to hear and see, for men, women, and even children, made up this seething mass. As I was above the crowd I could see hats, caps, bonnets and shawls wherever there was a bit of space visible. Men and women were bareheaded in consequence, the hair of the women streaming about their faces, and as agony and fear were depicted on these faces, it was a sight of terror never to be forgotten. It seemed a cruel thing, too, to drive those who were not there to fight, and to hurry and frighten them in this manner. But that was no day for courtesy or chivalry. It was equally a curious thing that so many whose only motive was curiosity could place themselves in such circumstances of peril. As I was going back towards the New Road I saw the special constables forming a cordon on the left-hand side of the market-place. They did not strike me as a very valorous body, as they kept well away from the crowd being driven upwards by the soldiers. When the people got into the wider area up near Greenhead, they broke away as fast as their legs could carry them until they got into the New Road and the road leading to High Lane. Then they halted in broken groups to tell of escapes and sufferings, and to pour the lava of their wrath upon the powers that be. In want, in terror, and with a sense of the crushing injustice of the times, they cursed the land in which they had been born, and no fiercer words could have been uttered against the Duke of Alva and his brutal soldiers than were heard that day by English men and women who only wanted to work and to live a reasonable life by their labour. Such things seem now like a grim nightmare. Such things, we now thankfully recognise, are impossible. Lancashire has just closed a stubbornly-contested dispute of twenty weeks, and yet no riot, not even a single disturbance, has occurred. The fighters have mingled daily, and only verbal conflicts have ensued, and these lightened by pleasantry and badinage as to which side would win. This has come of juster laws, of wider popular rights, and of that softening of antagonistic interests by more Christian goodwill and the respect which comes from the knowledge that the people have power to maintain a good defence.

CHAPTER XIX

JOSEPH CAPPER AGAIN

FOLLOWING the riots came the trials, but with these I shall have nothing to do, except as they affected the man I knew and reverenced, "Old Capper." His arrest and imprisonment were among the cruellest things ever done in the name of law. This man was never seen near a riot, nor ever commended one. He left the Crown Bank at Hanley on the Monday morning, and was soon busy in his blacksmith's shop. He was busy there too on the Tuesday and Wednesday while such tumult was going on in Hanley and Burslem. By no word, fairly interpreted, had he ever encouraged a resort to force. With such evidence as was brought against him he could not be convicted of sedition to-day. Yet the law of sedition, I suppose, is the same now as it was then. The fact is, it was not the judge who tried him who interpreted the law. It was the overpowering sentiment of the middle and upper classes that something must be done, that some signal retribution must be inflicted upon every man who had been at the front in this time of agitation, however sacred his motives, and however noble his endeavours to guide this movement to true patriotic issues. A purer and a more loyal patriot did not live in the Queen's realms than "Old Capper." A more God-fearing and man-loving man could not be found in the whole area of the British dominions. Yet this venerable man was taken from his peaceful home and quiet industry as if he were a murderous villain. It was such conduct as this, next to the prevailing want of the people, which made them so fiercely disaffected. It was a foolish and wicked thing to sack and burn property, as in those riots, but this infamy was only surpassed by that wild injustice which, in the name of the law, swept into its cruel meshes such men as "Old Capper," and hundreds who were as innocent as he was. He was not the man to shrink from the clear issues of what he advocated. But in all the stormy time from 1830 until now his arm had never been raised against any man, nor had he even injured any man's property. If he had believed in physical force and given effect to it, he would never have commanded the respect of his law-abiding neighbours and his political opponents. He was wildly accused with having said in his address of June 26th, "The noble-minded Chartists of Yorkshire and Lancashire have armed themselves, do you likewise, follow their example. Those who cannot afford to get guns must get pikes, and those who cannot afford to get either must get torches." Such words the old man solemnly denied having ever used, and he was able to prove that they were false, and sheer misconstructions of what he had really said. But these perversions were born of heated hostility and of heated imagination, given over to work ruin for the man whose crime was a patriotic sympathy with the great mass of his suffering countrymen. But such malicious mis-statement shows the kind of temper then prevailing on the part of prosecutors.

"Old Capper" was put on his trial in October, and was tried and sentenced to two years' imprisonment for sedition. Again, in 1843, he was put on his trial for conspiracy, along with Cooper and Richards. The old man defended himself on each occasion, knowing the integrity of his cause, and shrinking from employing anyone who would resort to mere legal artifices to effect his release. When he appeared on his second trial, it was seen what ravages had been wrought by the imprisonment he had already undergone, and yet he had only served six months of his two years. He told the Court he had been seriously ill, and that the prison diet "scoured" his inside. Skilly in these days did scour. He complained in this second trial of the great injustice which had been done him on the first trial. He had brought fourteen witnesses to Stafford, and had kept them here for a fortnight to prove that the witnesses against him were forsworn. These witnesses, however, owing to the great expense of his maintaining them so long, and as his case came on the last, were obliged to return home. This misfortune deprived the old man of the evidence of those who knew him well, and who knew what he had said and done. He feelingly complained of this injustice done to him on his first trial. As to his preaching from the text "To your tents, O Israel," he did not deny it, but he had dealt with the matter scripturally and not as stated by the witnesses against him. For thirty years he had tried in his humble way to do that sort of work, and had never received a sixpence for his service. Referring touchingly to his old friend and neighbour, Dr Davenport, he said, when he saw him in the witness-box, he could not question him as to his (Capper's) character, as he had been so kind to his wife while he had been in prison. He admitted Dr Davenport was an honourable man and a Tory, while he was a Radical. As to the witness Smallwood, he said he had talked of arms, but the only arms he had referred to were arms of flesh and blood, and then the old man, in grave and simple eloquence, referred to what the arms of English workmen had accomplished in every province of industrial activity.

As to his opinions of a reform in Parliament, although he had a vote and two tenants who had votes, yet he thought it wrong that men had not votes instead of houses. He was getting old himself; but he wanted to leave the world better than he found it. He had a poor, aged wife who had gone with him through all his troubles, and whom he esteemed more than all the world. Many other things he said forcibly and pathetically, and then drawing himself together for a full and final asseveration, he said he would leave his case now in the hands of the jury. This he would say, he knew nothing of the proceedings of Cooper and Richards and Ellis, nor had he joined them in any conspiracy. All his meetings had been in public, and he had gone to them openly. This simple and sincere eloquence powerfully affected many in the court, and moved some to tears. Of course a verdict was given against him as well as against Cooper and Richards, though Capper was recommended to mercy. A sentence of acquittal would have been a miracle of simple justice in such a time and with such a jury; but though virtually acquitted on his second trial, the injustice done him on his first trial was carried out. He served his two years in Stafford Gaol, and at the end of the time came out broken down in health, but strong as ever in the consciousness of his integrity. He was met as he came out of Stafford Gaol by a few friends, and he went on his way home through the Potteries triumphantly applauded by thousands who believed in his perfect innocence of the charge for which he had so cruelly suffered. In all the years of his life after this no man in Tunstall commanded more regard and honour and reverence. His kindliness, his rugged manliness, though now softened by suffering and long experience, won for him an unique position in the esteem of all who knew him. While poor Frith, the tailor, who had done him so much injury, was regarded with general contempt, this brave old man gathered more of regard and affection every year.

In the year 1850, when the Pope issued his famous Bull giving territorial titles to Roman Catholic bishops in this country, there sprang up an excitement all over the land difficult now to understand. Lord John Russell's "Durham letter" sent this excitement into the wildness of ecclesiastical delirium. Meetings were held all over the country, and valiant martyrs offered themselves on every hand to die on the altar of "No Popery." The fact is, if the Pope just then had had power to rule matters in England, he would have had to start many Smithfields to burn up these would-be martyrs that were ready for the stake. Fortunately, however, the only burning which ensued was that of the Pope's Bull. I remember a great meeting was held in the church school at Tunstall one night in the autumn of 1850. The incumbent of the town and other clergymen were there. Even the Wesleyan and Primitive Methodist ministers were invited to the rare privilege of sitting on the same platform. They must have felt quite in the Apostolic succession just then. The meeting was crammed with enthusiastic opponents of the Church of Rome. The people did not know then that it was the recent developments in the Church of England itself which had led the Pope to that act of aggressiveness now so widely resented. A strong resolution against Popery was brought before the meeting, and supported in varying keys of hysterical denunciation. I remember wondering how even the Pope could withstand this torrent of wrath, though the Pope was no more real to me, nor hundreds then present, than the Grand Llama of Thibet. A Wesleyan ministerial Boanerges, then stationed in the Tunstall circuit, was "the speaker of the evening." He had a great reputation in the district for his oratory, which was more powerful than finished. He fairly revelled in his subject that evening. He provoked rapturous applause by his rough sarcasm and his thunderous denunciation. Nothing that I remember in my life equalled it in terror and uselessness, except the incident recorded in *The Jackdaw of Rheims*. But the most dramatic and crowning event of that meeting was when "Old Capper" rose, amid loud and long-continued applause, "to burn the Pope's Bull." The old man stood with beaming face and shining silvery hair. Those ringing cheers were intended to convey more than approval of his present function. They were the triumphant endorsement, on the part of most there, of the noble and patriotic life he had lived. Here was a man who, eight years before, had been sentenced to imprisonment for sedition, against whom it had been solemnly sworn that he wished to destroy the Church of England, and yet this same man, six years after he had come out of Stafford Gaol, was received by clergymen and magistrates and the representatives of all the "respectable" people in the town, standing and applauding the old man. When this striking and significant ovation was over, the venerable man said a few simple and earnest words, conveying more than any oratory heard that evening in defence of the faith once delivered to the Saints. Then, holding up in one hand a copy of the Pope's Bull, and taking in the other hand a candle from the table, he applied the flame to the lower part of the paper. This flame suddenly rose, and so did the cheers of the people. The old blacksmith's hand never shrank from the thin flame of the paper. This was held till the last shred of it fell in a feeble flicker from between his finger and thumb. So also fell, in a short time, that sudden flame of ecclesiastical passion. This was "Old Capper's" last famous appearance in the town. On January 1860 he died, and was buried in the graveyard of the church he had helped to build, and whose adherents at one time had been his most relentless enemies. But he had no enemies now. He came to his end full of years, and honoured by the homage of all who knew him best. His life was simple; his aims were noble; and he gently passed in the light of eventide " to where, beyond these voices, there is peace."

The old blacksmith little thought, as he stroked the head of the little waif who was his neighbour, that the boy he told to " be good " would remember, nearly seventy years after, his struggles for liberty and the betterment of his down-trodden countrymen. I am sorry the record is so poor and scant. I have never met a man who did more to enrich England with simple ideals of progress, freedom and goodness. In a stormy and terrible time, he never said a word or performed an act which could be challenged to-day. He told men, who were driven to madness by their wrongs, neither to injure any other man nor destroy his property. He urged them to be sober and industrious. He urged them, by the great memories of England's worthies in the past, to carry forward their noble work, to make their country great and free and good. He was a workman who believed labour to be worship. He was a neighbour who believed in charity. He was a patriot who believed the good of his fellow-countrymen was the surest source of their welfare and strength. He was a citizen who saw the greatness and glory of his country must spring from its freedom, its industry and its character. Such were his ideals. To realise them he gave a full-hearted, simple and heroic life, and for all this his country, in a mad hour of frenzy and distortion, banned him, denounced him and imprisoned him. Its injustice shattered a strong constitution. It broke his heart through his sorrow for his aged wife in her loneliness, and though he came, in his last days, to the goodwill of his townsmen, his years were burdened and shortened. He knew he had been misunderstood, slandered and unjustly punished, but he was now calmly content to stand among those whom his fellow-prisoner, Thomas Cooper, had described—

"The free
Of soul with quenchless zeal must ever glow
To spread the freedom which their own minds know."

CHAPTER XX

SOME SPECIAL INDUSTRIAL AND SOCIAL CONDITIONS THEN PREVAILING IN THE POTTERIES

I HAVE told the story of these riots as I saw them in part, and in part as I heard of them and have read of them.

The history may be imperfect in some details, but I have tried to give a truthful account of the incidents I saw, and of the general feeling of the time among the people.

After these alarming events there was a distinct backwash of depression, which prevailed for some years throughout the district. There was a sullen, passive reign of distrust among the people. The Reform Bill had disappointed them. All their trade conflicts had ended in failure. Even the resounding attacks against the Corn Laws, then beginning to fill the country, excited little interest among the working classes, and so they gave little response. Betrayal and failure had made them sad and hopeless.

There was a marked difference between the Pottery working people and the miners who had invaded their towns from the outside districts like a storm-flood. While having sympathy with them in their sufferings and wrongs, they were mutely appalled by their violence. The Pottery people have not the grit which makes revolutions, nor successful riots, nor even masterful trade combinations.

Visitors from the northern counties of England, where labour organisations have been so pronounced and effective, have always spoken of the working classes of the Potteries as being too obsequious in their bearing and wanting in self-assertion. I know what this means, but I know what is called obsequiousness covers qualities which are becoming too rare in the atmosphere of democratic arrogance. I have seen other working populations, and lived among them for many years, but have never met with the same moral aroma in the relations between different classes. I have seen more strength, more dominance and more aggressiveness in the working classes in other parts of England, but not an indefinable something which seemed to lean towards the old feudal tie, but which, whatever its origin, carries a charm. Perhaps the concentration of the Pottery towns, and their long seclusion from the aggressive forces of modern industry and progress, may account in some way for the long retention of the quality I have spoken of.

The Manchester Guardian, in reviewing a book lately published, *The Staffordshire Potter*, says, " The wonder is how a body of workers of singular skill, holding a virtual monopoly of a great trade, in what is virtually a single town, should have failed so signally to do for themselves what artisans under more exacting conditions have generally managed to achieve. The stamp of futility is set on everything these unfortunate potters touch." These are strong and vivid words, nor am I surprised at the contrast between "these unfortunate potters and other artisans." These latter, all through their industrial history, have been achieving while the "unfortunate potters" have always been failing in a more or less marked degree.

There must be some special reason for so signal a contrast. These potters are Englishmen, and are as keenly alive to their great heritage, as such, as any of their countrymen. The causes of difference must be mainly local, and acting persistently upon a population untouched by the flowing currents of movements in the larger centres of English life. These causes, it seems to me, are various in their character and operate mainly "in what is virtually a single town." I think I can describe some of these causes as I saw them in operation fifty to sixty years ago. I did not understand then how they were giving "the stamp of futility," then seen only by a few, but in later years seen by many.

I write now, after many years of observation of the working classes in Lancashire and Yorkshire, and where I have seen suggestive contrasts in modes of labour and in asserting the claims of labour.

I believe one of the causes of the potters'

"futility" has been the want of discipline in his daily work.

Machinery means discipline in industrial operations. In the Potteries there was no such discipline, and very little of any other. I write of what I saw, and of conditions under which I and others worked. Owing, as I believe, to the absence of machinery, there was no effective economical management of a pot-works. Economical occupation of the premises was hardly ever thought of. "Cost of production," as determined by all the elements of production, was as remote as political economy in Saturn. There was only the loosest daily or weekly supervision of the workpeople, in their separate "shops," and working by "piece-work," they could work or play very much as they pleased. The weekly production of each worker was not scanned as it was in a cotton mill.

Hundreds of workpeople never did a day's work for the first two days of the week, and laxity abounded. Drinking or pure idleness were seen and winked at by the bailees and employers. It was never considered that if a week's work had to be done in four days it must be scamped to a great extent. If a man worked for these four days until ten o'clock at night, or began at four or five o'clock in the morning, this did not concern the "master," for each man found his own candle. There was loss, of course, in the use of coal for these extra hours, but this disturbed no sense of economy, for it did not exist. A man might begin to do his work on Wednesday morning, half asleep or half drunk, after two or three days' debauch, and "the bailee" might never notice him, or, if he did, he would throw out some contemptuous sneer, or some menacing words which meant nothing.

There was in all the places I knew even a premium put upon the early idleness of the week. If a man had only done about four days' work by the end of the week he might have "an old horse," that is, he would be credited with a certain amount of work which had to be done the following week. This was a sort of pawnshop method of doing business, and it was done at one of the largest pot-works in the town of Burslem. So far as I know, too, it was done more or less in every Pottery town.

Nothing can more strongly mark the absence of every economical element than such a condition, and the consequent demoralisation of the workers in the matter of production.

Now, if there had been a governing power like machinery, and if a steam-engine had started every Monday morning at six o'clock, the workers would have been disciplined to the habit of regular and continuous industry, and employers would have seen that this was necessary to economise the power of the steam-engine and the machinery.

The first scare of machinery came in my early years, and it scared not only the workpeople but the masters themselves. "Futility" breathed upon them as well as on their operatives, and after

SOME SPECIAL CONDITIONS 187

a while even some of the largest employers fled from the introduction of machinery as from a ghost.

In Lancashire and Yorkshire the same thing produced a determined struggle, but the struggle developed a fibre in both employer and workman which has been worth all it cost. It nurtured an independence whose face has scared futility from almost every province of their lives.

Further, many of the pot-works sixty years ago were rambling, ramshackle conglomerations of buildings, as if a stampede of old cottages had been arrested in their march.

Some of the " banks " had very few square yards of open spaces. There were tortuous ways round "hovels" and under archways, and in some even "purgatories," so-called, so that many of the workshops were separated one from one another as if, virtually, they were miles apart. This condition hindered any common rivalry in production, and led to many forms of dissipation and idleness which could never have occurred with larger intercourse.

It also prevented any effective inspection by the bailee of the habits of the workpeople in each shop. Many of these shops were on the ground floor, and the floors were often thick with wasted clay, of which little, if any, notice was taken. The shops on a second storey were equally available for methods of killing time without any fixed purpose to waste it. I remember in one of such shops in which I worked there were two hollow-ware pressers, one was a Methodist local preacher and the other was "a burgess" from Newcastle-under-Lyne. There was a cup-maker who was a Methodist class leader, and a saucer-maker who wanted to be one, and myself, as a "muffin-maker." These men were engaged in discussions all the day long. In the former part of the week these would turn on the sermons preached at the Wesleyan Methodist Chapel on the previous Sunday. One of the hollow-ware pressers, the cup-maker and the saucer-maker attended the same chapel, but they rarely, if ever, agreed about the sermons preached or the man who had preached them. They would dispute about questions of delivery, and whether the preachers had been simple and sound in doctrine.

Ordinarily these discussions, though earnest and absorbing, would pass pleasantly enough. Sometimes, however, their temper and tone would not have suited a class meeting, and I have seen these men leave their work benches to demonstrate in the middle of the shop floor, and sometimes lift their fists, not to fight (as a casual observer would have thought), but to give effect to their views. Usually, when this state of things arrived, "the burgess" from Newcastle-under-Lyne, who was both the "Punch" and the "wicked man" of the shop, would begin laughing or singing some political ditty, or would jump up and begin talking, as if to another "burgess" in an election dispute, and would stamp and mouth until the other three disputants would smile themselves into an abashed silence.

This burgess was not a religious man, never

went to chapel or church, except to attend a funeral at the latter. He always boasted that he voted, red or blue, for the man who gave him most sovereigns. He was fond of tobacco, and being a "hail fellow well met," he was often applied to for "a bit o' 'bacca." But his generosity was drawn upon too often, and to meet the emergency he kept an empty "'bacca box" on his bench, and if anyone came to beg or borrow, he would say, "Ay, lad," and open this empty box. Then he would exclaim in well-affected surprise, "Bless me, I havena a bit i' th' world." He had christened this empty box "the world," and by this device saved his "bacca" and his reputation. Yet this man was always the one to bring angry disputes to a ludicrous but quiet close in that shop.

I give this as a typical interior view of the waste of time in the ordinary life of one of these workshops. If the bailee or "the master" came, there was immediate silence, at a given signal. "The master" of this particular bank seemed to have no purpose in marching through a few of his workshops except to air his dignity by holding his hands under his swallow-tail coat and look loftily all round at nothing, and he generally saw it. I have referred before to waste of time by drinking and feasting in shops. Sometimes, however, there was fighting. In another workshop I once saw a fight between two boys under ten years of age, poor half-starved lads who had no quarrel of their own, but were "egged on" by some half-drunken men in the shop to fight. There were two other shops opening into this one, in which worked three or four "turners" and one "thrower." Altogether some twelve to fifteen people, men and women, were observers of this fight, and so had left their work. The women were all averse to what was going on, but were rudely rebuffed for their protests. The fight went on for fifty minutes. Boxing at that time was in great favour in the Potteries, for there were several well-known prize fighters in the district. These two lads fought according to the usual rules, in set rounds, and only by fists. In Lancashire such a fight would have been over in ten minutes, as both clogs and fists would have been used. These boys got a rest after each round, and so were able to keep on for so long a time. Noses bled, and eyes began to grow black; the fighters, too, lost all their flush, and got pale and weary. At last a big Yorkshire woman who worked in one of the shops, and who had married a potter, rushed to the lads and separated them, and stood in front of the men and defied them. She was a tall woman with a large head and face, and great brawny arms, which had not yet paled by Pottery workshops. Her eyes flashed, her brow was clouded, and her arms were held out as if for business if required. The men slunk away in their coward shame, and the other women in the shops came to her side and cheered her. The women took the lads and washed their faces, and then warmly kissed them.

SOME SPECIAL CONDITIONS 191

I don't describe this scene for its moral bearing, but to show how impossible economy was in a trade so loosely conducted. It would have been better for employers and workpeople if they had been in the disciplinary grip of machinery.

I have noticed, too, that machinery seems to lead to habits of calculation. The Pottery workers were woefully deficient in this matter; they lived like children, without any calculating forecast of their work or its result. In some of the more northern counties this habit of calculation has made them keenly shrewd in many conspicuous ways. Their great co-operative societies would never have risen to such immense and fruitful development but for the calculating induced by the use of machinery. A machine worked so many hours in the week would produce so much length of yarn or cloth. Minutes were felt to be factors in these results, whereas in the Potteries hours, or even days at times, were hardly felt to be such factors. There were always the mornings and nights of the last days of the week, and these were always trusted to make up the loss of the week's early neglect.

Their trades-unionism always presented a marked contrast to that of Lancashire. Though the latter, fifty years ago, had not the masterly organisation seen in the present day, yet it was on the lines of the present development. It had elements within it of calculation and shrewd foresight. But the trades-unionism of the Potteries was haphazard, feebly and timidly followed. It was surrounded by suspicion, for even many of those whose interests demanded its protection looked at it with misgiving and spoke of it with bated breath.

Somehow this form of self-defence and protection was regarded as tainted with the idea of moral perversion or political disaffection. I can remember men who were spoken of as trades-unionists in the same spirit and tone as others were spoken of as " poachers." This was one of the most blighting influences which fell upon all attempts at trades-union organisation.

Moreover, I know in Tunstall, many working men were Methodists, even among the poorest, and most long-suffering. The same condition prevailed, too, more or less, in other towns. Now Methodism in those days always frowned upon trades unionism as much as on " poaching." Even a working man, though suffering himself from palpable injustice, if he were a class leader or local preacher, would warn his fellows against the " wiles of the devil." These " wiles " were often supposed to be found in trades unionism, but never in the tyranny and injustice of the " masters." There was, too, a leaven of religious feeling in those days in the Pottery towns, which it is difficult to realise in these days. The Sunday schools mainly fed this feeling. Though few could write, many could read, and in the Sunday schools the habit of reading the Bible was strongly fostered. Through reading, the sympathy and habit of the " man in the street," though he did not attend a place of worship, were in favour of religion. That "man in the street" would not stand brazenly in "the public ways" as now, when church and chapel-goers were going to their places of worship. The multitudinous and maudlin cheap literature of this day has brought forth after its own kind—flaunting impudence and stolid defiance. In the days I speak of, working potters who were not Methodists were yet under an influence which made them distrustful of all associations which were condemned by religious people.

I remember *The Potter's Examiner* (though I have never seen one for over fifty years) was steeped in the forms and methods of biblical expression. I remember letters addressed to certain "masters" in the style of "The Book of Chronicles," but there was no license and no irreverence in this form of address. To the bulk of the readers of the *Examiner* the rebukes were all the more weighty and scathing because of the Biblical form in which they were presented.

It will be seen how this dominant feeling militated against any successful trades-union.

There were two other elements which helped this "futility" in any combination.

One was in the relation of the workmen to each other, and further, in their relation to their employers.

There was a deep and wide division between one class of workmen on a pot-bank and another. The plate-makers, slip-makers, and some odd branches were regarded as a lower caste than hollow-ware pressers, throwers, turners and printers.

The former were the hardest worked and the worst paid. The latter class had an easier employment, were better dressed and better paid. There were black sheep among these, as can be easily imagined, but I am speaking of them as a class. In this class were found many local preachers, class leaders, and church and chapel-goers.

Even those who did not regularly attend places of worship would be seen on the Sabbath "in their Sunday best."

The poor plate-makers and their kind would be seen, if seen at all, furtively running from their wretched homes, when the beer-shops were open, in their working clothes.

Now in any attempt at union, trade or otherwise, it was impossible to unite classes which differed so widely in sentiment and habit. Two men might work in the same shop and be friendly enough in their intercourse, but if you could have seen these two men on the Sunday, or at a holiday time, you might have taken the one to be the employer of the other. I have never met with such contrasts and separation among working men anywhere else as those seen sixty years ago among the workers on a pot bank. Another hindering element of the success of trade unionism was the relation of the workpeople to "the master." He was always "the master," regarded with awe and fear on the bank, and meekly and deferentially passed in the street, though often not seeing those who diffused this token of conventional regard. The spirit of feudalism must have saturated the Pottery district as in no other industrial district. This perhaps was helped too by the fact that up to the time of the introduction of the railway, just over fifty years ago, the people were shut up to themselves. I remember hearing "an invader" from Lancashire about 1842 telling in our street of a strike from which he and others were suffering. But the way in which he denounced the employers of those days shocked the simpler Pottery people. They hadn't much to give, but his violence soon closed many hearts and many doors.

This fear of "the master," this overweening deference undermined all true independence of character and proper self-regard. If these elements had not existed the workpeople would never have so long tolerated their "annual hiring," their "allowance of twopence or threepence or fourpence in the shilling," "good from oven," and the "truck system." These were carried out in abusive forms and measures, such as no other industrial population in the country would have tolerated for so many years. I saw then their demoralising and cruel results.

I saw the sufferings of the Lancashire working-people during the American War. I saw both food and clothing rejected which would have been eagerly accepted in the Potteries between 1840 and 1850. I was on more than one relief committee, where the committees were harangued by the men because the food was not up to the quality desired, and I have seen women refuse new linsey petticoats and demand flannel ones. On such occasions my memory always went back to Tunstall market-place and the rubbish I had seen given out there. "Futility!" Yes, any true inner history of the Pottery working-people will account for the absence of a beneficent co-operative movement and an effective trades-union. There was a want of economical discipline in their work and life.

CHAPTER XXI

"AN OUT" TO TRENTHAM AT TUNSTALL WAKES

THIS was the greatest and brightest holiday of the year. For the children it was "the maddest, merriest time of all the glad new year." There were no trip trains in those days. The full sociality of the people, undivided, was given to its enjoyment. On the Monday the market-place was thronged. Shows, flying boats, hobby-horses, board and canvas theatres, with "the finest company in the world," "Aunt Sally," gingerbread stalls and other things ministered in their different ways to the great festival. On Tuesday there were the Sunday school "outs" to Trentham. "Treats" had not then come in. These have been born of the later socialistic sympathy abroad. They were much more needed then than now, for "fares" were a serious business for mothers, low as they were. These "outs" to Trentham meant a ride there and back in a canal boat, for which fourpence had to be paid. The boat usually started about five o'clock in the morning, and it took four or five hours to make the journey to Trentham from Tunstall. Hundreds of bundles were to be seen on that morning, these bundles containing bread and butter, perhaps a small meat pie and a currant bun or two. In some cases, perhaps, there was a small parcel of tea and sugar, but this only for those who could afford to pay for "hot water" at a cottage. The largest number drank all they needed at a fountain near the park entrance, or at the well in the wood. I have rarely missed drinking from that well for the last fifty years, and the water comes to my lips with the same freshness "as when I was a boy."

The journey in the boat was a pleasant tumult from beginning to end. There was little to be seen that was new until we passed Stoke. We used to stay at this "port" an unconscionably long time. It, more than another place, should have been christened Long-port. The delay was occasioned by the locks there, and the boats waiting to get through them. This port of Stoke was just as attractive then as now. Its squalor and jumble, however, were little heeded by the waiters in the boats. The grand sensation was to be enclosed within two narrow, slimy stone walls, and to sink or rise as the case might be.

On the first journey a youngster was filled with wondering fear at this new experience, and was only saved from a feeling of terror by the gaiety and boisterousness of his "veteran" companions who had been once or twice before. When the top of the lock was reached, after the inrush of water, or the level of the canal gained after the outrush of water, there was a ringing shout or clapping of hands. Some of the bigger boys would indulge in rolling the boat by rushing from side to side; and some of the mothers would declare if they didn't stop they should be sea-sick. In these and other ways the journey rarely seemed a long one to most of those present. When the port was gained at Trentham there was a general hurry-scurry to get on the high road, to look on the astonishing greenery of field and wood, and to breathe the inspiring air, so fresh compared with what had been left behind, where hovels and furnaces abounded. The march to the park was a merry revel—fun and song and laughter making the "welkin ring." The cottages so bright and trim on the way, with such clean, sweet flowers, called forth repeated outbursts of admiration and wonder. The cottagers, old and young, looked with wonder too on the pale faces, now so merry and gleeful. As there was then no Factory Act, this was the day of sunshine and fresh air for those youngsters. Since then, what with trips and—well, say more confidence, those cottagers or their successors don't look with very kindly interest now upon their young visitors. Trentham is visited by thousands, and if it is necessary for this to be so that there should be a duke, may the duke live for ever, whatever may become of the House of Lords. That park has been " a thing of beauty and of joy" for many weary thousands for many years. If the dukes of the last two generations have known what simple bliss they have ministered to so many pinched lives by their generous allowance of the free use of the park, they must have had some happy moments even in spite of the heavy cares of vast wealth and property. I should not be surprised if, on "the Great Day to come," those dukes are surprised to hear the words, "Inasmuch as ye did it unto one of the least of these My brethren, ye have done it unto Me."

Rank will then be a poor remembrance compared with a rich recognition of goodness whose "sweet smell" passes even up to Heaven.

When the youngsters used to enter the park, supposing the day was fine, there was a hurried scamper to the trees, those grand trees whose ample branches and rich foliage afforded such broad shelter from sun or shower. There the many wanderers rested. The bundles were untied, and the simple fare they contained was readily devoured in part. The different condition of things between those days and now could not be more vividly shown than by the sight of the leavings after a meal then and now. A squirrel (and there were squirrels then on the trees) could hardly have found a crumb at the bottom of the tree; but now it seems sometimes as if as much had been thrown away as had been eaten. Prodigality is not the special privilege of wealth.

After this simple feast, the park was scoured in all directions in ever-varying groups. The startled deer, rushing into the woods, gave immense delight and fun, when some unwinged juvenile Mercury vowed he would catch one. His speed and the speed of the deer excited roars of laughter by the contrast.

After a general survey of the park, you would see ringed groups assembling under the trees, especially of those who were beginning to be conscious of a soft down on the upper lip, and of the gentler sex of the same age. Perhaps it would not be going beyond the fact to say that on no green spot in England have more kissing-rings been formed than in Trentham Park. If they could all have been marked, as the rings were marked where the fairies used to dance in Robin Hood's time, they would now look more curious than the wave-undulations on some strata. Yes, these young folks, without intending it, kissed themselves into courtship and marriage, and the link which widened and brightened out into many a domestic circle was first formed in a kissing-ring under the trees in Trentham Park. For better and for worse this was done, but let us hope that in the simplicity of those days it was mainly for the better.

The afternoon was chiefly devoted to wandering through the wood as far as "the well," and up to the monument, which was then always accessible. After tea (for those who could afford tea to the remainder of food in their bundles) there would be a slow walk back through the village to the canal boat, contrasting with the elasticity and hilarity of the morning.

Most of these children were leaving a paradise which they would not see again for a whole year. They knew it. The thought of it made some of them pensive as they pursued their way to the boat. They were going back to hard toil and to long, weary hours in stifling workshops. They were going back to hardship, to oaths and curses and brutalities in many cases. The one glad, free, bright day was nearly gone. Except on Sundays, they would never have anything like it for a whole year. Soon the black, bitter winter would come, and through sludge and storm, and only half-clad, they would travel from home to "the bank," and from the bank home, never seeing the latter in daylight for many months, except at week-ends. With so much that was bright and beautiful behind, and so much that was hard and chilling before, is there any wonder that some of the more thoughtful were pensive on their way to the boat? If England's legislators could have seen these children passing out of the sweet sunshine and fresh air into the darkness and hardship of their daily lives, they would not have allowed them and their successors to continue in those toils and cruelties for twenty-five more years. "Knowledge comes, but wisdom lingers," and no wisdom seems to linger so much as that of statesmanship where vested interests are in the way. But thank God time doesn't linger, and "throughout the ages one increasing purpose runs, and the thoughts of men" (and the privileges of men) "are widened by the process of the suns."

Many of those children, as they afterwards sang in their Sunday schools of " sweet fields beyond the swelling flood stand dressed in living green," would associate that bright and hopeful vision with what they had seen in Trentham Park. And the soft twilight comes on as the boat is steered on its homeward journey. The boat is now full of jollity, for numbers spread the contagion of joy. The stars come out, as if to view with smiling, pensive interest these happy children. Trentham with its wooded heights fades in the distance, but to many in this boat its memory will be a sweet vision and an inspiring hope amid the sad and sorrowful toils of the year.

CHAPTER XXII

A CONTRAST BETWEEN THIS AND THE GENERATION OF MY EARLY YOUTH

AFTER the riots my mind became acutely alive to political and social questions for one so young. There was a premature development of fear of public turmoil in the shape of other riots, or public trouble in the want of work or food. Sixty years after, though we have had epochs of material prosperity by "leaps and bounds," I cannot yet free myself from this oppression of misgiving when political movements are ominous. A sort of "chill" atmosphere surrounds me, and I dread for my country a repetition of the chilling and blighting touch of such trouble. I cannot describe how terribly this feeling has oppressed me since the Chancellor of the Exchequer has made his proposal to go back to Protection. I never thought such a thing possible in my time, and I seem to feel the chill and shadow of those early days, when lean, half-starved figures stood at our street corners waiting for work that did not come, and hungry for food they could not get. I have a sort of dull, deadening wonder whether history is going to repeat itself, and whether the first half of the twentieth century, through the burdens of war and the stupid burden of ignorance, is going to see as terrible nakedness in the land as in the first of the nineteenth century. This feeling comes over me, though it gets no sustenance from the general buoyancy and pursuits of pleasure seen on every side. This generation might be as far from the time of my youth as the age of the Sphinx. It seems to know as little, too, of the "Forties" in England as of the condition of Egypt in the time of the early Pharaohs. There might always have been Free Trade and Factory Acts as thorough as those which now forbid a child to begin to work before twelve years of age. There might always have been education as abundant as to-day and as free. There might have been Board schools as palatial and sanitary as now, and furnished with such graded and effective equipments, with a staff of teachers as able and devoted as we now possess.

Food and clothing might always have been as plentiful and as cheap as now.

The thunders of Carlyle might never have been heard against the "infernal" usage of the poor little toilers of his day. Fielden, Oastler and Lord Shaftesbury might be myths born of monstrosities in some industrial Sodom and Gomorrah.

This "age of intelligence" and prosperity and liberty has a glamour about it which blinds to all that went before. Our social history of the first half of the nineteenth century is walled up by halfpenny and penny novels, sporting papers, and "evening editions," read almost as quickly as flame could consume them.

There never was such a time, to use an old Methodist phrase, for "the giddy multitude" before this time. Yet this multitude is not separated more than two generations from those from whose loins they have descended, and of whose sorrows and woes they seem to know nothing. Perhaps this paper wall of "latest news," "sporting intelligence" and sensations may be rudely broken down, and by the time of the Forties of the twentieth century they may have as grim an outlook as their forefathers had a century before.

Such a condition no one would wish for, rather would we hope that every true patriot and reformer will say—

> "I will not cease from mental fight,
>   Nor shall my sword sleep in my hand,
> Till we have built Jerusalem
>   In England's green and pleasant land."

But the Nemesis of nations is not stayed by mere wishes or poetical sentiments. For ever nations and men reap as they sow, and if the wildest of "wild oats" are not now being flung into our national furrows of self-indulgence and waste and folly, then some deep misconception holds the minds of many.

In this I am sure, however, that the generation that lived about sixty to seventy years ago, though far less "educated" than this, had a deeper and stronger grip of the facts of life, and saw more of the potentialities latent in progress and liberty and righteousness. They were rude of speech. Many of them could hardly have read a halfpenny novel of the present day, and certainly would not have understood its flimsy and flaming sensations if they had. Its sickly descriptions of life, its immoral innuendoes and its fevered extravagance would have been as strange to them as Egyptian hieroglyphics.

What reading power they had they had got mostly at the Sunday school. They drank, however rarely, at the "well of English undefiled." Their thoughts were shaped by what they learnt from their Bible, probably helped by a teacher who knew little more than they knew, but whose heart God had touched. This teacher could not command a commentary. Sometimes he had heard of Dr Adam Clarke's *Commentary*, but that seemed to him something as distant and as awful as Mount Sinai, and he kept away from it as if its light would blind him. But he had heard "a still, small voice" within his own soul. He gave its whispers reverently, sweetly and modestly to his scholars. As I write I have such a teacher in my mind's eye. If he met with "a bid word" he always looked pathetically towards the smartest lad in the class for help, yet, with all his defects and stumblings in literary matters, he commanded the regard and love of his scholars, and breathed a savour which kept their lives sweeter when they were separated from him. It is a too little specialised coincidence in our national history that, just when "the new industry" was beginning to draw young people from their homes to the factories, Providence inspired Robert Raikes to draw them into Sunday schools. Factories rose in the Midland and Northern Counties, and so did Sunday schools with equal rapidity. The kindliest and finest elements of our social life were drawn to those schools. These in turn kindled self-help on the part of those who had been scholars. Hundreds and thousands of young men and women, who had to work long hours at hard labours, readily, cheerfully, and with heroic self-sacrifice, would give the hours of "the day of rest" to toil for the children under their care. Self-help! There never was a more glorious manifestation in the history of England, or of any other country, than that shown in the early history of our Sunday schools. Their spell and charm, too, were seen in many social ways.

I will try to describe "a Charity Sunday." It is typical in many ways of most others, but in the instance I am going to give more pronounced, because connected with one of the largest Sunday schools in Tunstall. I am referring to the Primitive Methodist "Charity Sunday." This was the phrase used to describe the Sunday school anniversary. The term "charity" came down from the time of Raikes and the schools he founded.

To prepare for "Charity Sunday" was a serious, or delightful, or anxious time for teachers, scholars and parents. For teachers, because ' the collections" for the day were all-important for the welfare of the school, and for scholars, because it was "the maddest, merriest day" of all the year. No "May Queen" looked forward with keener joy to "May Day" than boys and girls to Charity Sunday. This meant new clothes, it meant, too, walking through the streets on Sunday morning in procession, so that everybody would see the new clothes. Besides these things, many would be chosen as "little singers," to stand on a stage apart, surrounding the pulpit, "the observed of all observers," the girls in their white dresses, looking as lovely as a bed of lilies. The boys, though a contrast in dress, had faces and hands as clean as soap and water could make them, and hair shining with whatever lustre nature and hair-oil could give. Though not so charming as the girls in their white dresses and ribbons, they were attractive by an unusual elateness, by a dignity compelled by the honour and joy of the occasion.

If you had seen some of those boys and girls coming home from their work on the Saturday afternoon, with the smudge of clay on their clothes and faces, some too in patches and rags, you would not have known them again as you saw them "on the stage" on Charity Sunday. I have said this Sunday in its coming was an anxious time for parents. New clothes had to be found for the children, and this out of scant resources. Perhaps some of them had only just wiped off obligations incurred by clothes for the last Charity Sunday.

Yet the parents were under a gracious and compelling motive to get their children the best they could. They had memories of their own childhood, and even after the wreck of many hopes and the experience of many bitter disappointments, they had golden moments of memory when they, too, were Sunday scholars, and for their children not to have the joy which they once had was not to be thought of. They were inspired to a self-sacrifice which gave nobility even to their poverty. Not only was carefulness carried into the least possible expenditure for food for weeks, but it was well known at the time that even fathers who had given way to drunkenness would keep themselves sober for weeks before " Charity Sunday." On that day the poorest parents were proud as their children passed their door in the procession of scholars. There was a throb that brought smiles and tears to their faces, if only for a few moments. They were back in the softness and joy of their youth, and on this day, though skies might be clouded or sunny, it rained many precious drops on the hearts of parents who had long been separated by poverty or folly from the sweet hopes of their youth.

The " Charity Sunday " has now come, but soon after its sun rose many young eyes opened, not to look at the glory on the hills or in the fields, but at their " new clothes," which careful mothers had laid about their beds and bedrooms. Those poor children knew nothing of " Santa

Claus." His day had not yet come for the children of the poor; but no Santa Claus ever scattered his gifts with more excitement of surprise than that brought by the sight of new clothes.

These had not been seen in many instances before the children went to bed. They had to be fetched by fathers and mothers, after a late wage had been paid, from the dressmakers or milliners, or tailors, or boot and shoemakers.

Not much breakfast is required that morning, nor would there be time to prepare much even if there was much to prepare. The children want "to be got off," and the streets are streaming with hurrying feet and happy faces.

There is a murmur of joy over the whole town. Groups of observers are gathering together at the corners of streets, or wandering slowly towards the point of departure. Doors are open in every street, with eager observers on the steps. At last the procession is on the move, and a flowing radiance of bright faces is seen, lovelier than a "lane of beams athwart the sea." The "big singers" walk apart from the procession, and stop to sing in some public place or at some "patron's house."

A trumpet gives the the keynote, and then follows a burst of song from hearts elated and inspired by all the expectations and hopes of the day.

If the day happened to be a sunny one, no lovelier sight could have been seen in all England.

Hundreds of children with shining "morning faces" and throbbing "morning hearts." And such a morning! The very glory and summit of all the year's mornings. All smiling and all gladsome, with clothing so unusual for so many of them, it might have been brought by Ceres and her attendants from fields and gardens of Elysium and cast upon the children as they passed along the streets. The air, too, filled with the music of "the singers," and the melodious murmurs of the eager, watchful multitude. If the great bulk of those children could have been seen on Saturday, returning from their week's work, weary, pale, ragged, splashed and daubed with clay, with broken boots and shoes, as dirty white as their clay-stained clothes, and now seen on this Sunday morning, no "staged" transformation scene could ever have equalled this. The paleness, the weariness, the smudginess, the rags were all gone. Bright faces, rippling with laughter and joy, as if their glad lightness never left those faces; shining forms of dress, flimsy perhaps in substance, as they had been low in cost, but lending illusion and transport to the bright day. Then there was the movement of all the happy throng, rhythmical, measured, and yet so full of soul. All these things made up sights and sounds that "guardian angels" might stay to watch and listen to with joy. But a thought intrudes much below this celestial one.

Those children belonged to the Primitive Methodist Sunday School, then gathering together the poorest in the town. But they would raise that day, by the help of friends, some £170 to £180 to educate those children in their Sunday school, teach them to read, while the Government of that day was not giving as many shillings to educate all the children in the town as these poor people were giving to educate their own poor. "Sunday schools are England's glory" is a line which causes many superior persons "to curl up their lip" at the thought of what they deem the singing cant of a few fanatics. But that line covers a substratum of fact and truth never matched by any Government policy, to help the children of England for some sixty or seventy years, after the Sunday schools had been pouring out their beneficence for over two generations. After the happy tumult of the morning, there was movement again in the early afternoon for the service. Little girls were seen flitting about the streets, as if they had just come below the clouds for "a pop visit," but these were the "little singers," really the biggest attraction of the day. If the choir and the preacher could have seen the true perspective and proportion in which the popular imagination drew them and the "little singers," the former would have hidden their diminished heads.

Carts and traps from country districts many miles away began to enter the town in the morning, and continued into the afternoon. This was to the Primitive Methodists of the districts a veritable coming up to Mount Zion, as real in its gladness as the joy inspired by the sight of Jerusalem in the tribes who went up to its Temple. One striking incident was to be witnessed in the old chapel in those days.

A pew on each side of the gallery clock was reserved. If you looked, you would see twelve or fourteen men enter these pews; they came in quietly without any air of swagger, and yet with assurance. They knew they were expected and welcome. They were mostly young men, strong, active, and with an exceptionally virile look about them. They all wore neckerchiefs, according to the fashion of the time, about three inches deep, with the ends tied in little bows in front. The speciality of these neckerchiefs was that they were all made of dark blue silk, with small white spots. You saw no other class but the class these men represented with these neckties on.

It may surprise some to learn that some of these men were well-known prize-fighters or celebrated footracers and their abettors. It was well known many of these men had been scholars in the Sunday school in their earlier years. It is equally well known that they, in their way, were deeply attached to the school. It is well known, too, that on this "Charity Sunday" it was a common bond that all should give liberally.

I saw those men on many occasions in those services, and I have seen many far more irreverent worshippers. Perhaps anything like this would shock the conventional order and pious form of this day, and yet those Primitive Methodists of that day had some of the most devout and saintly men and women I have ever known.

I don't know whether this "laxity" in so indulging these men had any direct, injurious or demoralising influence, but I do know that that Primitive Methodist church got hold of the "vilest of the vile" in that town. It was the refuge of the outcast. It was "the House of Mercy" to which many fled who would never have sought the more "correct" churches of the town.

Though "the little singers" were the chief attraction, as I have indicated, the "big singers" were much admired, especially as "Dan Stubbs," with his first violin, was the practical manager of the whole business. There was "a leading singer," as he was then called (not choirmaster as now), but to those who knew Dan, another leader beside himself was unthinkable, and nobody ever attempted to think of it. He was a master with his own violin, he had an ear for choral effects as wonderful as his own manipulation of his violin.

Any singer or instrumentalist who strayed in tone or time got a withering glance, and sometimes a vocable, more out of harmony with the place where it was spoken than the slip Dan Stubbs was rebuking. He was aided by a few instrumentalists of very rare ability, though only local amateurs. Dan Stubbs was only an amateur. That is the pity of it, for he seemed to have the possibility of a Joachim of later days in him.

But his faculty was pitifully environed. If his amateurs had not been men of marked ability, they would not have been with him.

The singing too was wonderful, considering most of the singers could not read music, but the practising went on for two or three months, and the singers always knew that at some particular practice they would have to meet Dan Stubbs. For a few "practices" some hard words were uttered, and a terrific stamping of a foot too. But all was more than forgotten on the great day. The burst of joyful sound, varied by rhythmic cadences, and the rushing swell of some exultant harmony made all one to-day. Even Handel, Haydn and Mozart would have been surprised to hear those pale-faced potters, male and female, give such sweet-voiced expression to their choruses.

Perhaps the least powerful factor of the day, though he seemed the central one, was the preacher. What was he, standing as in a garden of flowers, when those children in bright dresses and faces surrounded the pulpit? What was his voice—earnest and pleading it might be—in rivalry with the mass of melodious and harmonious voices behind him? I have heard many of those preachers, but their most powerful moment seemed to come when they pleaded for the collection. If, after the evening collection, the money obtained was not enough, another pleading and another collection was made. If even this failed, a third pleading and a third collection followed, and then, if this was not successful, Dan Stubbs and the orchestra would give the "Hallelujah Chorus" in a manner which would close that day in a triumph of sound and memory and achievement.

CHAPTER XXIII

THE PURSUIT OF KNOWLEDGE UNDER DIFFICULTIES

I HAVE not, as yet, given any particular description of the methods of my own educational development. I think I have let it be seen that the Sunday school was the most powerful factor in giving any education to poor children. There were scholars who could go into day schools, but the bulk of the little workers on the pot banks got no education after being six or seven years old, except in the Sunday school. As a scholar under George Kirkham, I got great assistance and stimulus for so young a boy. This led me to read all I could. We had a few books in our small Sunday school library which attracted my attention. I read *Robinson Crusoe* and a few other favourite boys' books, but there were not many there. After these the most readable book I could find was Rollin's *Ancient History*. I was somehow drawn by it. His narratives opened a new world, but I never supposed that world had anything to do with the one in which I was then living. It might have been a world whose development took place on some other planet. I regarded it as remote from Tunstall and England as those other worlds I read of in Dick's *Christian Philosopher*, which book I found in the library too.

This book was a real charm and inspiration. Scientific matters were put before me with such new vividness and interest, I felt far more interest in this than in Rollin's *History*. Nature, from sods to stars, became to me a temple. The religious tone of the book entranced, and the sublimities of the heavens which it unfolded awoke in me imaginings which thrilled my soul. Then I read Milton's *Paradise Lost*, Klopstock's *Messiah*, and, later on, Pollock's *Course of Time*, and Gilfillan's *Bards of the Bible*.

These books may look now a strange assortment for such a boy of fourteen or fifteen to read, but they were no assortment at all. They just happened to fall into my hands, and though I might have read more elementary and educative books, these could not have moved the passion in me which these other books did. All this time, however, I had learned very little writing and arithmetic. I always felt then a strange indifference to these things, and I suppose this must account for my not learning to write at the Sunday school. Reading had been my main passion so far, but my very reading now led me to feel more and more my need of the power to write. I began to feel a desire to express myself about the things I read, and certain forms of expression lingered in my ear as well as entranced my eye. This, I imagine, was the first movement of a literary instinct. I read these expressions again and again, and their rhythm became a sort of new music in my ears. I remember my first efforts at composition were made on a slate. I could better manage a slate pencil than a pen. I tried a pen and a copy-book now and then, but the exercise proved a weariness to the hand and arm and an irritation to the mind. I had an old friend who was a boot and shoemaker. He was a well-read man, and one who thought deeply on many subjects, as I thought then and have known since. I spent many hours near his bench while he was cobbling. I found, too, he liked me to go to his house and encouraged me to go. He undertook to give me lessons in writing and arithmetic two nights a week. These exercises always went on slowly and irksomely, but the conversation pleasantly. Sometimes, when this became absorbing, both teacher and pupil forgot the more mechanical work on which I should have been engaged. However, after about two years' drill, I could scrawl a little, beyond which I have never been able to go. I was a little better in arithmetic, but always kept even this well inside the range of vulgar fractions.

About this time I began to develop a taste for reciting, as it was one of the chief items in the Sunday school entertainments. No tea-meeting would have been complete without recitations.

I had as companions two friends who had been much more highly educated than myself, and they had acquired rare elocutionary power. One of them especially developed such a faculty in this direction that he would have chosen the stage for his profession in life, but his father, a Wesleyan local preacher, sternly forbade this, and spoiled his son's life.

He went afterwards to America, with the bitterness of a broken purpose and a lost ideal, and was lost among the roaming thousands of the West, whose occupations in those days may be described as "various." But my association with these youths gave me a distinct mental uplift. I began to enjoy the literary charms of certain recitations, not only when reciting them in public, but they sent their music through my daily drudgery. In the midst of this, when opportunity served, I recited a few verses or lines aloud, and found they were always more inspiring when I heard them than when I simply said them to myself.

When I was about eighteen years of age a few more youths and myself formed, in connection with our Sunday school, a "Young Men's Mutual Improvement Society." These institutions in England's educational barrenness were as oases in the desert.

Our wise Governments of those days were only just beginning to lead the children out of the desert of neglect, but for growing youths there was only then the desert, except they had opportunity or ability to pay for attendance at a Mechanics' Institute.

Most of the youths who belonged to our Society had neither the one nor the other. What a "Cockerton judgment" has done in these days was then done silently and effectively by official apathy. The time of figs was not yet come, so no "Cockerton" blight could fall upon them. What was amusing, as now seen, was, that in our Mutual Improvement Society we never dreamt of any elementary pursuit of knowledge. There was a most comfortable and consummate assumption that this was not required. We met to discuss and criticise all things in heaven and earth, and sometimes even a far deeper province of the universe.

This habit was not born of our conceit—it was the pure birth of our simplicity. We could expatiate about the universe when an examination in the geography of England would have confounded us. We could discuss astronomy (imaginatively) when a sum in decimals would have plucked us from our soaring heights into an abyss of perplexity. We could discuss the policies of governments and nations, and the creeds and constitutions of churches, while we would have been puzzled to give a bare outline of our country's history. The audacity and simplicity of young men in such societies in those days cannot be understood in these more disciplined days. "The schoolmaster has been abroad" since then, and by examinations, and even by "cramming," has scared away all such lofty flights.

But we had the freedom of the universe, and such lesser matters as nations and churches, policies and creeds, statesmen and preachers, came easily under our purview. It was well our "essays" were not published and our discussions not reported, and so of most other such meetings in those days. The world has no doubt lost what would have been a moving source of wonder and amusement; but while it has lost this, it has also lost a chance of great misinterpretation. For in these more self-conscious days it would have been almost impossible not to have seen bombastic pretence where only simplicity and sincerity were the impelling forces.

I think I may say this, that when our society had got much enlarged by growth and by amalgamation with another society, no members of the "Imperial Parliament" ever go with a prouder joy to their great "House" than we went on Saturday nights to our meetings. There was a hum, a bustle and an interest when we first met, as if the fate of a nation depended on that night's debate. The reader of the essay was a man of mark for the occasion. Who else would become a man of mark that night was an uncertain quantity. The subject determined variety in development. Sometimes a man who had been hitherto comparatively unknown would surprise by his essay, or his criticism of another, sometimes there was much excitement over a subject, and intense feeling, but I never remember any abiding bitterness. It was well understood that all was for our mutual improvement, and this was mainly the issue. When I had got fairly in the grip of these meetings, I set myself to prepare for them as much as possible by a more determined course of study.

We had in our house a small room over "an entry." This "entry" afforded a passage from the street to the backyards of the cottages.

This room was about three to four feet wide, the widest part being a recess near the window, the other part of the room being narrowed by the chimney. I got a small iron stove to warm the room on cold nights, and I fixed up a small desk against the wall, and two small shelves for my few books. I don't know what a university atmosphere is. I have dreamt of it, but I know when I entered this little room at night I was in another world. I seemed to leave all squalor and toil and distraction behind. I felt as if I entered into converse with presences who were living and breathing in that room. I had not read many authors then, but such as I had seemed to meet me with an unspoken welcome every night. My life there was strangely and sweetly above what it had been during the day. It was often from nine o'clock to half-past before I could enter this room after walking from my work and getting my tea-supper, the only meal since half-past twelve at noon.

But, usually, as soon as I entered that room, I was as a giant refreshed with new wine. Its silence was as refreshing as dew, and exhausted energies seemed refilled with vigour and pulsed along with eager ardour. Unfortunately, I never acquired much in the way of knowledge. As I have since found out, I was on the wrong tack, and had no one to guide me. But what I failed to get in acquisition I got in inspiration and communion with some of those "sceptred sovrans who still sway our spirits from their urns." I made the mistake of climbing trees for golden fruit when I should have been employed in the simpler and more needed pursuits of digging and delving in the soul.

It was my misfortune to live in a town where there was not then one public institution to help those who had either taste or ambition to rise above their environments. Not only was there no local public spirit to create such an institution, but the Government of the country had no idea of the mental possibilities of enrichment in industry and commerce, and art and literature, which lay in the growing youths of that day. These youths wanted cheap and easy facilities for the development of their powers and tastes, but as these were not provided, the powers lay in lethargy and paralysis. Probably the country's neglect in this matter has lost more wealth than the mines of the Transvaal will ever yield. And yet the Government is lingering in this matter sixty years after. The youth of the country, in the hours after their day's labour, are not tempted or charmed by such facilities as would probably enrich their country in the future beyond the dreams of avarice. Party politics fill up our horizon. We see nothing else, and are striving for nothing more, while other countries are training their young men and women as soldiers in a bloodless conflict, but in which defeat means a deeper and more abiding disaster than defeat in arms ever brings. The flow of our national virility, in our "evening classes" for the improvement of the young, is arrested by "a Cockerton Judgment," and then we try to compensate for this by a measure which proposes to lay waste one of the most fruitful provinces of our educational system.

Verily, then, I have no need to groan over the folly and neglect which smote my opportunities sixty years ago. The same foolish smiting is going on to-day. When will the nation come to see that the first potency of all its wealth and character is in the minds of its children. It is not she who rocks the cradle who rules the world. It is the wise policy which seeks for "hid treasure" in the minds of "the rising generation," rising not simply in years, but in faculty and power and achievement.

This diversion from my immediate purpose in this chapter is the result of an outburst of feeling against "my time," and yet even "our time," great as it seems to us, and proud as we are of it in many ways, may look to our grandchildren a time of amazing crassness, dulness, and ineptitude. They may see how we allowed rich tides of possibility to pass, by "taking" which we might have been carried on to "fortune" beyond our dreams, whereas they may find themselves crippled by misfortunes, the legacies of our apathy and neglect. I said it was my misfortune to lack guidance at a critical period in my history, but I had to seek what came by groping. Groping is better than standing still, but pathetic tragedies and failures strew the lives of individuals and nations, which might have been avoided if the light of guidance had shone in place of the shadows of groping.

I know it may be said, and said proudly, that England has done some masterful groping. So it has. "The rule of thumb" has done wonderful things in our country's history, but it has required very strong thumbs; and though all men may be born with "great toes," all are not born with great thumbs in this sense. It is better, in the main, to organise the weakness of the many into strength, rather than rest upon the strength of the few.

These even will be more powerful in a soil of potency than in one of weakness. So that "Cockerton Judgments," and all such hindering and blundering policies, want sweeping away by the tide of a true national wisdom.

I look back pensively and gratefully, however, upon what I did in my little room. I might have done much more in much less time if I had had a guiding mind. Sometimes I read and wrote on till two or three o'clock in the morning, and a mother's eye in the next room, seeing the light of my candle through the chink of the door, she would often call persuasively or chidingly for me "to get into bed."

Much of this was wasted time, but groping is not only a slow process, but it misses much in the process. How much then has the country missed through not lending its guiding hand to its youth in past generations?

Mutual Improvement Societies, like the one I was connected with, though crude and blundering in many ways, did much to provide social workers in the next generation, when the bounds of freedom were made wider still in many social and municipal ways. Some of the members of our society rendered good service in these ways in their native town, or in other districts, some as widely remote as Canada and Australia.

Without knowing it, our poor little society was preparing to help in empire-building. Our contributions never became the elements of reckless and unscrupulous aggression. So far as I know, they only became quiet fruitful factors of those forces which give to the empire its most assured strength.

When I left my native town I was presented with a volume of tracts by "Benjamin Parsons of Ebley," Stroud. They contained some of the most vigorous and sane writing then extant for "the people," who had just then been moved by the great stir produced by "The People's Charter."

I mention the book only to show the trend of many of our discussions, and also that it was presented to me as "a memento of a consistent and efficient membership of more than four years."

The book was in very humble form, but its inscription was loaded with an adulation which I dare not quote. The writer, who was a collier, would have surprised Johnson by his Johnsonese style. But what matter, a man who toiled amid the perils and hardships of a collier's life in those days, and won the culture of literary expression, even if a little too rotund, had done something altogether noble, and had done it by the bravery of his own self-help.

So much then for lowly Mutual Improvement Societies in the barren times of the Forties and Fifties of the nineteenth century.

CHAPTER XXIV

LOCAL PREACHERS: HOW I BECAME ONE

THE next important movement in my life was taken when I began to prepare to become a local preacher.

The local preacher is no insignificant factor in our national life, and what he has done in our English religious life for more than a hundred years has never yet been fully realised or described. Perhaps it never can be fully described in sufficiently vivid detail and living force. But unquestionably he has been an immense power in the best life of the nation among its humbler classes. He has carried "sweetness and light" where only bitterness and darkness would otherwise have prevailed. He has fertilised activity and aspiration in "hard times," and amid scantiness and ignorance and injustice in many provinces of our industrial and social life. Villages and small towns, in former days, found him almost the only herald of better things, such as they could understand. He spoke in his own language the wonderful works of God. The worst men and women heard of a mercy which could embrace even their condition of despair. The social leper knew that even he could be made clean, and felt the warm breath of a love, through a human brother's voice and heart, which drove away the chill of his hopelessness. Men were drawn away from the ranks of devilry and recklessness to which their hard lot in life had often driven them. The poor heard of riches unsearchable which could be obtained without money and without price, and whose enrichment brought them freedom and hope and joy such as the world knew not of. In "the waste howling wilderness" of their "mean lives" they heard of a "Promised Land" to which they could travel by a path which shone brighter and brighter unto the perfect day.

These views and voices sent a charm through their lives, and lifted them into "societies" whose fellowship was at once a source of safety and an ever-recurring inspiration. Multitudes who would have been evil forces in the State, and sources of degeneracy in their social centres, were rescued from these dread possibilities, and if they did not become the purest and highest exemplars of virtue and grace, were yet forces "which made for righteousness." Their influence went for national stability in times of tumult and unrest, and probably did more to "exalt" the nation than many other loudly boasted movements. If there is a true, deep conservatism in the pursuit of goodness, deeper far than any political party ever gives, then these multitudes stood on the side of orderly development in our national progress.

While they looked up to heaven as their final goal, they shed a sweeter sanctity upon the common things of earth. I must say that, though I did not belong to the Primitive Methodist body, I saw most of its activity in Tunstall, my native town, and in the district round about. This was the first great and successful centre of Primitive Methodism. It was there that Hugh Bourne and William Clowes first began to work. I once heard both these men in a Great Camp Meeting held in "Booth's Field," then a large unoccupied piece of land, but now in the middle of the town.

I saw the spell these men cast upon the multitudes to whom they spoke, by their simplicity, their rough energy, softened by their all-pervading compassion and their great theme. These men themselves, in a sense, were never anything but local preachers. They went far and wide into other localities, but they carried with them the dominant mark of the local preacher. There was nothing clerical about them. They were simply "sinners saved by grace," telling in homely language how it had been done. This "telling how it had been done" was the source of their commanding power and their simple eloquence. This had no accent of culture, so that between them and the ordinary local preacher there was no gulf. They stood on common ground. They sought common aims, and the common people loved to have it so. For this reason they were ever welcome in all the villages and towns of the district. The people not only "took knowledge of them that they had been with Jesus," but understood their language and were subdued by their influence. So "the word of God grew and multiplied." I knew some of their local preachers to be men of the humblest position and abilities. I don't wish to make any invidious comparison with other Methodist bodies. They had local preachers too, humble both in position and ability, and whose devotion and self-sacrifice were beyond praise, but the Primitive Methodists, as I knew them, took in men as local preachers of a lower degree in both elements, but their wonderful success showed they were " owned " both by God and the people.

I must say the marvel has grown through all the years of my life that the men I remember could do so much in their time. It must have been that they carried a "consecration" truer than was ever carried by the dogma of "Apostolic Succession." If England had never had its local preachers, and had been left only to the high-claiming "successors of the Apostles," I hesitate to say what would have been the condition of England in the stormy revolutions which swept over Europe, and what would have been its lack in purifying and uplifting forces if these had not been so zealously disseminated by the local preachers in almost all quarters of our country. I said it had never been told what the local preacher has done in our English religious life, and time would fail, and power too, for any man to tell of "brother" Smith, and Brown, and Jones, and Robinson, who through faith and self-sacrifice did so much to win a good report by a devotion as beneficent in its issues as it was lowly in its operation. I must confess here, in the first place, that I have been led away from my direct purpose in this chapter by my admiration for a body of men who have done such widespread and fruitful work in our nation's life. Of this work and that of our Sunday school teachers I know no movements of high self-help on the part of humble classes of the people comparable to theirs in any age or nation. If the nation retains such moral virility as this in the future, and if the passion for athletics does not drain this away, then our country will carry the assurance of its own stability and progress in its own spiritual pursuits. The second reason for going away from my direct purpose in this chapter is, that my admiration has deepened through all the years of my life for the Primitive Methodists, as I knew them in my youth. The breath of their intense activity and their fervent simplicity, which were so near to me from childhood to my young manhood, have been about me like an atmosphere all through my life. Their wonderful prosperity as a denomination has been no surprise to me. They laid hold of the primal source of Divine Power from the first, as the disciples did on the Day of Pentecost. They trusted neither in ecclesiasticism nor learning. These matters were incidental and secondary. Their supreme resource in all their work was found in the promise, "the Holy Ghost shall teach you in the same hour what ye ought to say."

I must now more directly relate how I became a local preacher. Indirectly, and all unconsciously, my connection with the Mutual Improvement Society was leading to this. I had become connected in my youth with the Methodist New Connexion Sunday School, and from the gracious impulses received from my teacher, George Kirkham, I gained a strong religious bent in my early youth. This inward bent had been strengthened by all my associations with the Sunday school and the chapel. At the last this feeling was brought to full expression and form by what was called "a Revival," a spiritual awakening which spread over the Hanley Circuit, of which Tunstall was a part.

My connection with the Mutual Improvement Society fostered regular habits of study, as far as possible, and gave me increasing power of expression. These things were noticed, as they usually are in Methodism at large, and it was suggested by friends that I should prepare to take the position of a local preacher. These suggestions changed somewhat the course of my study. I began to read more in theology, but lacked resources and guidance. By some means I became possessed of Dwight's *Theology*, a book not at all adapted to one as crude as I was. Whatever else it may be, it is not a satisfactory "handbook" of theology.

I was soon afterwards lent Richard Watson's *Institutes*, but for elementary guidance in theology for one like myself, an office-boy in a lawyer's office might as well have been told to read *Coke upon Lyttleton*. I then read Dr Cooke's *Theology*, but in all I found diffuseness, rhetorical amplification and elaborate arguments; in fact, everything but such a precise and simple statement of matters as I then needed.

My theological studies were therefore somewhat bewildering and uninforming. I am afraid I learnt more in this direction from Milton's *Paradise Lost* and *Paradise Regained*, and Dick's *Christian Philosopher*, and Gilfillan's *Bards of the Bible*. My theology therefore was made up of a very curious blend. It had less of dogma in it than imagination and rhetoric. So I kept well away from definitions in my first sermons and dealt much in description. In this way I could go up Mount Moriah with Abraham, and freely describe what probably he never saw.

I could stand with Moses overlooking the Red Sea, and sway his rod over that sea, in imagination, with a mastery and sublimity he never thought of under the burden of his responsibility. I could ride in Elijah's chariot of fire, and describe too the Great Day of Wrath, with rolling thunders and falling mountains, and the cries of sinners to be hidden by them. I could do this too with a faith as real as if all were visibly passing before my eyes. No film of doubt had then settled upon "the eye of faith." That eye was then as a clear mirror, responsive to every image from Genesis to Revelation. All was true from "the bottomless pit" to "the heights of glory." No critical faculty in relation to faith had begun to grow. It had not even the promise then of "first the blade and then the ear." There was just faith's simplicity and supremacy of assurance, and I have yet to learn, in later years, after much reading of "learning" and of books, that there is anything under these heavens more truly heavenly. I have come more and more to believe that the child-trust taught by our Saviour is the one bright, pure and peaceful centre of our life on earth.

If I could only have known this before, what maelstroms, what "moors" and "fens" and "crags" and "torrents" would have been avoided?

I have one or two of my early sermons left, and I don't know at which most to be amazed, their rhetoric or their faith, but I do know which I most admire.

Whatever was the secret of it, I have this most distinct recollection, that middle-aged and old people most admired my sermons. Whilst young folks could smile, the older ones always listened and looked. Benedictions in Methodist circles were more common in those days than now, and I used to get my share of them. And somehow they cheered and sustained, and led to stronger resolves to deserve them. They were not like the flimsy flatteries of a later time. They didn't stop in the ear and sing like a syren. They went into the very heart. They warmed its very blood, and they inspired a mood, an upward look, to which flattery never yet lifted a human soul.

I well remember preaching in a place called "Hot Lane," just outside the town of Burslem, one Sunday afternoon. I don't know why the place was called Hot Lane, but it was very hot for me that afternoon. The service was held in a cottage, and a very humble one too. I remember part of the congregation was made up of four or five hens, quietly parading about on the hearth. The cottage was fairly well filled with people in years, who could not attend the more distant chapels. The pulpit was a chair with a step on the bottom part of its back legs, and with a board to fit on the top of its back.

This was my first visit, and while I was nervous, I could see my congregation was curious. They saw "the lad," and they were evidently eager to hear him. I got through the opening part of the service very well, for the brother who led the singing was hearty and apt in his choice of tunes, and there was a refreshing rain of "answers" all over the cottage. I took for my text words which will seem strange to modern eyes as the text of a mere boy. They were, however, "The great day of His wrath is come, and who shall be able to stand?"

While dealing with this appalling theme in some lurid rhetoric and vivid realism, I came to a sudden stop. I might have been stunned by a piece from one of the falling rocks I was describing. While looking dazed at the faces near me, the singing brother of whom I have spoken jumped to his feet and said in a cheery voice, "Come, friends, let us sing while our young friend finds hisself." His tone and manner, and the long hymn he and the people sang, enabled me to find myself and to finish my sermon, and the great day with which I was dealing. If all the methods by which local preachers have been evolved could be described, though the pursuit was serious enough, the incidents would make a rich theme of comicality.

Gargoyles and Gothic architecture go together, and they may be taken as symbolic of the laughable and serious minglings seen in human life.

I must give a personal and social phase in local preaching. There was one altogether pleasant and recurring episode in a local preacher's life—that was when he had an appointment some five or six miles away in the country on some spring or summer day. Supposing him to be a young potter, he has been moiling late and early in the dust of a potter's workroom all the week. He has breathed the thick, heavy smoke in the air, and through its black canopy has hardly ever seen the sun while he has been about. But on Sunday morning he starts off to his "country appointment." He knows he is going to be the guest of a rubicund, jolly, big-hearted farmer, but who is as devout as he is hearty.

The morning is bright and the air is sweet. As the pale-faced young preacher walks along country lanes and through field paths he meets the fragrance of flowers, which makes his nostrils expand with joy. His eye brightens with the sight of hedgerows shimmering in dewy green and the fields decked with flowers. He is in a devout mood within himself, in view of the work before him. He is in a gladsome mood by all things without.

It seems to him as if heaven and earth were pouring into his soul their best and highest influence, and to enter the Lord's house in due course to see there "the beauty of holiness" seems to him the fitting issue of such a morning.

It was always wise when going to such an appointment to go in good time, especially if thirsty, and more especially if hungry. And in the times of which I am writing all local preachers were not "well fed." New milk, curds and whey, and "butter of kine" were not to be seen and enjoyed every morning. Nor was the music of such a welcome to be heard every day, as when the farmer would say, "Come in, Brother Smith," or "Come in, my young friend, and welcome. Just have a mouthful before we go to chapel, and get a good drink of that new milk."

We talk sometimes about this and that "giving tone to a service." In those days of which I am writing tone was often given to a service by a good man's hospitality. Nor was this tone confined to the service or even the day. Many a pale-faced young fellow carried a bloom on his cheeks into the day following, from the country air and from the rich yet simple hospitality he had shared.

One man I remember was always anxious for his

visitor to have a good supper, before returning home, of roast apples out of his own orchard, with a plentiful supply of bread and butter and milk.

One farmer in Cheshire would be delighted beyond expression if, when he asked you what you would have for supper before starting back home, you happened to say, "Toasted cheese, please." He would pat you on the back fondly, and say, "Now you've got some good sense. There is nothing better for a journey than toasted cheese." His question would be asked before the evening service, and when you got back you would be amazed at the "Benjamin's mess" of toasted cheese which would be set before you.

If I didn't "grow in grace" by these simple and hearty hospitalities, I grew in wisdom and observation. Such kindliness never checked the growth of the grace, while it did very much to brighten many a monotonous course of life. The time came round when I had to preach my "trial sermon" before coming on "full plan," as the Methodist phrase puts it. To pass from "being on trial" to "full plan" is the sign and seal of your acceptance as a fully accredited local preacher.

This "trial sermon" gave security against the entrance on " the plan" of anyone who thought he could preach. The preacher's character was looked after in other ways. This was simply to see what sort of mental calibre the preacher had, and whether he had power or promise to deliver himself so as to edify and impress a congregation. The trial sermon may have been " a strait gate" to some, but it has not been quite strait enough at times. Sometimes men have passed through with what, rhetorically speaking, has seemed like "a goodly Babylonish garment," but, "alas, Master, it was borrowed," or had even been "stolen." Yet sometimes even "borrowed plumes" have passed when the judges did not know the bird to whom the plumes belonged. This trial sermon was "a trial" to me. My poor little study witnessed many a struggle to get at a subject, and to get at clearness when the subject was found. I consulted my old friend "the shoemaker," but I could get no more than generalities in counsel from him. The one note he pressed continuously upon me was, "Do your best." I only knew afterwards the emphasis he had put on the first word. Before I preached this trial sermon a most unexpected episode occurred. I had an invitation to pay a visit to Glasgow and Edinburgh. I should beforehand as soon have expected an invitation to go to Pekin. However, the way was open, and as my mind was alert and eager about preachers and preaching, I welcomed the opportunity to hear the great Scotch preachers of that day.

I shall relate in the following chapter what I saw and heard in Scotland, and I shall now close the account of my becoming a local preacher.

The trial sermon was not preached until after my return from Scotland. No doubt my visit had led to its being something different from what it would have been if that visit had not happened.

LOCAL PREACHERS

However, I preached it, and in the discussion which followed, the most noticeable thing, as I was told, was that the superintendent minister said it was not my own sermon. In the history of preaching this was not a new incident. My old friend the shoemaker asked the minister if he could tell whose sermon it was? He avowed he could not do this, but was sure it was not my own.

My friend was equally sure it was, and told the minister if he were to lock me up in a room with no book but the Bible, I could have written another as good. I once thought that a bold statement, but I don't now. I happen to possess the sermon yet, and if it was not my own, when I look into it, I wonder whose it was, and how I came to possess it. My shrewd shoemaker friend had evidently seen into its weakness when he said I could produce another as good. The minister, on the other hand, did not know of the inspiration I had brought back from Scotland. However, I was " passed on to full plan," and so was permitted to join a great brotherhood of lay preachers, whose account in social, national and religious matters is not the least glorious in the history of the nineteenth century.

CHAPTER XXV

CLOSING INCIDENTS

UP to the time of my visit to Scotland I had rarely had the privilege of hearing much preaching, excepting from local preachers. Our church was one of those feeble ones which, but for their labours, could not have existed. Some of these local preachers were men of mark in their sphere, and for working men, as most of them were, I have often wondered how they prepared to do what they did, considering their lack of time and the few opportunities of culture they had enjoyed. But some of them had a refreshing individuality, and in this feature they stand in contrast to the same class of men to-day. Two men stand out in my recollection as preachers of "high degree"—Dr Newton and Dr Beaumont. These celebrated men came occasionally to preach at the Wesleyan Chapel at Tunstall.

Of Dr Newton all has faded from my memory except his great presence in the pulpit, and his voice, which rolled like subdued thunder through the chapel. I have the memory of the sound, but of nothing of what was said. I have the feeling that if the voice had been "let go" it could have shaken the place where we were assembled. Of Dr Beaumont I have a much more vivid recollection. He, too, had a fine presence, but there was the play upon his face of far more varied emotions. His voice was peculiar at times, but it was a reservoir of many intonations which gave remarkable effects to many things he said. I heard him afterwards, and it seemed sometimes when these variations of voice came as if two or three men were in the pulpit.

I remember the text the first time I heard him. "Thus saith the Lord, The heaven is My throne, and the earth is My footstool," etc. I shall never forget the delivery of the words, "Thus saith the Lord," and then the marvellous change of voice in giving the following words. The first words were given in a loud tone of dominant proclamation, as if you must and should hear. The words which followed were delivered with a quiet, sustained majesty, which seemed to fill the congregation with awe, as if God Himself were in the "place," and "they knew it not" until that moment. From that moment, too, the preacher had the congregation in the hollow of his hand. I remember when I returned home I was asked what I thought of the preacher, and I instantly avowed I had never heard a preacher before. I found out afterwards, on several occasions, that Dr Beaumont captured his congregation in a few moments. I remember one striking occasion of this in the Wesleyan Chapel at Burslem. The words of the text were, "And when He was come into Jerusalem all the city was moved, saying, Who is this?" He asked the question of the people in the body of the chapel, then of those to his right hand in the gallery, then of those in the front of the gallery, and then of those to the left of the gallery. This was done in changing voices, and with such eagerness that they seemed to come " like a rushing mighty wind " from a moving multitude. Then there was a pause. The stillness both astonished and awed, and from that moment the congregation was as clay in the hands of the potter.

We have got beyond these oratorical triumphs now, but all is not loss. We have our gains. Those " great sermons " in delivery in those days were often " poor stuff" to read, whereas now we may have the poorest delivery, and yet pearls and gems of thought to read in quiet hours. It seems a pity the best elements of the two periods cannot be blended.

We have oratory, too, in these times—what I should call vocative oratory, a blend of blatancy and egotism, and " the people will have it so." The louder the noise and the self-inflation, the more garish the pomp and show heralding the oratorical exploitations, the larger the crowds.

We have, too, and never more so, pearls quietly thrown out, which are not only symbolic of the Kingdom of Heaven, but are of its very grace and beauty. We have a great and suggestive counsel as to where these pearls are not to be " cast," and so as long as " the fit " are " the few" the many will follow the noisy. With this Scotch journey before me my mind was full of expectation, but I was fortunate enough to realise more than I expected.

My first Sunday was spent in Glasgow. I failed to hear Dr Ralph Wardlaw, then one of the celebrities of that city. I heard, however, a Dr William Anderson, also a celebrity. I was specially struck with his mastery of his subject. He seemed to have it, as the saying is, at his finger ends. I was struck most, however, with the number and nicety of his divisions, and the circumstance that with each division and sub-division he took up a snuff-box which lay on the pulpit at his right hand. For the moment the preaching was suspended. The lid of the snuff-box was deliberately and gently rapped, and as deliberately a pinch of snuff was taken with a soft hushing sound. When this was done, the theme or argument was resumed until another division came, with the deliberate details of the snuff-taking ceremony.

This was all very strange to my "Southron" ideas, and to my simple Methodist notions. Still I was not shocked, and have even the memory of a charm resting upon me from the sermon. I say from the sermon, for the service was so bald, so rigid, and the psalms sounded to me so uncouth that the service itself cast no element of grace upon my mind. I can imagine how a perfectly similar strangeness would fall upon a Highlander who should hear the hymns of a

Methodist service for the first time. The following Sunday I was in Edinburgh. I must say nothing here of the wonder which fell upon me when I first beheld that picturesque old city with its enchanting contrast of old and new. Princes Street, with the towering heights of the old part of the city opposite, crowned by the castle, to a youth who had lived mainly among the dingy towns of the Potteries, was a thrilling marvel.

But Dr Guthrie was then in the height of his fame, and as a preacher was then the great attraction of the city. He was its most immediate and commanding attraction to me. On Sunday morning, with two friends, I was early at his kirk. But there was a momentary disappointment when I learned that his co-pastor, Dr Hanna, was the preacher. But the disappointment passed away as a light cloud when I came under the spell of the preacher. There was to me the same baldness in the service as I had experienced in Glasgow the Sunday before. But the preacher soon gripped me with his thoughtfulness and simplicity combined. These gave both inspiration and refreshment, and left upon me an unusual sense of elevation. I had never heard a sermon so well compacted and so full of suggestion, and all done with intense quietness.

My friends and I were told that Dr Guthrie would preach in the afternoon, and that if we wanted to secure seats, we must be back in half an hour after the morning service. We just took a walk into the cemetery to see Dr Chalmers's grave, eating a bun each, which one of my friends had provided. When we returned the kirkyard was full of people. Soon after the doors were opened, and we were, fortunately, able to secure good seats. The kirk was soon full, and it was full too of the hum of a great expectation. There was not the silence I had been accustomed to even in a great congregation in England. I noticed especially the free conversation which went on in what I suppose was the elders' pew, just under the pulpit.

I was very much struck by the entrance into this pew of a tall, powerful-looking man, who walked into it with his hat on, and who sat down before taking it off. He seemed to survey the great audience with interest, and seemed as if he had forgotten that he had his hat on. This gave a little shock to my Southern notions. He had, too, a walking stick which seemed big enough for a shepherd's crook. When he sat down he rested his chin on his hands, looking intently at his congregation. Then he put one of his hands into his waistcoat pocket and brought out a big snuff-box, and from this took what seemed to me a mighty pinch of snuff for each nostril. This made my first shock much deeper on account of the prominence given to the whole process.

The service was opened by Dr Hanna, and during this period the big man, who had so attracted my attention, disappeared. Soon after this I saw, with a start, this man ascending the pulpit stairs in his gown. Then for the first time I knew he was Dr Guthrie. I had conceived a slight repugnance for him as I had seen him at first, but not many words passed from his lips before all this was changed into an absorbing wonder.

He preached on Peter in prison, and gave a thrilling account of Peter's courage in standing up in the very city in which he had so recently denied his Lord. The climax of his sermon, however, came when he described Peter sleeping on the prison floor, chained between two soldiers, and the angel touching him, his chains falling off his hands. All this was done with such vividness, with such intensity, that all eyes were turned towards the elders' pew, to which the great preacher pointed, as if all had taken place there. As far as I could see, there was an involuntary rising from seats and craning of necks on the part of the congregation to see the living wonder the preacher's imagination had created. Then there was a falling back to the seats and a loud breathing after some moments of strong suspense. I never saw or heard anything approaching this before or since. That prison scene has lived in my mind ever since, and when I read the narrative yet, it comes to me with all the vividness with which Dr Guthrie described it. I saw him the next day in the city with a number of children following him, taking hold of his hand, and if I had seen the angel who liberated Peter I could not have felt more of awe and of gratitude.

That week had a store of unexpected events

CLOSING INCIDENTS 251

and privileges for me. On the following evening, I think, I heard Sheridan Knowles, the dramatist, preach. I don't remember much about his sermon, except the robust earnestness with which it was delivered, but the dramatist was infinitely away from Dr Guthrie in dramatic action.

The night following, I believe, I attended a great meeting called to protest against the imprisonment of a Scotch lady, a Miss Cunningham, I think, by the Duke of Tuscany, for reading the Bible to some poor Italian peasants. I don't remember where the meeting was held, but it was in a very large hall. This was densely crowded, and the spirit of John Knox seemed to throb in every man and woman present.

It was well for the Duke of Tuscany that the thunder and lightning in that protest and in that meeting did not reach him at once. If it had, his poor throne would have gone down tumbling into contempt and confusion a few years sooner than it did. This was nearly fifty years ago. The wrath then aroused in Scotland and England by the indignity done to a Scotch lady, engaged in a work of mercy, was as terrible as it was august.

But fifty years can dissipate many things. I have lived into a time when Miss Hobhouse, engaged in an equally merciful mission, through the uprising of an abnormal party passion, has been held back from that mission by England's Government. This, too, not only without a national protest, but she has been howled at and denounced even when gently telling the story of her gracious mission. How far we are from the Duke of Tuscany's time; yet how near the spirit of his time. Truly, Freedom may come to its own and its own receive it not. Wrongs, though modern, can be as grim and terrible as ancient ones. The week I spent in Edinburgh proved to be the one in which a great Peace Conference was held there in October 1853. I knew nothing of this until I got there, for newspapers were then comparatively rare, and pennies were not as plentiful as now. Moreover, I knew very little about newspapers then.

I attended several of the sessions of this Conference for two or three days. Men were there whom I have known better since than I knew before. Public life outside the Potteries was then almost unknown to me. The great event of the Conference, however, was its last meeting, held, I think, on the Thursday night. At that time rumours of war were heard, and afterwards there came the Crimean War. I am giving matters here as I remember them; I have read nothing about the meeting I am going to describe, or even the Conference. I am not writing a history, but simply my own recollections. I think the meeting must have been held in the same hall where the meeting to protest against Miss Cunningham's imprisonment was held.

But there was a rare sensation for that meeting in the announcement that Admiral Sir Charles Napier was to appear as an opponent of peace proposals. The two other chief speakers were Richard Cobden and John Bright. I don't remember who the chairman was, but I do remember that Mr Samuel Bowly, a staunch member of the Peace Society, made a short speach. I think Mr Cobden made the first principal speech, with the lucidity and persuasiveness and restrained strenuousness I so often heard in after years. He held the meeting in a grip as strong as it was gentle, though hostile elements were present. Then the Admiral came, with all the frankness and bluffness of a sailor. He spoke with vigour and real earnestness. He stormed in his declamation, as he did afterwards with his guns at Bomarsund, and with equal futility. He had the fair play which frankness and sincerity should always command, but the great mass of those present were unconvinced. Then Mr Bright followed. He was then in his prime, in the fulness of his power, and moved evidently by a mighty inspiration. His presence would have been attractive then, if his name had been unknown. His handsome face and massive head and his voice were strong elements in his favour.

I am not going to describe what he said. That can be ascertained elsewhere. I am only going to describe the effect as I saw its living expression.

A short time after he began the audience was in his hands. Those peculiar, thrilling tones of his voice, as if a soft, weird, metallic vibration were among them, soon held the people spellbound,

I heard those tones many times afterwards, and never heard them from any other speaker. Humour, argument, the play of fine sarcasm, and high and earnest pleading followed each other, until the intensity of interest seemed almost too great to bear. Then came the peroration, sublime in its restraint, but carrying a most passionate appeal for peace. Then there came a most remarkable coincidence. Just as Mr Bright's peroration excited a storm of applause the guns of the Castle went booming over the city, as if applauding the eloquent apostle of peace. The fact was, that just then the Queen and Prince Albert and the Royal Family were entering the city on their return from Balmoral. It was an incongruous coincidence. Applause for such a purpose and booming of guns. But this is typical of much that goes on every day. Things apparently near each other are yet separated by deep and awful gulfs. The resounding acclamations of a peace policy were followed in a few months by the roar of cannons to support a policy of war with Russia. So came the Crimean War, a war now seen to be as useless and as mistaken as it was disastrous. But the disastrousness of it lies fifty years away, though it brought the dread time when you seemed to hear the beating of the wings of the "angel of death" in almost every part of Europe. Distance, however, lends disenchantment to sorrow, and thus we can hear a great statesman of the present day say, that enormous tragedy of error was simply " putting

CLOSING INCIDENTS 255

money on the wrong horse." The language of the Turf suits now to pass over to a sort of comical limbo what was once an appalling and wasting conflict.

I am reminded again that the great protest against war was made in Edinburgh fifty years ago. Not only did it fail in its own day, but even with the useless tragedy of the Crimean War before us it has failed to keep us in the paths of peace. I have lived to see a war wildly welcomed mainly, and welcomed too, not against a great power which was clothed with the bad traditions of long hatred and villifying ignorance, as Russia was. There is the saving mercy we did not proclaim this war, but who will say it was not acclaimed as eagerly as if we had spoken the first word.

There is one thing we do proclaim, however, "an unaggressive policy" for our Empire. We want "no territory and no gold." It is somewhat remarkable to see a fair-looking avowal transmuted into what looks like lust of territory and gold, and "unaggressiveness" to show fangs as strong as those of ancient plunder.

Verily, we need to look again into "the law of liberty," to wash our eyes in its beauty and justice, as did our forefathers "in the great days of old."

> "England, the time is come when thou shouldst wean
> Thy heart from its emasculating food ;
> The truth should now be better understood,
> Old things have been unsettled ; we have seen

WHEN I WAS A CHILD

Fair seed-time, better harvest might have been,
But for thy trespasses . . .
Therefore the wise pray for thee, tho' the freight
Of thy offences be a heavy weight;
Oh grief! that earth's best hopes rest all with thee."
WORDSWORTH.

INDEX

Balfour and the "first third" of the 19th century, Mr, 21, 22.
Beaumont, Dr, 245.
Beer-selling, facilities for, 130.
Bright, John, 253-255.
Brougham, on Charity, Lord, 113.
Burslem, 121, 160-171, 186, 238.

Capper, Joseph, 141, 154, 172-181.
"Caste" among workpeople, 193, 194.
"Charity Sunday," 208-217.
Chartism, 142, 143, 150, 156, 157.
Child labour, 12-17, 54-56, 58, 59, 64, 65.
Children in factories, treatment of, 17, 54-62, 65, 189, 190.
Cobblers, the public activity of, 167.
Cobden, Richard, 43, 253.
Comparisons between present time and sixty years ago, 129, 132, 133, 155, 171, 204-208, 246.
Constables, old-time, 31-33.
Cooper, Thomas, 142, 14 , 158, 160, 176.

Corn Laws, 43-45, 182.

Democracy, the apparent failure of, 131-133.
Destitution, general, 42-45, 94.

Edinburgh, 248-255.
Etruria, 122.
"Examiner, the Potter's," 34, 193.

Factory life during early part of 19th century, 14-16, 25, 74, 75, 81-83.
Fenton, 159.

Glimpses of social want and degradation, 121, 122, 127, 128.
Guthrie, Dr, 248-251.

Hanley, 151, 155, 158, 159.
"Hooliganism," 37-39.
Hughes, Tom, 132.

Idiots, the treatment of, 39, 40, 72.
Industrial conditions in the Potteries, 184-187.
Intemperance, 49, 51.

INDEX

JOKING, practical, 37, 52, 53, 73.

KIRKHAM, George, 138-140, 218, 235.

LEAD poisoning, 80.
Leek, 162.
Longton, 159.
Lowell, Russell, 166.

MASTER Potter, A, 22-26, 30.
Methodism, 144, 192, 193.
Methodist New Connexion, 138, 235.
Morality in Factories sixty years ago, 49-51.

NAPOLEON BONAPARTE, 125, 126.
Newton, Dr, 244.

PLEASURES and recreations, 7, 31, 190, 197-203, 209.
Pottery people, characteristics of, 182-196.
Powys, Major, 162-165.
Primitive Methodism, 144, 208, 213, 215, 232-234.

RECREATIONS and pleasures, 7, 31, 190, 197-203, 209.
Reform agitation, 147-149.
Religion and ethics, 25, 69, 129.

Riots, 143, 158-171.
Roman Catholicism, 177.
Ruskin, John, 29.
Russell, Lord John, 177.

SCHOOL life, 1-6.
School, the Workhouse, 100.
Schools and their influence, Sunday, 6-9, 134, 140, 192, 207.
Sheridan Knowles, 251.
Smith of Coalville, George, 3-4.
Stoke-on-Trent, 158, 198.
Strikes, 33, 34, 90, 91, 142, 155.

TOYMAKING, 118, 119, 125.
Trades unionism, 33, 34, 183, 184, 191-195.
Trentham Park, 197-203.
Tunstall, 27-45, 140, 145.

WAKES, the annual, 31, 197.
Ward's *History of Stoke-on-Trent*, 143, 159, 160.
Wedgwood, Josiah, 122.
Workhouse, the, 83-85, 96-98.
Workhouse discipline, 109-112.
Workshops, condition of, 47, 48, 63.

THE END

Colston & Coy. Limited, Printers, Edinburgh

A CATALOGUE OF BOOKS AND ANNOUNCEMENTS OF METHUEN AND COMPANY PUBLISHERS : LONDON 36 ESSEX STREET W.C.

CONTENTS

	PAGE		PAGE
ANNOUNCEMENTS,	2	LEADERS OF RELIGION,	29
GENERAL LITERATURE,	8-26	SOCIAL QUESTIONS OF TO-DAY,	29
METHUEN'S STANDARD LIBRARY,	26	UNIVERSITY EXTENSION SERIES,	30
BYZANTINE TEXTS,	27	COMMERCIAL SERIES,	30
LITTLE LIBRARY,	27	CLASSICAL TRANSLATIONS,	30
LITTLE GUIDES,	27	METHUEN'S JUNIOR SCHOOL-BOOKS,	31
LITTLE BIOGRAPHIES,	28	SCHOOL EXAMINATION SERIES,	31
LITTLE BLUE BOOKS	28	TEXTBOOKS OF TECHNOLOGY,	31
LIBRARY OF DEVOTION,	28	FICTION,	31-39
WESTMINSTER COMMENTARIES,	28	THE FLEUR DE LIS NOVELS,	39
HANDBOOKS OF THEOLOGY,	28	BOOKS FOR BOYS AND GIRLS,	40
CHURCHMAN'S LIBRARY,	29	THE NOVELIST,	40
CHURCHMAN'S BIBLE,	29	METHUEN'S SIXPENNY LIBRARY,	40

FEBRUARY 1903

Messrs. Methuen's
ANNOUNCEMENTS

BY COMMAND OF THE KING

THE CORONATION OF EDWARD VII. By J. E. C. BODLEY, Author of 'France.' *Demy 8vo.*

This important book is the official history of the Coronation, and has been written by the distinguished author of 'France,' by command of the King himself. The Coronation is the central subject, and of it a detailed account is given. But the book is in no sense an occasional volume, and the Ceremony is treated, not as an isolated incident, but as an event belonging to European and Imperial history. At the end of the work there will be an appendix containing official list of all the persons invited to the Abbey, and also lists drawn up with some historical detail of the Colonial and Indian troops who assisted at the Ceremony. It will therefore be an historical document of permanent value and interest.

THE COMPLETE WORKS OF CHARLES LAMB. Edited by E. V. LUCAS. With numerous Illustrations. *In Seven Volumes. Demy 8vo. 7s. 6d. each.*

This new edition of the works of Charles and Mary Lamb, in five volumes (to be followed by two volumes containing the Letters), will be found to contain a large quantity of new matter both in prose and verse—several thousand words in all. Mr. E. V. Lucas, the editor, has attempted in the notes, not only to relate Lamb's writings to his life, but to account for all his quotations and allusions—an ideal of thoroughness far superior to any that previous editors have set before themselves. A Life of Lamb by Mr. Lucas will follow in the autumn.

THE LIFE AND LETTERS OF OLIVER CROMWELL. By THOMAS CARLYLE. With an Introduction by C. H. FIRTH, M.A., and Notes and Appendices by Mrs. S. C. LOMAS. *Three Volumes. 6s. each.* [*Methuen's Standard Library.*]

This edition is brought up to the standard of modern scholarship by the addition of numerous new letters of Cromwell, and by the correction of many errors which recent research has discovered.

CRITICAL AND HISTORICAL ESSAYS. By LORD MACAULAY Edited by F. C. MONTAGUE, M.A. *Three Volumes. Crown 8vo. 6s. each.* [*Methuen's Standard Library.*]

The only edition of this book completely annotated.

A SHORT HISTORY OF FLORENCE. By F. A. HYETT. *Demy 8vo. 7s. 6d.*

This work is intended to occupy a middle position between the Guides and Histories of Florence. It tells the story of the rise and fall of the Republic consecutively, but more succinctly than the works of Napier, Trollope, or Villari, while it treats of Florentine Art and Letters parenthetically but more systematically than has been done by either of these writers.

DAVID COPPERFIELD. With Introduction by GEORGE GISSING, Notes by F. G. KITTON, and Illustrations by E. H. NEW. *Two Volumes. Crown 8vo. 3s. 6d. each.*
[The Rochester Dickens.

THIRTY YEARS IN AUSTRALIA. By Mrs. CROSS (ADA CAMBRIDGE). *Demy 8vo. 7s. 6d.*

A highly interesting account of a generation in Australia by a distinguished writer. Mrs. Cross's style is picturesque, and the book is more attractive than many novels. The early difficulties of Australian settlers, life in the towns and life on the farms are vividly described.

LETTERS FROM A SELF-MADE MERCHANT TO HIS SON. By GEORGE HORACE LORIMER. *Crown 8vo. 6s.*

This book is a masterpiece of humour and sound sense. It purports to be a collection of letters written by J. Graham, head of a great packing company in Chicago, to his son Pierrepont, and it describes in a racy and interesting form the secrets of success in business and in life.

WHEN I WAS A CHILD. By AN OLD POTTER BOY. *Crown 8vo. 6s.*

A BOOK OF THE COUNTRY AND THE GARDEN. By H. M. BATSON. Illustrated by F. CARRUTHERS GOULD and A. C. GOULD. *Demy 8vo. 10s. 6d.*

SHAKESPEARE'S GARDEN. By the Rev. J. H. BLOOM. With Illustrations. *Fcap. 8vo. 3s. 6d.; leather, 3s. 6d. net.*

A CONCISE HANDBOOK OF HERBACEOUS PLANTS. By H. M. BATSON. *Fcap. 8vo. 3s. 6d.*

A very complete and concise guide in alphabetical order.

THE LAND OF THE BLACK MOUNTAIN. Being a description of Montenegro. By R. WYON and G. PRANCE. With 40 Illustrations. *Crown 8vo. 6s.*

A BOOK OF EXMOOR. By F. J. SNELL. Illustrated. *Crown 8vo. 6s.*

This book deals with a variety of topics, embracing legend, folklore, dialect, sport, biography, history, and natural history, and renders accessible to the public a mass of particulars hitherto attainable only in expensive monographs or in scattered periodicals. The author has been at immense pains to consult every known source of information, both printed and oral; and his aim has been to produce, not so much a guide-book, but something more satisfying and substantial, viz. an exhaustive account of the matters in question. There are numerous illustrations.

THE DEVOTIONS OF BISHOP ANDREWES. By F. E. BRIGHTMAN, M.A., of Pusey House, Oxford. *Crown 8vo. 6s.*

This elaborate work has been in preparation for many years, and is the most complete edition that has ever been published of the famous devotions. It contains a long Introduction, with numerous Notes and References.

THE SPIRIT AND ORIGIN OF CHRISTIAN MONASTICISM. By JAMES O. HANNAY, M.A. *Crown 8vo. 6s.*

THE SATIRES OF JUVENAL. Translated by S. G. OWEN. *Crown 8vo. 2s. 6d.*
[Classical Translations.

THE ENGLISH SUNDAY. By E. R. BERNARD, M.A., Canon of Salisbury. *Fcap. 8vo. 1s. 6d.*

The Little Library

Pott 8vo, cloth, 1s. 6d. net; leather, 2s. 6d. net each volume.

ROMANY RYE. By GEORGE BORROW. With Notes and an Introduction by JOHN SAMPSON.

ESMOND. By W. M. THACKERAY. Edited by STEPHEN GWYNN.

CHRISTMAS BOOKS. By W. M. THACKERAY. Edited by STEPHEN GWYNN.

CHRISTMAS BOOKS. By CHARLES DICKENS. Edited by STEPHEN GWYNN. *Two Volumes.*

A LITTLE BOOK OF ENGLISH SONNETS. Edited by J. B. B. NICHOLS.

THE SCARLET LETTER. By NATHANIEL HAWTHORNE.

The Arden Shakespeare

General Editor—W. J. CRAIG.

OTHELLO. Edited by H. C. HART. *Demy 8vo.* 3s. 6d.

CYMBELINE. Edited by EDWARD DOWDEN. *Demy 8vo.* 3s. 6d.

Little Biographies

Cloth, 3s. 6d.; leather, 4s. net.

THE YOUNG PRETENDER. By C. S. TERRY. With 12 Illustrations.

ROBERT BURNS. By T. F. HENDERSON. With 12 Illustrations.

CHATHAM. By A. S. M'DOWALL. With 12 Illustrations.

TENNYSON. By A. C. BENSON, M.A. With 12 Illustrations. *Fcap. 8vo.*

The Little Guides

Pott 8vo, cloth, 3s.; leather, 3s. 6d. net.

CORNWALL. By A. L. SALMON. Illustrated by B. C. BOULTER.

KENT. By G. CLINCH. Illustrated by F. D. BEDFORD.

HERTFORDSHIRE. By H. W. TOMPKINS, F.R.H.S. Illustrated by E. H. NEW.

ROME. By C. G. ELLABY. Illustrated by B. C. BOULTER.

The Library of Devotion

Pott 8vo, cloth, 2s.; leather, 2s. 6d. net.

GRACE ABOUNDING. By JOHN BUNYAN. Edited by S. C. FREER, M.A.

BISHOP WILSON'S SACRA PRIVATA. Edited by A. E Burn, B.D.

THE DEVOTIONS OF ST. ANSELM. Edited by C. C. J. Webb, M.A.

LYRA SACRA: A Book of Sacred Verse. Selected and edited by H. C. Beeching, M.A., Canon of Westminster.

Educational Books

AN INTRODUCTION TO THE STUDY OF TEXTILE FABRICS AND TEXTILE DESIGN. By Aldred F. Barker, Author of 'Pattern Analysis,' etc. With numerous Diagrams and Illustrations. *Demy 8vo.*

AGRICULTURAL GEOLOGY. By J. E. Marr, F.R.S. With numerous Illustrations. *Crown 8vo.*

MENSURATION. By C. T. Millis, M.I.M.E., Principal of the Borough Polytechnic College. With Diagrams. *Crown 8vo.*

THE ACTS OF THE APOSTLES. Edited by A. E. Rubie, M.A., Headmaster Royal Naval School, Eltham. *Crown 8vo.* 2s. [*Methuen's Junior School Books.*

A JUNIOR FRENCH GRAMMAR. By L. A. Sornet and M. J. Acatos, Modern Language Masters at King Edward's School, Birmingham. [*Methuen's Junior School Books.*

THE STUDENTS' PRAYER BOOK. Part I. Morning and Evening Prayer and Litany. Edited by W. H. Flecker, M.A., D.C.L., Headmaster of the Dean Close School, Cheltenham. *Crown 8vo.* 2s. 6d.

Fiction

LORD LEONARD THE LUCKLESS. By W. E. Norris. *Crown 8vo.* 6s.

THE BETTER SORT. By Henry James. *Crown 8vo.* 6s.

ANTHEA'S WAY. By Adeline Sergeant. *Crown 8vo.* 6s.

OUTSIDE AND OVERSEAS. By G. Makgill. *Crown 8vo.* 6s.

THE SQUIREEN. By Shan. F. Bullock. *Crown 8vo.* 6s.

AUNT BETHIA'S BUTTON. By J. Randal. *Crown 8vo.* 6s.

MESSRS. METHUEN'S ANNOUNCEMENTS

LOVE IN A LIFE. By ALLAN MONKHOUSE. *Crown 8vo. 6s.*

A MIXED MARRIAGE. By Mrs. F. E. PENNY. *Crown 8vo. 6s.*

THE SWORD OF AZRAEL, a Chronicle of the Great Mutiny. By R. E. FORREST. *Crown 8vo. 6s.*

A FREE LANCE OF TO-DAY. By HUGH CLIFFORD. *Crown 8vo. 6s.*

A STRETCH OFF THE LAND. By C. STEWART BOWLES. *Crown 8vo. 6s.*

THE KNIGHT PUNCTILIOUS. By ARTHUR MOORE. *Crown 8vo. 6s.*

THE POET'S CHILD. By EMMA BROOKE. *Crown 8vo. 6s.*

THE DIVERTED VILLAGE. By GRACE RHYS and ANOTHER. With Illustrations by DOROTHY GWYN JEFFRIES. *Crown 8vo. 6s.*

THE RED HOUSE. By Mrs. E. BLAND (E. NESBIT). Illustrated. *Crown 8vo. 6s.*

WORLD'S PEOPLE. By JULIEN GORDON. *Crown 8vo. 6s.*

THE CYNIC AND THE SYREN. By J. W. MAYALL. *Crown 8vo. 6s.*

A BRANDED NAME. By J. BLOUNDELLE BURTON. *Crown 8vo. 6s.*

SILENT DOMINION. By Mrs. E. W. TRAFFORD-TAUNTON. *Crown 8vo. 6s.*

THE MACHINATIONS OF THE MYO-OK. By CECIL LOWIS. *Crown 8vo. 6s.*

ABRAHAM'S SACRIFICE. By GUSTAF JANSON. *Crown 8vo. 6s.*

PLAIN AND VELDT. By J. H. M. ABBOT, Author of 'Tommy Cornstalk.' *Crown 8vo. 6s.*

BY A FINNISH LAKE. By PAUL WAINEMAN. *Crown 8vo. 6s.*

A LOST ESTATE. By M. E. MANN. A New Edition. *Crown 8vo. 6s.*

THE PARISH OF HILBY. By M. E. MANN. A New Edition. *Crown 8vo. 6s.*

LITTLE TU'PENNY. By S. BARING-GOULD. A New Edition *Crown 8vo. 6d.*

FOUR NOVELS TRANSFERRED

New Editions. Crown 8vo. 3s. 6d. each.

TALES OF SPACE AND TIME. By H. G. WELLS.
WHEN THE SLEEPER WAKES. By H. G. WELLS.
LOVE AND MR. LEWISHAM. By H. G. WELLS.
THE INVISIBLE MAN. By H. G. WELLS.

The Novelist

Messrs. METHUEN are issuing under the above general title a Monthly Series of Novels by popular authors at the price of Sixpence. Each Number is as long as the average Six Shilling Novel.

Jan. DRIFT. By L. T. MEADE.
Feb. THE MASTER OF BEECHWOOD. By ADELINE SERGEANT.
March. CLEMENTINA. By A. E. W. MASON.
April. THE ALIEN. By F. F. MONTRESOR.
May. THE BROOM SQUIRE. By S. BARING-GOULD.
June. HONEY. By HELEN MATHERS.
July. THE FOOTSTEPS OF A THRONE. By MAX PEMBERTON.

Additional Volumes and Reprints

III. THE INCA'S TREASURE. By ERNEST GLANVILLE. *Reprint.*
IX. A FLASH OF SUMMER. By Mrs. W. K. CLIFFORD, *in place of* 'The Adventure of Princess Sylvia.'

Methuen's Sixpenny Library

New Volumes 1903.

Jan. A STATE SECRET. By B. M. CROKER.
Feb. SAM'S SWEETHEART. By HELEN MATHERS.
March. HANDLEY CROSS. By R. S. SURTEES.
April. ANNE MAULEVERER. By Mrs. CAFFYN.
May. THE ADVENTURERS. By H. B. MARRIOT WATSON.
THE CEDAR STAR. By M. E. MANN.
June. MASTER OF MEN. By E. P. OPPENHEIM.
July. THE TRAIL OF THE SWORD. By GILBERT PARKER.

A Catalogue of Messrs. Methuen's Publications

Part I.—General Literature

Jacob Abbot. THE BEECHNUT BOOK. Edited by E. V. Lucas. Illustrated. *Square Fcap 8vo. 2s. 6d.*
[Little Blue Books.

W. F. Adeney, M.A. See Bennett and Adeney.

Æschylus. AGAMEMNON, CHOEPHOROE, EUMENIDES. Translated by Lewis Campbell, LL.D., late Professor of Greek at St. Andrews. 5s.
[Classical Translations.

G. A. Aitken. See Swift.

William Alexander, D.D., Archbishop of Armagh. THOUGHTS AND COUNSELS OF MANY YEARS. Selected from the writings of Archbishop Alexander. *Square Pott 8vo. 2s. 6d.*

Aristophanes. THE FROGS. Translated into English by E. W. Huntingford, M.A., Professor of Classics in Trinity College, Toronto. *Crown 8vo. 2s. 6d.*

Aristotle. THE NICOMACHEAN ETHICS. Edited, with an Introduction and Notes, by John Burnet, M.A., Professor of Greek at St. Andrews. *Demy 8vo. 15s. net.*
'We have seldom, if ever, seen an edition of any classical author in which what is held in common with other commentators is so clearly put, and what is original is of such value and interest.'—*Pilot.*

J. B. Atkins. THE RELIEF OF LADYSMITH. With 16 Plans and Illustrations. *Third Edition. Crown 8vo. 6s.*

J. B. Atlay. See R. H. Barham.

St. Augustine, THE CONFESSIONS OF. Newly Translated, with an Introduction and Notes, by C. Bigg, D.D., late Student of Christ Church. *Third Edition. Pott 8vo. Cloth, 2s; leather, 2s. 6d. net.*
[Library of Devotion.
'The translation is an excellent piece of English, and the introduction is a masterly exposition. We augur well of a series which begins so satisfactorily.'—*Times.*

Jane Austen. PRIDE AND PREJUDICE. Edited by E. V. Lucas. *Two Volumes. Pott 8vo. Each volume, cloth, 1s. 6d.; leather, 2s. 6d. net.* [Little Library.

NORTHANGER ABBEY. Edited by E. V. Lucas. *Pott 8vo. Cloth, 1s. 6d.; leather, 2s. 6d. net.* [Little Library.

Constance Bache. BROTHER MUSICIANS. Reminiscences of Edward and Walter Bache. With 16 Illustrations. *Crown 8vo. 6s. net.*

R. S. S. Baden-Powell, Major-General. THE DOWNFALL OF PREMPEH. A Diary of Life in Ashanti, 1895. With 21 Illustrations and a Map. *Third Edition. Large Crown 8vo. 6s.*

THE MATABELE CAMPAIGN, 1896. With nearly 100 Illustrations. *Fourth and Cheaper Edition. Large Crown 8vo. 6s.*

Graham Balfour. THE LIFE OF ROBERT LOUIS STEVENSON. *Second Edition. Two Volumes. Demy 8vo. 25s. net.*
'Mr. Balfour has done his work extremely well—done it, in fact, as Stevenson himself would have wished it done, with care and skill and affectionate appreciation.'—*Westminster Gazette.*

S. E. Bally. A FRENCH COMMERCIAL READER. With Vocabulary. *Second Edition. Crown 8vo. 2s.*
[Commercial Series.
FRENCH COMMERCIAL CORRESPONDENCE. With Vocabulary. *Third Edition. Crown 8vo. 2s.*
[Commercial Series.
A GERMAN COMMERCIAL READER. With Vocabulary. *Crown 8vo. 2s.*
[Commercial Series.
GERMAN COMMERCIAL CORRESPONDENCE. With Vocabulary. *Crown 8vo. 2s. 6d.* [Commercial Series.

Elizabeth L. Banks. THE AUTOBIOGRAPHY OF A 'NEWSPAPER

GIRL.' With Portrait of the Author and her Dog. *Crown 8vo.* 6s.

'A picture of a strenuous and busy life, perhaps the truest and most faithful representation of the ups and downs of a lady journalist's career ever given to the public. A very lively and interesting book.'—*Daily Telegraph.*

'A very amusing, cheery, good-natured account of a young lady's journalistic struggle in America and London.'—*Times.*

R. H. Barham. THE INGOLDSBY LEGENDS. Edited by J. B. Atlay. *Two Volumes. Pott 8vo. Each volume, cloth, 1s. 6d. net; leather, 2s. 6d. net.*
[The Little Library.

S. Baring-Gould, Author of 'Mehalah,' etc. THE LIFE OF NAPOLEON BONAPARTE. With over 450 Illustrations in the Text, and 12 Photogravure Plates. *Gilt top. Large quarto.* 36s.

'The main feature of this gorgeous volume is its great wealth of beautiful photogravures and finely-executed wood engravings, constituting a complete pictorial chronicle of Napoleon I.'s personal history.'—*Daily Telegraph.*

THE TRAGEDY OF THE CÆSARS. With numerous Illustrations from Busts, Gems, Cameos, etc. *Fifth Edition. Royal 8vo.* 15s.

'A most splendid and fascinating book on a subject of undying interest. It is brilliantly written, and the illustrations are supplied on a scale of profuse magnificence.' —*Daily Chronicle.*

A BOOK OF FAIRY TALES. With numerous Illustrations and Initial Letters by ARTHUR J. GASKIN. *Second Edition. Crown 8vo. Buckram.* 6s.

OLD ENGLISH FAIRY TALES. With numerous Illustrations by F. D. BEDFORD. *Second Edition. Cr. 8vo. Buckram.* 6s.

'A charming volume.'—*Guardian.*

THE CROCK OF GOLD. Fairy Stories. *Crown 8vo.* 6s.

'Twelve delightful fairy tales.'—*Punch.*

THE VICAR OF MORWENSTOW: A Biography. A new and Revised Edition. With Portrait. *Crown 8vo.* 3s. 6d.

A completely new edition of the well-known biography of R. S. Hawker.

DARTMOOR: A Descriptive and Historical Sketch. With Plans and numerous Illustrations. *Crown 8vo.* 6s.

'A most delightful guide, companion and instructor.'—*Scotsman.*

THE BOOK OF THE WEST. With numerous Illustrations. *Two volumes.* Vol. I. Devon. *Second Edition.* Vol. II. Cornwall. *Second Edition. Crown 8vo.* 6s. each.

'Bracing as the air of Dartmoor, the legend weird as twilight over Dozmare Pool, they give us a very good idea of this enchanting and beautiful district.'—*Guardian.*

A BOOK OF BRITTANY. With numerous Illustrations. *Crown 8vo.* 6s.

Uniform in scope and size with Mr. Baring-Gould's well-known books on Devon, Cornwall, and Dartmoor.

BRITTANY. Illustrated by Miss J. WYLIE. *Pott 8vo. Cloth, 3s.; leather, 3s. 6d. net.*
[The Little Guides.

'A dainty representative of "The Little Guides."'—*Times.*

'An excellent little guide-book.'—*Daily News.*

OLD COUNTRY LIFE. With 67 Illustrations. *Fifth Edition. Large Cr. 8vo.* 6s.

AN OLD ENGLISH HOME. With numerous Plans and Illustrations. *Cr. 8vo.* 6s.

HISTORIC ODDITIES AND STRANGE EVENTS. *Fifth Edition. Cr. 8vo.* 6s.

YORKSHIRE ODDITIES AND STRANGE EVENTS. *Fifth Edition. Crown 8vo.* 6s.

STRANGE SURVIVALS AND SUPERSTITIONS. *Second Edition. Cr. 8vo.* 6s.

A GARLAND OF COUNTRY SONG: English Folk Songs with their Traditional Melodies. Collected and arranged by S. BARING-GOULD and H. F. SHEPPARD. *Demy 4to.* 6s.

SONGS OF THE WEST: Traditional Ballads and Songs of the West of England, with their Melodies. Collected by S. BARING-GOULD, M.A., and H. F. SHEPPARD, M.A. In 4 Parts. *Parts I., II., III.,* 3s. *each. Part IV.,* 5s. In One Volume, French Morocco, 15s.

'A rich collection of humour, pathos, grace, and poetic fancy.'—*Saturday Review.*

W. E. Barnes, D.D. ISAIAH. *Two Volumes. Fcap. 8vo.* 2s. *net each.* Vol. I. With Map. [Churchman's Bible.

Mrs. P. A. Barnett. A LITTLE BOOK OF ENGLISH PROSE. *Pott 8vo. Cloth, 1s. 6d. net; leather, 2s. 6d. net.*
[Little Library.

R. R. N Baron, M.A. FRENCH PROSE COMPOSITION. *Crown 8vo.* 2s. 6d. Key, 3s. net.

H. M. Barron, M.A., Wadham College, Oxford. TEXTS FOR SERMONS. With a Preface by Canon SCOTT HOLLAND. *Crown 8vo.* 3s. 6d

C. F. Bastable, M.A., Professor of Economics at Trinity College, Dublin. THE COMMERCE OF NATIONS. *Second Edition. Crown 8vo* 2s. 6d.
[Social Questions Series.

H. M. Batson. See Edward FitzGerald.

A Hulme Beaman. PONS ASINORUM; OR, A GUIDE TO BRIDGE. *Second Edition.* *Fcap. 8vo.* 2s.

W. S. Beard, Headmaster Modern School, Fareham. JUNIOR ARITHMETIC EXAMINATION PAPERS. *Fcap. 8vo.* 1s. [Junior Examination Series.

Peter Beckford. THOUGHTS ON HUNTING. Edited by J. Otho Paget, and Illustrated by G. H. Jalland. *Demy 8vo.* 10s. 6d.

William Beckford. THE HISTORY OF THE CALIPH VATHEK. Edited by E. Denison Ross. *Pott 8vo. Cloth,* 1s. 6d. *net; leather,* 2s 6d. *net.* [Little Library.

F. D. Bedford. See E. V. Lucas.

H. C. Beeching, M.A. See Tennyson.

Jacob Behmen. THE SUPERSENSUAL LIFE. Edited by Bernard Holland. *Fcap. 8vo.* 3s. 6d.

Hilaire Belloc. PARIS. With Maps and Illustrations. *Crown 8vo.* 6s.

H. H. L. Bellot, M.A. THE INNER AND MIDDLE TEMPLE. With numerous Illustrations. *Crown 8vo.* 6s. *net.*
'A vast store of entertaining material.'—*Liverpool Mercury.*
'A delightful and excellently illustrated book; a real encyclopædia of Temple history.'—*Pilot.*

W. H. Bennett, M.A. A PRIMER OF THE BIBLE. *Second Edition.* *Crown 8vo.* 2s. 6d.
'The work of an honest, fearless, and sound critic, and an excellent guide in a small compass to the books of the Bible.'—*Manchester Guardian.*

W. H. Bennett and W. F. Adeney. A BIBLICAL INTRODUCTION. *Crown 8vo.* 7s. 6d.
'It makes available to the ordinary reader the best scholarship of the day in the field of Biblical introduction. We know of no book which comes into competition with it.'—*Manchester Guardian.*

A. C. Benson, M.A. THE LIFE OF LORD TENNYSON. With 12 Illustrations. *Fcap. 8vo. Cloth,* 3s. 6d.; *Leather,* 4s. *net.* [Little Biographies.

R. M. Benson. THE WAY OF HOLINESS: a Devotional Commentary on the 119th Psalm. *Crown 8vo.* 5s.

M. Bidez. See Parmentier.

C. Bigg, D.D. See St. Augustine, À Kempis, and William Law.

C. R. D. Biggs, B.D. THE EPISTLE TO THE PHILIPPIANS. Edited by. *Fcap. 8vo.* 1s. 6d. *net.* [Churchman's Bible.
'Mr. Biggs' work is very thorough, and he has managed to compress a good deal of information into a limited space.'—*Guardian.*

T. Herbert Bindley, B.D. THE OECUMENICAL DOCUMENTS OF THE FAITH. With Introductions and Notes. *Crown 8vo.* 6s.
A historical account of the Creeds.

William Blake. See Little Library.

B. Blaxland, M.A. THE SONG OF SONGS. Being Selections from St. Bernard. *Pott 8vo. Cloth,* 2s.; *leather,* 2s. 6d. *net.* [Library of Devotion.

George Body, D.D. THE SOUL'S PILGRIMAGE: Devotional Readings from his published and unpublished writings. Selected and arranged by J. H. Burn, B.D. *Pott 8vo.* 2s. 6d.

Cardinal Bona. A GUIDE TO ETERNITY. Edited with an Introduction and Notes, by J. W. Stanbridge, B.D., late Fellow of St. John's College, Oxford. *Pott 8vo. Cloth,* 2s.; *leather,* 2s. 6d. *net.* [Library of Devotion.

F. C. Boon, B.A. A COMMERCIAL GEOGRAPHY OF FOREIGN NATIONS. *Crown 8vo.* 2s.
Commercial Series.

George Borrow. LAVENGRO. Edited by F. Hindes Groome. *Two Volumes. Pott 8vo. Each volume, cloth,* 1s. 6d. *net; leather,* 2s. 6d. *net.* [Little Library.

J. Ritzema Bos. AGRICULTURAL ZOOLOGY. Translated by J. R. Ainsworth Davis, M.A. With an Introduction by Eleanor A. Ormerod, F.E.S. With 155 Illustrations. *Cr. 8vo.* 3s. 6d.

C. G. Botting, B.A. JUNIOR LATIN EXAMINATION PAPERS. *Fcap. 8vo.* 1s. [Junior Examination Series.
EASY GREEK EXERCISES. *Cr. 8vo.* 2s.

E. M. Bowden. THE EXAMPLE OF BUDDHA: Being Quotations from Buddhist Literature for each Day in the Year. *Third Edition.* *16mo.* 2s. 6d.

E. Bowmaker. THE HOUSING OF THE WORKING CLASSES. *Crown 8vo.* 2s. 6d. [Social Questions Series.

F. G. Brabant, M.A. SUSSEX. Illustrated by E. H. New. *Pott 8vo. Cloth,* 3s.; *leather,* 3s. 6d. *net.* [Little Guides.
'A charming little book; as full of sound information as it is practical in conception.'—*Athenæum.*

THE ENGLISH LAKES. Illustrated by E. H. New. *Pott 8vo. Cloth,* 4s.; *leather,* 4s. 6d. *net.* [The Little Guides.

Miss M. Brodrick and Miss Anderson Morton. A CONCISE HANDBOOK OF EGYPTIAN ARCHÆOLOGY. With many Illustrations. *Crown 8vo.* 3s. 6d.

E. W. Brooks. See F. J. Hamilton.

C. L. Brownell. THE HEART OF JAPAN. Illustrated. *Crown 8vo.* 6s.
'These lively pages are full of portraits from the life.'—*Morning Post.*

'It is the work of one who has lived in Japan among the people.'—*Athenæum*.

'A more readable and interesting book about Japan has not been written.'
—*Scotsman*.

Robert Browning. SELECTIONS FROM THE EARLY POEMS OF. With Introduction and Notes by W. HALL GRIFFIN. *Pott 8vo.* 1s. 6d. *net* ; *leather*, 2s. 6d. *net*. [Little Library.

O. Browning, M.A. A SHORT HISTORY OF MEDIÆVAL ITALY, A.D. 1250-1530. *In Two Volumes. Crown 8vo.* 5s. *each*.
VOL. I. 1250-1409.—Guelphs and Ghibellines.
VOL. II. 1409-1530.—The Age of the Condottieri.

J. Buchan. See Isaak Walton.

Miss Bulley. See Lady Dilke.

John Bunyan. THE PILGRIM'S PROGRESS. Edited, with an Introduction, by C. H. FIRTH, M.A. With 39 Illustrations by R. ANNING BELL. *Cr. 8vo.* 6s.
'The best "Pilgrim's Progress."'—
Educational Times.

G. J. Burch, M.A., F.R.S. A MANUAL OF ELECTRICAL SCIENCE. With numerous Illustrations. *Crown 8vo.* 3s. [University Extension Series.

Gelett Burgess. GOOPS AND HOW TO BE THEM. With numerous Illustrations. *Small 4to.* 6s.

A. E. Burn, B.D., Examining Chaplain to the Bishop of Lichfield. AN INTRODUCTION TO THE HISTORY OF THE CREEDS. *Demy 8vo.* 10s. 6d. [Handbooks of Theology.
'This book may be expected to hold its place as an authority on its subject.'—*Spectator*.

J. H. Burn, B.D., F.R.S.E. A MANUAL OF CONSOLATION FROM THE SAINTS AND FATHERS. *Pott 8vo.* Cloth, 2s. ; *leather*, 2s. 6d. *net*. [Library of Devotion.

Robert Burns. THE POEMS OF ROBERT BURNS. Edited by ANDREW LANG and W. A. CRAIGIE. With Portrait. *Second Edition. Demy 8vo, gilt top.* 6s.

J. B. Bury, LL.D. See Gibbon.

Alfred Caldecott, D.D. THE PHILOSOPHY OF RELIGION IN ENGLAND AND AMERICA. *Demy 8vo.* 10s. 6d. [Handbooks of Theology.
'A lucid and informative account, which certainly deserves a place in every philosophical library.'—*Scotsman*.

D. S. Calderwood, Headmaster of the Normal School, Edinburgh. TEST CARDS IN EUCLID AND ALGEBRA. In three packets of 40, with Answers. 1s. each. Or in three Books, price 2d., 2d., and 3d.

E. F. H. Capey. THE LIFE OF ERASMUS. With 12 Illustrations. *Cloth*, 3s. 6d. *net* ; *leather*, 4s. *net*. [Little Biographies.

Thomas Carlyle. THE FRENCH REVOLUTION. Edited by C. R. L. FLETCHER, Fellow of Magdalen College, Oxford. *Three Volumes. Crown 8vo.* 6s. each. [Methuen's Standard Library.
'This last edition, or annotation, may be said to be final. It will be impossible to produce any other in which the notes shall be more thorough, in which every point will be more accurately noted, or in which the correctness of date, locality, and every other detail will be better preserved. The work has been done once for all, it cannot be done again.'—*Speaker*.

R. M. and A. J. Carlyle, M.A. BISHOP LATIMER. With Portrait. *Crown 8vo.* 3s. 6d. [Leaders of Religion.

C. C. Channer and M. E. Roberts. LACE-MAKING IN THE MIDLANDS, PAST AND PRESENT. With 16 full-page Illustrations. *Crown 8vo.* 2s. 6d.
'An interesting book, illustrated by fascinating photographs.'—*Speaker*.

Lord Chesterfield, THE LETTERS OF, TO HIS SON. Edited, with an Introduction, by C. STRACHEY, and Notes by A. CALTHROP. *Two Volumes. Crown 8vo.* 6s. *each*. [Methuen's Standard Library.

F. W. Christian. THE CAROLINE ISLANDS. With many Illustrations and Maps. *Demy 8vo.* 12s. 6d. *net*.

Cicero. DE ORATORE I. Translated by E. N. P. MOOR, M.A. *Crown 8vo.* 3s. 6d. [Classical Translations.

SELECT ORATIONS (Pro Milone, Pro Murena, Philippic II., In Catilinam). Translated by H. E. D. BLAKISTON, M.A., Fellow and Tutor of Trinity College, Oxford. *Crown 8vo.* 5s. [Classical Translations.

DE NATURA DEORUM. Translated by F. BROOKS, M.A., late Scholar of Balliol College, Oxford. *Crown 8vo.* 3s. 6d. [Classical Translations.

DE OFFICIIS. Translated by G. B. GARDINER, M.A. *Crown 8vo.* 2s. 6d. [Classical Translations.

F. A. Clarke, M.A. BISHOP KEN. With Portrait. *Crown 8vo.* 3s. 6d. [Leaders of Religion.

E. H. Colbeck, M.D. DISEASES OF THE HEART. With numerous Illustrations. *Demy 8vo.* 12s.

W. G. Collingwood, M.A. THE LIFE OF JOHN RUSKIN. With Portraits. *Cheap Edition. Crown 8vo.* 6s.

J. C. Collins, M.A. See Tennyson.

W. E. Collins, M.A. THE BEGINNINGS OF ENGLISH CHRISTIANITY. With Map. *Crown 8vo.* 3s. 6d. [Churchman's Library.

A. M. Cook, M.A. See E. C. Marchant.

R. W. Cooke-Taylor. THE FACTORY SYSTEM. *Crown 8vo. 2s. 6d.*
[Social Questions Series.

Marie Corelli. THE PASSING OF THE GREAT QUEEN: A Tribute to the Noble Life of Victoria Regina. *Small 4to. 1s.*

A CHRISTMAS GREETING. *Sm. 4to. 1s.*

Rosemary Cotes. DANTE'S GARDEN. With a Frontispiece. *Second Edition. Fcap. 8vo. cloth 2s. 6d.; leather, 3s. 6d. net.*

Harold Cox, B.A. LAND NATIONALIZATION. *Crown 8vo. 2s. 6d.*
[Social Questions Series.

W. J. Craig. See Shakespeare.

W. A. Craigie. A PRIMER OF BURNS. *Crown 8vo. 2s. 6d.*

Mrs. Craik. JOHN HALIFAX, GENTLEMAN. Edited by ANNIE MATHESON. *Two Volumes. Pott 8vo. Each Volume, Cloth, 1s. 6d. net; leather, 2s. 6d. net.* [Little Library.

Richard Crashaw, THE ENGLISH POEMS OF. Edited by EDWARD HUTTON. *Pott 8vo. Cloth, 1s. 6d. net; leather, 2s. 6d. net.* [Little Library.

F. G. Crawford. See Mary C. Danson.

C. G. Crump, M.A. See Thomas Ellwood.

F. H. E. Cunliffe, Fellow of All Souls' College, Oxford. THE HISTORY OF THE BOER WAR. With many Illustrations, Plans, and Portraits. *In 2 vols. Vol. I., 15s.*

E. L. Cutts, D.D. AUGUSTINE OF CANTERBURY. With Portrait. *Crown 8vo. 3s. 6d.* [Leaders of Religion.

The Brothers Dalziel. A RECORD OF FIFTY YEARS' WORK. With 150 Illustrations. *Large 4to. 21s. net.*
The record of the work of the celebrated Engravers, containing a Gallery of beautiful Pictures by F. Walker, Sir J. Millais, Lord Leighton, and other great Artists. The book is a history of the finest black-and-white work of the nineteenth century.

G. W. Daniell, M.A. BISHOP WILBERFORCE. With Portrait. *Crown 8vo. 3s. 6d.* [Leaders of Religion.

Mary C. Danson and F. G. Crawford. FATHERS IN THE FAITH. *Small 8vo. 1s. 6d.*

Dante Alighieri. LA COMMEDIA DI DANTE. The Italian Text edited by PAGET TOYNBEE, Litt.D., M.A. *Demy 8vo. Gilt top. 8s. 6d. Also, Crown 8vo. 6s.*
[Methuen's Standard Library.

THE INFERNO OF DANTE. Translated by H. F. CARY. Edited by PAGET TOYNBEE, Litt.D., M.A. *Pott 8vo. Cloth, 1s. 6d. net; leather 2s. 6d. net.*
[Little Library.

THE PURGATORIO OF DANTE. Translated by H. F. CARY. Edited by PAGET TOYNBEE, Litt.D., M.A. *Pott 8vo. Cloth, 1s. 6d. net; leather, 2s. 6d. net.*
[Little Library.

THE PARADISO OF DANTE. Translated by H. F. CARY. Edited by PAGET TOYNBEE, Litt.D., M.A. *Post 8vo. Cloth, 1s. 6d. net; leather, 2s. 6d. net.*
[Little Library.

See also Paget Toynbee.

A. C. Deane. Edited by. A LITTLE BOOK OF LIGHT VERSE. *Pott 8vo. Cloth, 1s. 6d. net; leather, 2s. 6d. net.*
[Little Library.

Percy Dearmer. See N. Hawthorne.

Leon Delbos. THE METRIC SYSTEM. *Crown 8vo. 2s.*
A theoretical and practical guide, for use in schools and by the general reader.

Demosthenes: THE OLYNTHIACS AND PHILIPPICS. Translated upon a new principle by OTHO HOLLAND. *Crown 8vo. 2s. 6d.*

Demosthenes. AGAINST CONON AND CALLICLES. Edited with Notes and Vocabulary, by F. DARWIN SWIFT, M.A. *Fcap. 8vo. 2s.*

Charles Dickens.
THE ROCHESTER EDITION.
Crown 8vo. Each Volume, cloth, 3s. 6d.
With Introductions by GEORGE GISSING, Notes by F. G. KITTON, and Topographical Illustrations.

THE PICKWICK PAPERS. With Illustrations by E. H. NEW. *Two Volumes.*

NICHOLAS NICKLEBY. With Illustrations by R. J. WILLIAMS. *Two Volumes.*

BLEAK HOUSE. With Illustrations by BEATRICE ALCOCK. *Two Volumes.*

OLIVER TWIST. With Illustrations by E. H. NEW.

THE OLD CURIOSITY SHOP. With Illustrations by G. M. BRIMELOW. *Two Volumes.*

BARNABY RUDGE. With Illustrations by BEATRICE ALCOCK. *Two Volumes.*

G. L. Dickinson, M.A., Fellow of King's College, Cambridge. THE GREEK VIEW OF LIFE. *Second Edition. Crown 8vo. 2s. 6d.* [University Extension Series.

H. N. Dickson, F.R.S.E., F.R.Met. Soc. METEOROLOGY. The Elements of Weather and Climate. Illustrated. *Crown 8vo. 2s. 6d.* [University Extension Series.

Lady Dilke, Miss Bulley, and **Miss Whitley.** WOMEN'S WORK. *Crown 8vo. 2s. 6d.* [Social Questions Series.

P. H. Ditchfield, M.A., F.S.A. ENGLISH VILLAGES. Illustrated. *Crown 8vo. 6s.*
'A book which for its instructive and pictorial value should find a place in every village library.'—*Scotsman.*

THE STORY OF OUR ENGLISH TOWNS. With Introduction by AUGUSTUS JESSOP, D.D. *Second Edition. Crown 8vo. 6s.*

OLD ENGLISH CUSTOMS: Extant at the Present Time. An Account of Local Observances, Festival Customs, and Ancient Ceremonies yet Surviving in Great Britain. *Crown 8vo. 6s.*

W. M. Dixon, M.A. A PRIMER OF TENNYSON. *Second Edition. Crown 8vo. 2s. 6d.*

'Much sound and well-expressed criticism. The bibliography is a boon.'—*Speaker.*

ENGLISH POETRY FROM BLAKE TO BROWNING. *Second Edition. Crown 8vo. 2s. 6d.* [University Extension Series.

E. Dowden, Litt.D. See Shakespeare.

J. Dowden, D.D., Lord Bishop of Edinburgh. THE WORKMANSHIP OF THE PRAYER BOOK: Its Literary and Liturgical Aspects. *Second Edition. Crown 8vo. 3s. 6d.* [Churchman's Library.

S. R. Driver., D.D., Canon of Christ Church, Regius Professor of Hebrew in the University of Oxford. SERMONS ON SUBJECTS CONNECTED WITH THE OLD TESTAMENT. *Crown 8vo. 6s.*

'A welcome companion to the author's famous "Introduction."'—*Guardian.*

S. J. Duncan (MRS. COTES), Author of 'A Voyage of Consolation.' ON THE OTHER SIDE OF THE LATCH. *Second Edition. Crown 8vo. 6s.*

J. T. Dunn, D.Sc., **and V. A. Mundella.** GENERAL ELEMENTARY SCIENCE. With 114 Illustrations. *Crown 8vo. 3s. 6d.* [Methuen's Science Primers.

The Earl of Durham. A REPORT ON CANADA. With an Introductory Note. *Demy 8vo. 7s. 6d. net.*

A reprint of the celebrated Report which Lord Durham made to the British Government on the state of British North America in 1839. It is probably the most important utterance on British colonial policy ever published.

W. A. Dutt. NORFOLK. Illustrated by B. C. BOULTER. *Pott 8vo. Cloth, 3s.; leather, 3s. 6d. net.* [Little Guides.

Clement Edwards. RAILWAY NATIONALIZATION. *Crown 8vo. 2s. 6d.* [Social Questions Series.

W. Douglas Edwards. COMMERCIAL LAW. *Crown 8vo. 2s.* [Commercial Series.

H. E. Egerton, M.A. A HISTORY OF BRITISH COLONIAL POLICY. *Demy 8vo. 12s. 6d.*

'It is a good book, distinguished by accuracy in detail, clear arrangement of facts, and a broad grasp of principles.'—*Manchester Guardian.*

Thomas Ellwood, THE HISTORY OF THE LIFE OF. Edited by C. G. CRUMP, M.A. *Crown 8vo. 6s.* [Methuen's Standard Library.

This edition is the only one which contains the complete book as originally published. It has a long Introduction and many Footnotes.

E. Engel. A HISTORY OF ENGLISH LITERATURE: From its Beginning to Tennyson. Translated from the German. *Demy 8vo. 7s. 6d. net.*

W. H. Fairbrother, M.A. THE PHILOSOPHY OF T. H. GREEN. *Second Edition. Crown 8vo. 3s. 6d.*

Dean Farrar. See À Kempis.

Susan Ferrier. MARRIAGE. Edited by Miss GOODRICH FREER and Lord IDDESLEIGH. *Two Volumes. Pott 8vo. Each volume, cloth, 1s. 6d. net; leather, 2s. 6d. net.* [Little Library.

THE INHERITANCE. *Two Volumes. Pott 8vo. Each Volume, cloth, 1s. 6d. net.; leather, 2s. 6d. net.* [The Little Library.

C. H. Firth, M.A. CROMWELL'S ARMY: A History of the English Soldier during the Civil Wars, the Commonwealth, and the Protectorate. *Crown 8vo. 7s. 6d.*

An elaborate study and description of Cromwell's army by which the victory of the Parliament was secured. The 'New Model' is described in minute detail.

G. W. Fisher, M.A. ANNALS OF SHREWSBURY SCHOOL. With numerous Illustrations. *Demy 8vo. 10s. 6d.*

Edward FitzGerald. THE RUBAIYAT OF OMAR KHAYYAM. With a Commentary by H. M. BATSON, and a Biography of Omar by E. D. ROSS. *Crown 8vo. 6s.*

E. A. FitzGerald. THE HIGHEST ANDES. With 2 Maps, 51 Illustrations, 13 of which are in Photogravure, and a Panorama. *Royal 8vo. 30s. net.*

C. R. L. Fletcher. See Thomas Carlyle.

W. Warde Fowler. M.A. See Gilbert White.

J. F. Fraser. ROUND THE WORLD ON A WHEEL. With 100 Illustrations. *Fourth Edition Crown 8vo. 6s.*

'A classic of cycling, graphic and witty.'—*Yorkshire Post.*

J. H. Freese. See Plautus.

W. French, M.A., Principal of the Storey Institute, Lancaster. PRACTICAL CHEMISTRY. Part I. With numerous Diagrams. *Crown 8vo. 1s. 6d.* [Textbooks of Technology.

'An excellent and eminently practical little book.'—*Schoolmaster.*

Ed. von Freudenreich. DAIRY BACTERIOLOGY. A Short Manual for the Use of Students. Translated by J. R. AINSWORTH DAVIS, M.A. *Second Edition. Revised. Crown 8vo. 2s. 6d.*

H. W. Fulford, M.A. THE EPISTLE OF ST. JAMES. Edited by. *Fcap. 8vo.* 1s. 6d. *net.* [Churchman's Bible.

Mrs. Gaskell. CRANFORD. Edited by E. V. LUCAS. *Pott 8vo. Cloth,* 1s. 6d. *net*; *leather,* 2s. 6d. *net.* [Little Library.

H. B. George, M.A., Fellow of New College, Oxford. BATTLES OF ENGLISH HISTORY. With numerous Plans. *Third Edition. Crown 8vo.* 6s.

'Mr. George has undertaken a very useful task—that of making military affairs intelligible and instructive to non-military readers—and has executed it with a large measure of success.'—*Times.*

H. de B. Gibbins, Litt.D., M.A. INDUSTRY IN ENGLAND: HISTORICAL OUTLINES. With 5 Maps. *Second Edition. Demy 8vo.* 10s. 6d.

A COMPANION GERMAN GRAMMAR. *Crown 8vo.* 1s. 6d.

THE INDUSTRIAL HISTORY OF ENGLAND. *Eighth Edition.* Revised. With Maps and Plans. *Crown 8vo.* 3s. [University Extension Series.

THE ECONOMICS OF COMMERCE. *Crown 8vo.* 1s. 6d. [Commercial Series.

COMMERCIAL EXAMINATION PAPERS. *Crown 8vo.* 1s. 6d. [Commercial Series.

BRITISH COMMERCE AND COLONIES FROM ELIZABETH TO VICTORIA. *Third Edition. Crown 8vo.* 2s. [Commercial Series.

ENGLISH SOCIAL REFORMERS. *Second Edition. Crown 8vo.* 2s. 6d. [University Extension Series.

H. de B. Gibbins, Litt.D., M.A., and **R. A. Hadfield**, of the Hecla Works, Sheffield. A SHORTER WORKING DAY. *Crown 8vo.* 2s. 6d. [Social Questions Series.

Edward Gibbon. THE DECLINE AND FALL OF THE ROMAN EMPIRE. A New Edition, edited with Notes, Appendices, and Maps, by J. B. BURY, LL.D., Fellow of Trinity College, Dublin. *In Seven Volumes. Demy 8vo. Gilt top,* 8s. 6d. *each. Also, Crown 8vo.* 6s. *each.*

'At last there is an adequate modern edition of Gibbon. . . . The best edition the nineteenth century could produce.'—*Manchester Guardian.*

'A great piece of editing.'—*Academy.*

MEMOIRS OF MY LIFE AND WRITINGS. Edited, with an Introduction and Notes, by G. BIRKBECK HILL, LL.D. *Crown 8vo.* 6s.

'An admirable edition of one of the most interesting personal records of a literary life. Its notes and its numerous appendices are a repertory of almost all that can be known about Gibbon.'—*Manchester Guardian.*

E. C. S. Gibson, D.D., Vicar of Leeds. THE BOOK OF JOB. With Introduction and Notes. *Demy 8vo.* 6s. [Westminster Commentaries.

'Dr. Gibson's work is worthy of a high degree of appreciation. To the busy worker and the intelligent student the commentary will be a real boon; and it will, if we are not mistaken, be much in demand. The Introduction is almost a model of concise, straightforward, prefatory remarks on the subject treated.'—*Athenæum.*

THE XXXIX. ARTICLES OF THE CHURCH OF ENGLAND. With an Introduction. *Third and Cheaper Edition in One Volume. Demy 8vo.* 12s. 6d. [Handbooks of Theology.

'We welcome with the utmost satisfaction a new, cheaper, and more convenient edition of Dr. Gibson's book. It was greatly wanted. Dr. Gibson has given theological students just what they want, and we should like to think that it was in the hands of every candidate for orders.'—*Guardian.*

THE LIFE OF JOHN HOWARD. With 12 Illustrations. *Pott 8vo. Cloth,* 3s.; *leather,* 3s. 6d. *net.* [Little Biographies.

See also George Herbert.

George Gissing. See Dickens.

A. D. Godley, M.A., Fellow of Magdalen College, Oxford. LYRA FRIVOLA. *Third Edition. Fcap. 8vo.* 2s. 6d.

VERSES TO ORDER. *Cr. 8vo.* 2s. 6d. *net.*

SECOND STRINGS. *Fcap. 8vo.* 2s. 6d.

A new volume of humorous verse uniform with *Lyra Frivola.*

'Neat, brisk, ingenious.'—*Manchester Guardian.*

'The verse is facile, the wit is ready.'—*Daily Mail.*

'Excellent and amusing.'—*St. James's Gazette.*

Miss Goodrich-Freer. See Susan Ferrier.

P. Anderson Graham. THE RURAL EXODUS. *Crown 8vo.* 2s. 6d. [Social Questions Series.

F. S. Granger, M.A., Litt.D. PSYCHOLOGY. *Second Edition. Crown 8vo.* 2s. 6d. [University Extension Series.

THE SOUL OF A CHRISTIAN. *Crown 8vo.* 6s.

A book dealing with the evolution of the religious life and experiences.

E. M'Queen Gray. GERMAN PASSAGES FOR UNSEEN TRANSLATION. *Crown 8vo.* 2s. 6d.

P. L. Gray, B.Sc., formerly Lecturer in Physics in Mason University College, Birmingham. THE PRINCIPLES OF MAGNETISM AND ELECTRICITY: an Elementary Text-Book. With 181 Diagrams. *Crown 8vo.* 3s. 6d.

G. Buckland Green, M.A., Assistant Master at Edinburgh Academy, late Fellow of St. John's College, Oxon. NOTES ON GREEK AND LATIN SYNTAX. *Crown 8vo.* 3s. 6d.

Notes and explanations on the chief difficulties of Greek and Latin Syntax, with numerous passages for exercise.

E. T. Green, M.A. THE CHURCH OF CHRIST. *Crown 8vo.* 6s.
[Churchman's Library.

R. A. Gregory. THE VAULT OF HEAVEN. A Popular Introduction to Astronomy. With numerous Illustrations. *Crown 8vo.* 2s. 6d.
[University Extension Series.

W. Hall Griffin, M.A. See Robert Browning.

C. H. Grinling. A HISTORY OF THE GREAT NORTHERN RAILWAY, 1845-95. With Illustrations. *Demy 8vo.* 10s. 6d.

F. Hindes Groome. See George Borrow.

M. L. Gwynn. A BIRTHDAY BOOK. *Royal 8vo.* 12s.

This is a birthday-book of exceptional dignity, and the extracts have been chosen with particular care.

Stephen Gwynn. See Thackeray.

John Hackett, B.D. A HISTORY OF THE ORTHODOX CHURCH OF CYPRUS. With Maps and Illustrations. *Demy 8vo.* 15s. *net.*

A. C. Haddon, Sc.D., F.R.S. HEAD-HUNTERS, BLACK, WHITE, AND BROWN. With many Illustrations and a Map. *Demy 8vo.* 15s.

A narrative of adventure and exploration in Northern Borneo. It contains much matter of the highest scientific interest.

R. A. Hadfield. See H. de B. Gibbins.

R. N. Hall and W. G. Neal. THE ANCIENT RUINS OF RHODESIA. With numerous Illustrations. *Demy 8vo.* 21s. *net.*

F. J. Hamilton, D.D., **and E. W. Brooks.** ZACHARIAH OF MITYLENE. Translated into English. *Demy 8vo.* 12s. 6d. *net.*
[Byzantine Texts.

D. Hannay. A SHORT HISTORY OF THE ROYAL NAVY, FROM EARLY TIMES TO THE PRESENT DAY. Illustrated. *Two Volumes. Demy 8vo.* 7s. 6d. each. Vol. I. 1200-1688.

A. T. Hare, M.A. THE CONSTRUCTION OF LARGE INDUCTION COILS. With numerous Diagrams. *Demy 8vo.* 6s.

Clifford Harrison. READING AND READERS. *Fcap. 8vo.* 2s. 6d.

'An extremely sensible little book.'—*Manchester Guardian.*

Nathaniel Hawthorne. THE SCARLET LETTER. Edited by PERCY DEARMER. *Pott 8vo. Cloth*, 1s. 6d. *net; leather*, 2s. 6d. *net.*
[Little Library.

Sven Hedin, Gold Medallist of the Royal Geographical Society. THROUGH ASIA. With 300 Illustrations from Sketches and Photographs by the Author, and Maps. *Two Volumes. Royal 8vo.* 36s. *net.*

T. F. Henderson. A LITTLE BOOK OF SCOTTISH VERSE. *Pott 8vo. Cloth*, 1s. 6d. *net; leather*, 2s. 6d. *net.*
[Little Library.

See also D. M. Moir.

W. E. Henley. ENGLISH LYRICS. *Crown 8vo. Gilt top.* 3s. 6d.

W. E. Henley and C. Whibley. A BOOK OF ENGLISH PROSE. *Crown 8vo. Buckram, gilt top.* 6s.

H. H. Henson, M.A., Fellow of All Souls', Oxford, Canon of Westminster. APOSTOLIC CHRISTIANITY: As Illustrated by the Epistles of St. Paul to the Corinthians. *Crown 8vo.* 6s.

LIGHT AND LEAVEN: HISTORICAL AND SOCIAL SERMONS. *Crown 8vo.* 6s.

DISCIPLINE AND LAW. *Fcap. 8vo.* 2s. 6d.

George Herbert. THE TEMPLE. Edited, with an Introduction and Notes, by E. C. S. GIBSON, D.D., Vicar of Leeds. *Pott 8vo. Cloth*, 2s.; *leather*, 2s. 6d. *net.*
[Library of Devotion.

This edition contains Walton's Life of Herbert, and the text is that of the first edition.

Herodotus: EASY SELECTIONS. With Vocabulary. By A. C. LIDDELL, M.A. *Fcap. 8vo.* 1s. 6d.

W. A. S. Hewins, B.A. ENGLISH TRADE AND FINANCE IN THE SEVENTEENTH CENTURY. *Crown 8vo.*
[University Extension Series.

T. Hilbert. THE AIR GUN: or, How the Mastermans and Dobson Major nearly lost their Holidays. Illustrated. *Square Fcap. 8vo.* 2s. 6d.
[Little Blue Books.

Clare Hill, Registered Teacher to the City and Guilds of London Institute. MILLINERY, THEORETICAL, AND PRACTICAL. With numerous Diagrams. *Crown 8vo.* 2s.
[Textbooks of Technology.

Henry Hill, B.A., Headmaster of the Boy's High School, Worcester, Cape Colony. A SOUTH AFRICAN ARITHMETIC. *Crown 8vo.* 3s. 6d.

This book has been specially written for use in South African schools.

G. Birkbeck Hill, LL.D. See Gibbon.

Howard C. Hillegas. WITH THE BOER FORCES. With 24 Illustrations. *Second Edition. Crown 8vo.* 6s.

Emily Hobhouse. THE BRUNT OF THE WAR. With Map and Illustrations. *Crown 8vo.* 6s.

L. T. Hobhouse, Fellow of C.C.C., Oxford. THE THEORY OF KNOWLEDGE. *Demy 8vo.* 21s.

J. A. Hobson, M.A. PROBLEMS OF POVERTY: An Inquiry into the Industrial Condition of the Poor. *Fourth Edition. Crown 8vo.* 2s. 6d.
[Social Questions Series and University Extension Series.

THE PROBLEM OF THE UNEMPLOYED. *Crown 8vo.* 2s. 6d.
[Social Questions Series.

T. Hodgkin, D.C.L. GEORGE FOX, THE QUAKER. With Portrait. *Crown 8vo.* 3s. 6d. [Leaders of Religion.

Chester Holcombe. THE REAL CHINESE QUESTION. *Crown 8vo.* 6s.
'It is an important addition to the materials before the public for forming an opinion on a most difficult and pressing problem.'—*Times.*

Sir T. H. Holdich, K.C.I.E. THE INDIAN BORDERLAND: being a Personal Record of Twenty Years. Illustrated. *Demy 8vo.* 15s. *net.*
'Interesting and inspiriting from cover to cover, it will assuredly take its place as the classical work on the history of the Indian frontier.'—*Pilot.*

Canon Scott Holland. LYRA APOSTOLICA. With an Introduction. Notes by H. C. BEECHING, M.A. *Pott 8vo. Cloth,* 2s.; *leather,* 2s. 6d. *net.*
[Library of Devotion.

G. J. Holyoake. THE CO-OPERATIVE MOVEMENT TO-DAY. *Third Edition. Crown 8vo.* 2s. 6d.
[Social Questions Series.

Horace: THE ODES AND EPODES. Translated by A. GODLEY, M.A., Fellow of Magdalen College, Oxford. *Crown 8vo.* 2s. [Classical Translations.

E. L. S. Horsburgh, M.A. WATERLOO: A Narrative and Criticism. With Plans. *Second Edition. Crown 8vo.* 5s.
'A brilliant essay—simple, sound, and thorough.'—*Daily Chronicle.*

THE LIFE OF SAVONAROLA. With Portraits and Illustrations. *Fcap. 8vo. Cloth,* 3s. 6d.; *leather,* 4s. *net.*
[Little Biographies.

R. F. Horton, D.D. JOHN HOWE. With Portrait. *Crown 8vo.* 3s. 6d.
[Leaders of Religion.

Alexander Hosie. MANCHURIA. With Illustrations and a Map. *Demy 8vo.* 10s. 6d. *net.*

G. Howell. TRADE UNIONISM—NEW AND OLD. *Third Edition. Crown 8vo.* 2s. 6d. [Social Questions Series.

A. W. Hutton, M.A. CARDINAL MANNING. With Portrait. *Crown 8vo.* 3s. 6d. [Leaders of Religion.
See also TAULER.

Edward Hutton. See Richard Crashaw.

R. H. Hutton. CARDINAL NEWMAN. With Portrait. *Crown 8vo.* 3s. 6d. [Leaders of Religion.

W. H. Hutton, M.A. THE LIFE OF SIR THOMAS MORE. With Portraits. *Second Edition. Crown 8vo.* 5s.
WILLIAM LAUD. With Portrait. *Second Edition. Crown 8vo.* 3s. 6d.
[Leaders of Religion.

Henrik Ibsen. BRAND. A Drama. Translated by WILLIAM WILSON. *Third Edition. Crown 8vo.* 3s. 6d.

Lord Iddesleigh. See Susan Ferrier.

W. R. Inge, M.A., Fellow and Tutor of Hertford College, Oxford. CHRISTIAN MYSTICISM. The Bampton Lectures for 1899. *Demy 8vo.* 12s. 6d. *net.*
'It is fully worthy of the best traditions connected with the Bampton Lectureship.'—*Record.*

A. D. Innes, M.A. A HISTORY OF THE BRITISH IN INDIA. With Maps and Plans. *Crown 8vo.* 7s. 6d.
'Written in a vigorous and effective style . . . a thoughtful and impartial account.'—*Spectator.*

S. Jackson, M.A. A PRIMER OF BUSINESS. *Third Edition. Crown 8vo.* 1s. 6d. [Commercial Series.

F. Jacob, M.A. JUNIOR FRENCH EXAMINATION PAPERS. *Fcap. 8vo.* 1s. [Junior Examination Series.

J. Stephen Jeans. TRUSTS, POOLS, AND CORNERS. *Crown 8vo.* 2s. 6d.
[Social Questions Series.

E. Jenks, M.A., Professor of Law at University College, Liverpool. ENGLISH LOCAL GOVERNMENT. *Crown 8vo.* 2s. 6d. [University Extension Series.

C. S. Jerram, M.A. See Pascal.

Augustus Jessopp, D.D. JOHN DONNE. With Portrait. *Crown 8vo.* 3s. 6d.
[Leaders of Religion.

F. B. Jevons, M.A., Litt.D., Principal of Hatfield Hall, Durham. EVOLUTION. *Crown 8vo.* 3s. 6d. [Churchman's Library.

AN INTRODUCTION TO THE HISTORY OF RELIGION. *Second Edition. Demy 8vo.* 10s. 6d.
[Handbooks of Theology.
'The merit of this book lies in the penetration, the singular acuteness and force of the author's judgment. He is at once critical and luminous, at once just and suggestive. A comprehensive and thorough book.'—*Birmingham Post.*

Sir H. H. Johnston, K.C.B. BRITISH CENTRAL AFRICA. With nearly 200 Illustrations and Six Maps. *Second Edition. Crown 4to.* 18s. *net.*

H. Jones. A GUIDE TO PROFESSIONS AND BUSINESS. *Crown 8vo.* 1s. 6d.
[Commercial Series.

Lady Julian of Norwich. REVELATIONS OF DIVINE LOVE. Edited by GRACE WARRACK. *Crown 8vo.* 3s. 6d.

A partially modernised version, from the MS. in the British Museum of a book which Mr. Inge in his Bampton Lectures calls 'The beautiful but little known *Revelations*.'

M. Kaufmann. SOCIALISM AND MODERN THOUGHT. *Crown 8vo.* 2s. 6d. [Social Questions Series.

J. F. Keating, D.D. THE AGAPE AND THE EUCHARIST. *Crown 8vo.* 3s. 6d.

John Keble. THE CHRISTIAN YEAR. With an Introduction and Notes by W. LOCK, D.D., Warden of Keble College. Illustrated by R. ANNING BELL. *Second Edition. Fcap. 8vo.* 3s. 6d; *padded morocco,* 5s.

THE CHRISTIAN YEAR. With Introduction and Notes by WALTER LOCK, D.D., Warden of Keble College. *Second Edition. Pott 8vo. Cloth,* 2s.; *leather,* 2s. 6d. *net.* [Library of Devotion.

LYRA INNOCENTIUM. Edited, with Introduction and Notes, by WALTER LOCK, D.D., Warden of Keble College, Oxford. *Pott 8vo. Cloth,* 2s.; *leather,* 2s. 6d. *net.*
[Library of Devotion.

'This sweet and fragrant book has never been published more attractively.'—
Academy.

Thomas à Kempis. THE IMITATION OF CHRIST. With an Introduction by DEAN FARRAR. Illustrated by C. M. GERE. *Second Edition. Fcap. 8vo.* 3s. 6d. *net; padded morocco,* 5s.

THE IMITATION OF CHRIST. A Revised Translation, with an Introduction by C. BIGG, D.D., late Student of Christ Church. *Third Edition. Pott 8vo. Cloth,* 2s.; *leather,* 2s. 6d. *net.*
[Library of Devotion.

A practically new translation of this book which the reader has, almost for the first time, exactly in the shape in which it left the hands of the author.

THE SAME EDITION IN LARGE TYPE. *Crown 8vo.* 3s. 6d.

James Houghton Kennedy, D.D., Assistant Lecturer in Divinity in the University of Dublin. ST. PAUL'S SECOND AND THIRD EPISTLES TO THE CORINTHIANS. With Introduction, Dissertations and Notes. *Crown 8vo.* 6s.

J. D. Kestell. THROUGH SHOT AND FLAME: Being the Adventures and Experiences of J. D. KESTELL, Chaplain to General Christian de Wet. *Crown 8vo.* 6s.

C. W. Kimmins, M.A. THE CHEMISTRY OF LIFE AND HEALTH. Illustrated. *Crown 8vo.* 2s. 6d.
[University Extension Series.

A. W. Kinglake. EOTHEN. With an Introduction and Notes. *Pott 8vo. Cloth,* 1s. 6d. *net; leather,* 2s. 6d. *net.*
[Little Library.

Rudyard Kipling. BARRACK-ROOM BALLADS. 73*rd Thousand. Crown 8vo.* 6s.; *leather,* 6s. *net.*

'Mr. Kipling's verse is strong, vivid, full of character. . . . Unmistakable genius rings in every line.'—*Times.*

'The ballads teem with imagination, they palpitate with emotion. We read them with laughter and tears: the metres throb in our pulses, the cunningly ordered words tingle with life; and if this be not poetry, what is?'—*Pall Mall Gazette.*

THE SEVEN SEAS. 62*nd Thousand. Crown 8vo. Buckram, gilt top,* 6s.; *leather,* 6s. *net.*

'The Empire has found a singer; it is no depreciation of the songs to say that statesmen may have, one way or other, to take account of them.'—
Manchester Guardian.

F. G. Kitton. See Dickens.

W. J. Knox Little. See St. Francis de Sales.

Charles Lamb, THE ESSAYS OF ELIA. With over 100 Illustrations by A. GARTH JONES, and an Introduction by E. V. LUCAS. *Demy 8vo.* 10s. 6d.

'This edition is in many respects of peculiar beauty.'—*Daily Chronicle.*

ELIA, AND THE LAST ESSAYS OF ELIA. Edited by E. V. LUCAS. *Pott 8vo. Cloth,* 1s. 6d. *net; leather,* 2s. 6d. *net.*
[Little Library.

THE KING AND QUEEN OF HEARTS: An 1805 Book for Children. Illustrated by WILLIAM MULREADY. A new edition, in facsimile, edited by E. V. LUCAS. 1s. 6d.

This little book is a literary curiosity, and has been discovered and identified as the work of Charles Lamb by E. V. Lucas. It is an exact facsimile of the original edition, which was illustrated by Mulready.

Professor Lambros. ECTHESIS CHRONICA. Edited by. *Demy 8vo.* 7s. 6d. *net.* [Byzantine Texts.

Stanley Lane-Poole. THE LIFE OF SIR HARRY PARKES. *A New and Cheaper Edition. Crown 8vo.* 6s.

A HISTORY OF EGYPT IN THE MIDDLE AGES. Fully Illustrated. *Crown 8vo.* 6s.

F. Langbridge, M.A. BALLADS OF THE BRAVE: Poems of Chivalry, Enterprise, Courage, and Constancy. *Second Edition. Crown 8vo.* 2s. 6d.

'The book is full of splendid things.'—*World.*

William Law. A SERIOUS CALL TO A DEVOUT AND HOLY LIFE. Edited, with an Introduction, by C. BIGG, D.D., late Student of Christ Church. *Pott 8vo. Cloth,* 2s.; *leather,* 2s. 6d. *net.*

[Library of Devotion.

This is a reprint, word for word and line for line, of the *Editio Princeps.*

G. S. Layard. THE LIFE OF MRS. LYNN LINTON. Illustrated. *Demy 8vo.* 12s. 6d.

Captain Melville Lee. A HISTORY OF POLICE IN ENGLAND. *Crown 8vo.* 7s. 6d.

'A learned book, comprising many curious details to interest the general reader as well as the student who will consult it for exact information.'—*Daily News.*

V. B. Lewes, M.A. AIR AND WATER. Illustrated. *Crown 8vo.* 2s. 6d.

[University Extension Series.

W. M. Lindsay. See Plautus.

Walter Lock, D.D., Warden of Keble College. ST. PAUL, THE MASTER-BUILDER. *Crown 8vo.* 3s. 6d.

See also Keble and New Commentaries.

JOHN KEBLE. With Portrait. *Crown 8vo.* 3s. 6d. [Leaders of Religion.

E. V. Lucas. THE VISIT TO LONDON. Described in Verse, with Coloured Pictures by F. D. BEDFORD. *Small 4to.* 6s.

This charming book describes the introduction of a country child to the delights and sights of London. It is the result of a well-known partnership between author and artist.

'A beautiful children's book.'
Black and White.

'The most inimitable verses and interesting pictures.'—*Daily Chronicle.*

'Of quite unusual charm.'
Daily Telegraph.

See also Jane Austen and Mrs. Gaskell and Charles Lamb.

Lucian. SIX DIALOGUES (Nigrinus, Icaro-Menippus, The Cock, The Ship, The Parasite, The Lover of Falsehood). Translated by S. T. Irwin, M.A., Assistant Master at Clifton; late Scholar of Exeter College, Oxford. *Crown 8vo.* 3s. 6d.

[Classical Translations.

L. W. Lyde, M.A. A COMMERCIAL GEOGRAPHY OF THE BRITISH EMPIRE. *Third Edition. Crown 8vo.* 2s.

[Commercial Series.

Hon. Mrs. Lyttelton. WOMEN AND THEIR WORK. *Crown 8vo.* 2s. 6d.

'Thoughtful, interesting, practical.'—*Guardian.*

'The book is full of sound precept given with sympathy and wit.'—*Pilot.*

Lord Macaulay. CRITICAL AND HISTORICAL ESSAYS. Edited by F. C. MONTAGUE, M.A. *Three Volumes. Cr. 8vo.* 6s. *each.* [Methuen's Standard Library.

The only edition of this book completely annotated.

J. E. B. M'Allen, M.A. THE PRINCIPLES OF BOOKKEEPING BY DOUBLE ENTRY. *Crown 8vo.* 2s.

[Commercial Series.

J. A. MacCulloch. COMPARATIVE THEOLOGY. *Crown 8vo.* 6s.

[The Churchman's Library.

'Most carefully executed, readable and informing.'—*Scotsman.*

F. MacCunn. JOHN KNOX. With Portrait. *Crown 8vo.* 3s. 6d.

[Leaders of Religion.

A. M. Mackay. THE CHURCHMAN'S INTRODUCTION TO THE OLD TESTAMENT. *Crown 8vo.* 3s. 6d.

[Churchman's Library.

'The book throughout is frank and courageous.'—*Glasgow Herald.*

Laurie Magnus, M.A. A PRIMER OF WORDSWORTH. *Crown 8vo.* 2s. 6d.

J P. Mahaffy, Litt.D. A HISTORY OF THE EGYPT OF THE PTOLEMIES. Fully Illustrated. *Crown 8vo.* 6s.

F. W. Maitland, LL.D., Downing Professor of the Laws of England in the University of Cambridge. CANON LAW IN ENGLAND. *Royal 8vo.* 7s. 6d.

H. E. Malden, M.A. ENGLISH RECORDS. A Companion to the History of England. *Crown 8vo.* 3s. 6d.

THE ENGLISH CITIZEN: HIS RIGHTS AND DUTIES. *Crown 8vo.* 1s. 6d.

E. C. Marchant, M.A., Fellow of Peterhouse, Cambridge, and Assistant Master at St. Paul's School. A GREEK ANTHOLOGY. *Crown 8vo.* 3s. 6d.

E. C. Marchant, M.A., and **A. M. Cook,** M.A. PASSAGES FOR UNSEEN TRANSLATION. *Second Edition. Crown 8vo.* 3s. 6d.

'We know no book of this class better fitted for use in the higher forms of schools.'—*Guardian.*

J. E. Marr, F.R.S., Fellow of St. John's College, Cambridge. THE SCIENTIFIC STUDY OF SCENERY. *Second Edition.* Illustrated. *Crown 8vo.* 6s.

'A volume, moderate in size and readable in style, which will be acceptable alike to the student of geology and geography and to the tourist.'—*Athenæum.*

A. J. Mason. THOMAS CRANMER. With Portrait. *Crown 8vo.* 3s. 6d.
[Leaders of Religion.

George Massee. THE EVOLUTION OF PLANT LIFE: Lower Forms. With Illustrations. *Crown 8vo.* 2s. 6d.
[University Extension Series.

C. F. G. Masterman, M.A. TENNYSON AS A RELIGIOUS TEACHER. *Crown 8vo.* 6s.

'A thoughtful and penetrating appreciation, full of interest and suggestion.'—*World*.

Annie Matheson. See Mrs. Craik.

Emma S. Mellows. A SHORT STORY OF ENGLISH LITERATURE. *Crown 8vo.* 3s. 6d.

'A lucid and well-arranged account of the growth of English literature.'—*Pall Mall Gazette*.

L. C. Miall, F.R.S. See Gilbert White.

E. B. Michell. THE ART AND PRACTICE OF HAWKING. With 3 Photogravures by G. E. LODGE, and other Illustrations. *Demy 8vo.* 10s. 6d.

J. G. Millais. THE LIFE AND LETTERS OF SIR JOHN EVERETT MILLAIS, President of the Royal Academy. With 319 Illustrations, of which 9 are Photogravure. 2 vols. *Royal 8vo.* 20s. net.

'This splendid work.'—*World*.

'Of such absorbing interest is it, of such completeness in scope and beauty. Special tribute must be paid to the extraordinary completeness of the illustrations.'—*Graphic*.

J. G. Milne, M.A. A HISTORY OF ROMAN EGYPT. Fully Illustrated. *Crown 8vo.* 6s.

P. Chalmers Mitchell, M.A. OUTLINES OF BIOLOGY. Illustrated. *Second Edition. Crown 8vo.* 6s.

A text-book designed to cover the Schedule issued by the Royal College of Physicians and Surgeons.

D. M. Moir. MANSIE WAUCH. Edited by T. F. HENDERSON. *Pott 8vo. Cloth*, 1s. 6d. *net; leather*, 2s. 6d. *net*.
[Little Library.

F. C. Montague, M.A. See Macaulay.

H. E. Moore. BACK TO THE LAND: An Inquiry into the cure for Rural Depopulation. *Crown 8vo.* 2s. 6d.
[Social Questions Series.

W. R. Morfill, Oriel College, Oxford. A HISTORY OF RUSSIA FROM PETER THE GREAT TO ALEXANDER II. With Maps and Plans. *Crown 8vo.* 7s. 6d.

This history, is founded on a study of original documents, and though necessarily brief, is the most comprehensive narrative in existence. Considerable attention has been paid to the social and literary development of the country, and the recent expansion of Russia in Asia.

R. J. Morich, late of Clifton College. GERMAN EXAMINATION PAPERS IN MISCELLANEOUS GRAMMAR AND IDIOMS. *Sixth Edition. Crown 8vo.* 2s. 6d. [School Examination Series.

A KEY, issued to Tutors and Private Students only, to be had on application to the Publishers. *Second Edition. Crown 8vo.* 6s. *net*.

Miss Anderson Morton. See Miss Brodrick.

H. C. G. Moule, D.D., Lord Bishop of Durham. CHARLES SIMEON. With Portrait. *Crown 8vo.* 3s. 6d.
[Leaders of Religion.

M. M. Pattison Muir, M.A. THE CHEMISTRY OF FIRE. The Elementary Principles of Chemistry. Illustrated. *Crown 8vo.* 2s. 6d.
[University Extension Series.

V. A. Mundella, M.A. See J. T. Dunn.

W. G. Neal. See R. N. Hall.

H. W. Nevinson. LADYSMITH: The Diary of a Siege. With 16 Illustrations and a Plan. *Second Edition. Crown 8vo.* 6s.

J. B. B. Nichols. A LITTLE BOOK OF ENGLISH SONNETS. *Pott 8vo. Cloth*, 1s. 6d. *net; leather*, 2s. 6d. *net*.
[The Little Library.

James Northcote, R.A., THE CONVERSATIONS OF, WITH JAMES WARD. Edited by ERNEST FLETCHER. With many Portraits. *Demy 8vo.* 10s. 6d.

A. H. Norway, Author of 'Highways and Byways in Devon and Cornwall.' NAPLES: PAST AND PRESENT. With 40 Illustrations by A. G. FERARD. *Crown 8vo.* 6s.

Mrs. Oliphant. THOMAS CHALMERS. With Portrait. *Crown 8vo.* 3s. 6d.
[Leaders of Religion.

C. W. Oman, M.A., Fellow of All Souls', Oxford. A HISTORY OF THE ART OF WAR. Vol. II.: The Middle Ages, from the Fourth to the Fourteenth Century. Illustrated. *Demy 8vo.* 21s.

'The whole art of war in its historic evolution has never been treated on such an ample and comprehensive scale, and we question if any recent contribution to the exact history of the world has possessed more enduring value.'—*Daily Chronicle*.

Prince Henri of Orleans. FROM TONKIN TO INDIA. Translated by HAMLEY BENT, M.A. With 100 Illustrations and a Map. *Crown 4to, gilt top.* 25s.

R. L. Ottley, M.A., late Fellow of Magdalen College, Oxon., and Principal of Pusey House. THE DOCTRINE OF THE INCARNATION. *Second and cheaper Edition. Demy 8vo.* 12s. 6d.
[Handbooks of Theology.

'A clear and remarkably full account of the main currents of speculation. Scholarly precision . . . genuine tolerance . . . intense interest in his subject—are Mr. Ottley's merits.'—*Guardian*.

LANCELOT ANDREWES. With Portrait. *Crown 8vo.* 3s. 6d.
[Leaders of Religion.

J. H. Overton, M.A. JOHN WESLEY. With Portrait. *Crown 8vo.* 3s. 6d.
[Leaders of Religion.

M. N. Oxford, of Guy's Hospital. A HANDBOOK OF NURSING. *Crown 8vo.* 3s. 6d.
'The most useful work of the kind that we have seen. A most valuable and practical manual.'—*Manchester Guardian.*

W. C. C. Pakes. THE SCIENCE OF HYGIENE. With numerous Illustrations. *Demy 8vo.* 15s.
'A thoroughgoing working text-book of its subject, practical and well-stocked.'—*Scotsman.*

Prof. Léon Parmentier and M. Bidez. EVAGRIUS. Edited by. *Demy 8vo.* 10s. 6d. net. [Byzantine Texts.

Pascal, THE THOUGHTS OF. With Introduction and Notes by C. S. JERRAM. *Pott 8vo.* 2s.; *leather,* 2s. 6d. *net.*
[Library of Devotion.

George Paston. SIDELIGHTS ON THE GEORGIAN PERIOD. With many Illustrations. *Demy 8vo.* 10s. 6d.
'Touched with lightness and sympathy. We recommend this book to all who are tired with the trash of novels.'—*Spectator.*
'This book is the highly diverting product of research and compilation. It is a magazine of instructive and amusing information.'—*Academy.*

H. W. Paul. See Laurence Sterne.

E. H. Pearce, M.A. THE ANNALS OF CHRIST'S HOSPITAL. With many Illustrations. *Demy 8vo.* 7s. 6d.
'A well-written, copious, authentic history.'—*Times.*

R. E. Peary, Gold Medallist of the Royal Geographical Society. NORTHWARD OVER THE GREAT ICE. With over 800 Illustrations. *2 vols. Royal 8vo.* 32s. *net.*
'His book will take its place among the permanent literature of Arctic exploration.'—*Times.*

Sidney Peel, late Fellow of Trinity College, Oxford, and Secretary to the Royal Commission on the Licensing Laws. PRACTICAL LICENSING REFORM. *Second Edition. Crown 8vo.* 1s. 6d.

M. Perugini. SELECTIONS FROM WILLIAM BLAKE. *Pott 8vo.* Cloth, 1s. 6d. net; *leather,* 2s. 6d. net.
[Little Library.

J. P. Peters, D.D. THE OLD TESTAMENT AND THE NEW SCHOLARSHIP. *Crown 8vo.* 6s.
[Churchman's Library.

'Every page reveals wide reading, used with sound and scholarly judgment.'
—*Manchester Guardian.*

W. M. Flinders Petrie, D.C.L., LL.D., Professor of Egyptology at University College. A HISTORY OF EGYPT, FROM THE EARLIEST TIMES TO THE PRESENT DAY. Fully Illustrated. *In six volumes. Crown 8vo.* 6s. *each.*
'A history written in the spirit of scientific precision so worthily represented by Dr. Petrie and his school cannot but promote sound and accurate study, and supply a vacant place in the English literature of Egyptology.'—*Times.*

VOL. I. PREHISTORIC TIMES TO XVIth DYNASTY. *Fifth Edition.*
VOL. II. THE XVIIth AND XVIIIth DYNASTIES. *Third Edition.*
VOL. IV. THE EGYPT OF THE PTOLEMIES. J. P. MAHAFFY, Litt.D.
VOL. V. ROMAN EGYPT. J. G. MILNE, M.A.
VOL. VI. EGYPT IN THE MIDDLE AGES. STANLEY LANE-POOLE, M.A.

RELIGION AND CONSCIENCE IN ANCIENT EGYPT. Fully Illustrated. *Crown 8vo.* 2s. 6d.

SYRIA AND EGYPT, FROM THE TELL EL AMARNA TABLETS. *Crown 8vo.* 2s. 6d.

EGYPTIAN TALES. Illustrated by TRISTRAM ELLIS. *In Two Volumes. Crown 8vo.* 3s. 6d. *each.*

EGYPTIAN DECORATIVE ART. With 120 Illustrations. *Crown 8vo.* 3s. 6d.
'In these lectures he displays rare skill in elucidating the development of decorative art in Egypt.'—*Times.*

Philip Pienaar. WITH STEYN AND DE WET. *Second Edition. Crown 8vo.* 3s. 6d.
A narrative of the adventures of a Boer telegraphist of the Orange Free State during the war.

Plautus. THE CAPTIVI. Edited, with an Introduction, Textual Notes, and a Commentary, by W. M. LINDSAY, Fellow of Jesus College, Oxford. *Demy 8vo.* 10s. 6d. *net.*
For this edition all the important MSS. have been re-collated. An appendix deals with the accentual element in early Latin verse. The Commentary is very full.

THE CAPTIVI. Adapted for Lower Forms, by J. H. FREESE, M.A., late Fellow of St. John's, Cambridge. 1s. 6d.

J. T. Plowden-Wardlaw, B.A., King's College, Cambridge. EXAMINATION PAPERS IN ENGLISH HISTORY. *Crown 8vo.* 2s. 6d.
[School Examination Series.

Frank Podmore. MODERN SPIRITUALISM. *Two Volumes. Demy 8vo. 21s. net.*

A History and a Criticism.

'A complete guide to a very complex subject.'—*Academy.*

'Of great scientific value and considerable popular interest.'—*Scotsman.*

'A masterpiece of scientific analysis and exposition. There is no doubt it will hold the field for a long time.'—*Star.*

'The entire book is characterised by the greatest candour and fairness, and affords pleasant reading upon an entrancing theme.'—*Public Opinion.*

A. W. Pollard. OLD PICTURE BOOKS. With many Illustrations. *Demy 8vo. 7s. 6d. net.*

M. C. Potter, M.A., F.L.S. A TEXT-BOOK OF AGRICULTURAL BOTANY. Illustrated. *2nd Edition. Crown 8vo. 4s. 6d.* [University Extension Series.

G. Pradeau. A KEY TO THE TIME ALLUSIONS IN THE DIVINE COMEDY. With a Dial. *Small quarto. 3s. 6d.*

L. L. Price, M.A., Fellow of Oriel College, Oxon. A HISTORY OF ENGLISH POLITICAL ECONOMY. *Fourth Edition. Crown 8vo. 2s. 6d.* [University Extension Series.

"Q." THE GOLDEN POMP. A Procession of English Lyrics. Arranged by A. T. QUILLER COUCH. *Crown 8vo. Buckram. 6s.*

R. B. Rackham, M.A. THE ACTS OF THE APOSTLES. With Introduction and Notes. *Demy 8vo. 12s. 6d.* [Westminster Commentaries.

'A really helpful book. Both introduction and commentary are marked by common sense and adequate knowledge.'—*Guardian.*

B. W. Randolph, D.D., Principal of the Theological College, Ely. THE PSALMS OF DAVID. With an Introduction and Notes. *Pott 8vo. Cloth,* 2s.; *leather,* 2s. 6d. *net.* Library of Devotion.

A devotional and practical edition of the Prayer Book version of the Psalms.

Hastings Rashdall, M.A., Fellow and Tutor of New College, Oxford. DOCTRINE AND DEVELOPMENT. *Crown 8vo. 6s.*

W. Reason, M.A. UNIVERSITY AND SOCIAL SETTLEMENTS. *Crown 8vo. 2s. 6d.* [Social Questions Series.

Charles Richardson. THE ENGLISH TURF. With numerous Illustrations and Plans. *Demy 8vo. 15s.*

M. E. Roberts. See C. C. Channer.

A. Robertson, D.D., Principal of King's College, London. REGNUM DEI. The Bampton Lectures of 1901. *Demy 8vo. 12s. 6d. net.*

'A notable volume. Its chief value and interest is in its historic treatment of its great theme.'—*Daily News.*

'It is altogether a solid piece of work and a valuable contribution to the history of Christian thought.'—*Scotsman.*

Sir G. S. Robertson, K.C.S.I. CHITRAL: The Story of a Minor Siege. With numerous Illustrations, Map and Plans. *Second Edition. Demy 8vo. 10s. 6d.*

'A book which the Elizabethans would have thought wonderful. More thrilling, more piquant, and more human than any novel.'—*Newcastle Chronicle.*

J. W. Robertson-Scott. THE PEOPLE OF CHINA. With a Map. *Crown 8vo. 3s. 6d.*

A. W. Robinson, M.A. THE EPISTLE TO THE GALATIANS. Explained. *Fcap. 8vo. 1s. 6d. net.* [Churchman's Bible.

'The most attractive, sensible, and instructive manual for people at large, which we have ever seen.'—*Church Gazette.*

Cecilia Robinson. THE MINISTRY OF DEACONESSES. With an Introduction by the Lord Bishop of Winchester. *Crown 8vo. 3s. 6d.*

G. Rodwell, B.A. NEW TESTAMENT GREEK. A Course for Beginners. With a Preface by WALTER LOCK, D.D., Warden of Keble College. *Fcap. 8vo. 3s. 6d.*

Fred Roe. ANCIENT COFFERS AND CUPBOARDS: Their History and Description. With many Illustrations. *Quarto. £3, 3s. net.*

E. S. Roscoe. ROBERT HARLEY, EARL OF OXFORD. Illustrated. *Demy 8vo. 7s. 6d.*

This is the only life of Harley in existence.

Edward Rose. THE ROSE READER. With numerous Illustrations. *Crown 8vo. 2s. 6d. Also in 4 Parts. Parts I. and II. 6d. each; Part III. 8d.; Part IV. 10d.*

A reader on a new and original plan.

The distinctive feature of this book is the entire avoidance of irregularly-spelt words until the pupil has thoroughly mastered the principle of reading, and learned its enjoyment. The reading of connected sentences begins from the first page, before the entire alphabet is introduced.

E. Denison Ross, M.A. See W. Beckford

A. E. Rubie, M.A., Head Master of the Royal Naval School, Eltham. THE GOSPEL ACCORDING TO ST. MARK. Edited by. With three Maps. *Crown 8vo. 1s. 6d.* [Methuen's Junior School Books.

W. Clark Russell. THE LIFE OF ADMIRAL LORD COLLINGWOOD. With Illustrations by F. BRANGWYN. *Fourth Edition. Crown 8vo.* 6s.

'A book which we should like to see in the hands of every boy in the country.'—*St. James's Gazette.*

St. Anselm, THE DEVOTIONS OF. Edited by C. C. J. WEBB, M.A. *Pott 8vo. Cloth,* 2s.; *leather,* 2s. 6d. *net.*
[Library of Devotion.

Viscount St. Cyres. THE LIFE OF FRANÇOIS DE FENELON. Illustrated. *Demy 8vo.* 10s. 6d.

'We have in this admirable volume a most valuable addition to our historical portrait gallery.'—*Daily News.*

St. Francis de Sales. ON THE LOVE OF GOD. Edited by W. J. KNOX-LITTLE, M.A. *Pott 8vo. Cloth,* 2s.; *leather,* 2s. 6d. *net.*
[Library of Devotion.

A. L. Salmon. CORNWALL. Illustrated by B. C. BOULTER. *Pott 8vo. Cloth,* 3s.; *leather,* 3s. 6d. *net.* [The Little Guides.

J. Sargeaunt, M.A. ANNALS OF WESTMINSTER SCHOOL. With numerous Illustrations. *Demy 8vo.* 7s. 6d.

C. Sathas. THE HISTORY OF PSELLUS. *Demy 8vo.* 15s. *net.*
[Byzantine Texts.

H. G. Seeley, F.R.S. DRAGONS OF THE AIR. With many Illustrations. *Crown 8vo.* 6s.

A popular history of the most remarkable flying animals which ever lived. Their relations to mammals, birds, and reptiles, living and extinct, are shown by an original series of illustrations.

V. P. Sells, M.A. THE MECHANICS OF DAILY LIFE. Illustrated. *Crown 8vo.* 2s. 6d. [University Extension Series.

Edmund Selous. TOMMY SMITH'S ANIMALS. Illustrated by G. W. ORD. *Second Edition. Fcap. 8vo.* 2s. 6d.

'A quaint, fascinating little book: a nursery classic.'—*Athenæum.*

William Shakespeare.
THE ARDEN EDITION.
Demy 8vo. 3s. 6d. each volume. General Editor, W. J. CRAIG. An Edition of Shakespeare in single Plays. Edited with a full Introduction, Textual Notes, and a Commentary at the foot of the page.

'No edition of Shakespeare is likely to prove more attractive and satisfactory than this one. It is beautifully printed and paged and handsomely and simply bound.'—
St. James's Gazette.

HAMLET. Edited by EDWARD DOWDEN, Litt.D.

ROMEO AND JULIET. Edited by EDWARD DOWDEN, Litt.D.

KING LEAR. Edited by W. J. CRAIG.

JULIUS CAESAR. Edited by M. MACMILLAN, M.A.

THE TEMPEST. Edited by MORTON LUCE.

A. Sharp. VICTORIAN POETS. *Crown 8vo.* 2s. 6d. [University Extension Series.

J. S. Shedlock. THE PIANOFORTE SONATA: Its Origin and Development. *Crown 8vo.* 5s.

Arthur Sherwell, M.A. LIFE IN WEST LONDON. *Third Edition. Crown 8vo.* 2s. 6d. [Social Questions Series.

Evan Small, M.A. THE EARTH. An Introduction to Physiography. Illustrated. *Crown 8vo.* 2s. 6d.
[University Extension Series.

Nowell C. Smith, Fellow of New College, Oxford. SELECTIONS FROM WORDSWORTH. *Pott 8vo. Cloth,* 1s. 6d. *net; leather,* 2s. 6d. *net.*
[Little Library.

Sophocles. ELECTRA AND AJAX. Translated by E. D. A. MORSHEAD, M.A., Assistant Master at Winchester. 2s. 6d.
[Classical Translations.

R. Southey. ENGLISH SEAMEN (Howard, Clifford, Hawkins, Drake, Cavendish). Edited, with an Introduction, by DAVID HANNAY. *Second Edition. Crown 8vo.* 6s.

'A brave, inspiriting book.'—*Black and White.*

C. H. Spence, M.A., Clifton College. HISTORY AND GEOGRAPHY EXAMINATION PAPERS. *Second Edition. Crown 8vo.* 2s. 6d.
[School Examination Series.

W. A. Spooner, M.A., Fellow of New College, Oxford. BISHOP BUTLER. With Portrait. *Crown 8vo.* 3s. 6d.
[Leaders of Religion.

J. W. Stanbridge, B.D., Rector of Bainton, Canon of York, and sometime Fellow of St. John's College, Oxford. A BOOK OF DEVOTIONS. *Pott 8vo. Cloth,* 2s.; *leather,* 2s. 6d. *net.* [Library of Devotion.

'It is probably the best book of its kind. It deserves high commendation.'—*Church Gazette.*

See also Cardinal Bona.

'Stancliffe.' GOLF DO'S AND DONT'S. *Second Edition. Fcap. 8vo.* 1s.

A. M. M. Stedman, M.A.
INITIA LATINA: Easy Lessons on Elementary Accidence. *Sixth Edition. Fcap. 8vo.* 1s.

FIRST LATIN LESSONS. *Sixth Edition. Crown 8vo.* 2s.

FIRST LATIN READER. With Notes adapted to the Shorter Latin Primer and

Vocabulary. *Sixth Edition revised.* 18mo. 1s. 6d.

EASY SELECTIONS FROM CÆSAR. The Helvetian War. *Second Edition.* 18mo. 1s.

EASY SELECTIONS FROM LIVY. Part I. The Kings of Rome. 18mo. *Second Edition.* 1s. 6d.

EASY LATIN PASSAGES FOR UNSEEN TRANSLATION. *Eighth Edition.* Fcap. 8vo. 1s. 6d.

EXEMPLA LATINA. First Lessons in Latin Accidence. With Vocabulary. Crown 8vo. 1s.

EASY LATIN EXERCISES ON THE SYNTAX OF THE SHORTER AND REVISED LATIN PRIMER. With Vocabulary. *Ninth and Cheaper Edition, re-written.* Crown 8vo. 1s. 6d. KEY, 3s. *net. Original Edition.* 2s. 6d.

THE LATIN COMPOUND SENTENCE: Rules and Exercises. *Second Edition.* Crown 8vo. 1s. 6d. With Vocabulary. 2s.

NOTANDA QUAEDAM: Miscellaneous Latin Exercises on Common Rules and Idioms. *Fourth Edition. Fcap.* 8vo. 1s. 6d. With Vocabulary. 2s. Key, 2s. *net.*

LATIN VOCABULARIES FOR REPETITION: Arranged according to Subjects. *Eleventh Edition. Fcap.* 8vo. 1s. 6d.

A VOCABULARY OF LATIN IDIOMS. 18mo. *Second Edition.* 1s.

STEPS TO GREEK. *Second Edition, revised.* 18mo. 1s.

A SHORTER GREEK PRIMER. Crown 8vo. 1s. 6d.

EASY GREEK PASSAGES FOR UNSEEN TRANSLATION. *Third Edition, revised.* Fcap. 8vo. 1s. 6d.

GREEK VOCABULARIES FOR REPETITION. Arranged according to Subjects. *Third Edition. Fcap.* 8vo. 1s. 6d.

GREEK TESTAMENT SELECTIONS. For the use of Schools. With Introduction, Notes, and Vocabulary. *Third Edition.* Fcap. 8vo. 2s. 6d.

STEPS TO FRENCH. *Sixth Edition.* 18mo. 8d.

FIRST FRENCH LESSONS. *Sixth Edition, revised.* Crown 8vo. 1s.

EASY FRENCH PASSAGES FOR UNSEEN TRANSLATION. *Fifth Edition, revised.* Fcap. 8vo. 1s. 6d.

EASY FRENCH EXERCISES ON ELEMENTARY SYNTAX. With Vocabulary. *Second Edition.* Crown 8vo. 2s. 6d. KEY. 3s. *net.*

FRENCH VOCABULARIES FOR REPETITION: Arranged according to Subjects. *Tenth Edition. Fcap.* 8vo. 1s.

FRENCH EXAMINATION PAPERS IN MISCELLANEOUS GRAMMAR AND IDIOMS. *Twelfth Edition.* Crown 8vo. 2s. 6d. [School Examination Series.

A KEY, issued to Tutors and Private Students only, to be had on application to the Publishers. *Fifth Edition.* Crown 8vo. 6s. net.

GENERAL KNOWLEDGE EXAMINATION PAPERS. *Fourth Edition.* Crown 8vo. 2s. 6d. [School Examination Series.
KEY (*Second Edition*) issued as above. 7s. *net.*

GREEK EXAMINATION PAPERS IN MISCELLANEOUS GRAMMAR AND IDIOMS. *Sixth Edition.* Crown 8vo. 2s. 6d. [School Examination Series.
KEY (*Third Edition*) issued as above. 6s. *net.*

LATIN EXAMINATION PAPERS IN MISCELLANEOUS GRAMMAR AND IDIOMS. *Eleventh Edition.* Crown 8vo. 2s. 6d. [School Examination Series.
KEY (*Fourth Edition*) issued as above. 6s. *net.*

R. **Elliott Steel**, M.A., F.C.S. THE WORLD OF SCIENCE. Including Chemistry, Heat, Light, Sound, Magnetism, Electricity, Botany, Zoology, Physiology, Astronomy, and Geology. 147 Illustrations. *Second Edition.* Crown 8vo. 2s. 6d.

PHYSICS EXAMINATION PAPERS. Crown 8vo. 2s. 6d.
[School Examination Series.

C. **Stephenson**, of the Technical College, Bradford, and **F. Suddards**, of the Yorkshire College, Leeds. ORNAMENTAL DESIGN FOR WOVEN FABRICS. Demy 8vo. *Second Edition.* 7s. 6d.

J. **Stephenson**, M.A. THE CHIEF TRUTHS OF THE CHRISTIAN FAITH. Crown 8vo. 3s. 6d.

An attempt to present in clear and popular form the main truths of the Faith. The book is intended for lay workers in the Church, for educated parents and for teachers generally.

Laurence Sterne. A SENTIMENTAL JOURNEY. Edited by H. W. PAUL. Pott 8vo. Cloth, 1s. 6d. *net; leather,* 2s. 6d. *net.* [Little Library.

W. Sterry, M.A. ANNALS OF ETON COLLEGE. With numerous Illustrations. Demy 8vo. 7s. 6d.

Katherine Steuart. BY ALLAN WATER. *Second Edition.* Crown 8vo. 6s.
'A delightful mixture of fiction and fact, tradition and history. There is not a page which is not informing and not entertaining.' —*Spectator.*
'A charming book.'—*Glasgow Herald.*

'Has a unique charm.'—*Pilot.*
'A unique series of historical pictures.'—*Manchester Guardian.*

R. L. Stevenson. THE LETTERS OF ROBERT LOUIS STEVENSON TO HIS FAMILY AND FRIENDS. Selected and Edited, with Notes and Introductions, by SIDNEY COLVIN. *Sixth and Cheaper Edition. Crown 8vo. 12s.*

LIBRARY EDITION. *Demy 8vo. 2 vols. 25s. net.*

'Irresistible in their raciness, their variety, their animation . . . of extraordinary fascination. A delightful inheritance, the truest record of a "richly compounded spirit" that the literature of our time has preserved.'—*Times.*

VAILIMA LETTERS. With an Etched Portrait by WILLIAM STRANG. *Third Edition. Crown 8vo. Buckram. 6s.*

THE LIFE OF R. L. STEVENSON. See G. Balfour.

E. D. Stone, M.A., late Assistant Master at Eton. SELECTIONS FROM THE ODYSSEY. *Fcap. 8vo. 1s. 6d.*

Charles Strachey. See Chesterfield.

A. W. Streane, D.D. ECCLESIASTES. Explained. *Fcap. 8vo. 1s. 6d. net.*
[Churchman's Bible.
'Scholarly, suggestive, and particularly interesting.'—*Bookman.*

Clement E. Stretton. A HISTORY OF THE MIDLAND RAILWAY. With numerous Illustrations. *Demy 8vo. 12s. 6d.*

H. Stroud, D.Sc., M.A., Professor of Physics in the Durham College of Science, Newcastle-on-Tyne. PRACTICAL PHYSICS. Fully Illustrated. *Crown 8vo. 3s. 6d.*
[Textbooks of Technology.

Capt. Donald Stuart. THE STRUGGLE FOR PERSIA. With a Map. *Crown 8vo. 6s.*
'Is indispensable to any student of international politics in the Middle East.'—*Daily Chronicle.*

F. Suddards. See C. Stephenson.

Jonathan Swift. THE JOURNAL TO STELLA. Edited by G. A. AITKEN. *Crown 8vo. 6s.* [Methuen's Standard Library.

J. E. Symes, M.A. THE FRENCH REVOLUTION. *Crown 8vo. 2s. 6d.*
[University Extension Series.

Tacitus. AGRICOLA. With Introduction, Notes, Map, etc. By R. F. DAVIS, M.A., late Assistant Master at Weymouth College. *Crown 8vo. 2s.*

GERMANIA. By the same Editor. *Crown 8vo. 2s.*

AGRICOLA AND GERMANIA. Translated by R. B. TOWNSHEND, late Scholar of Trinity College, Cambridge. *Crown 8vo. 2s. 6d.*
[Classical Translations.

J. Tauler. THE INNER WAY. Being Thirty-six Sermons for Festivals by JOHN TAULER. Edited, with an Introduction. By A. W. HUTTON, M.A. *Pott 8vo. Cloth, 2s.; leather, 2s. 6d. net.*
[Library of Devotion.

E. L. Taunton. A HISTORY OF THE JESUITS IN ENGLAND. With Illustrations. *Demy 8vo. 21s. net.*
'A history of permanent value, which covers ground never properly investigated before, and is replete with the results of original research. A most interesting and careful book.'—*Literature.*

F. G. Taylor, M.A. COMMERCIAL ARITHMETIC. *Third Edition. Crown 8vo. 1s. 6d.* [Commercial Series.

Miss J. A. Taylor. SIR WALTER RALEIGH. With 12 Illustrations. *Fcap. 8vo. Cloth, 3s. 6d.; leather 4s. net.*
[Little Biographies.

T. M. Taylor, M.A., Fellow of Gonville and Caius College, Cambridge. A CONSTITUTIONAL AND POLITICAL HISTORY OF ROME. *Crown 8vo. 7s. 6d.*
'We fully recognise the value of this carefully written work, and admire especially the fairness and sobriety of his judgment and the human interest with which he has inspired his subject.'—*Athenæum.*

Alfred, Lord Tennyson. THE EARLY POEMS OF. Edited, with Notes and an Introduction, by J. CHURTON COLLINS, M.A. *Crown 8vo. 6s.*
[Methuen's Standard Library.
Also with 10 Illustrations in Photogravure by W. E. F. BRITTEN. *Demy 8vo. 10s. 6d.*
An elaborate edition of the celebrated volume which was published in its final and definitive form in 1853.

IN MEMORIAM, MAUD, AND THE PRINCESS. Edited by J. CHURTON COLLINS, M.A. *Crown 8vo. 6s.*
[Methuen's Standard Library.

MAUD. Edited by ELIZABETH WORDSWORTH. *Pott 8vo. Cloth, 1s. 6d. net; leather, 2s. 6d. net.* [Little Library.

IN MEMORIAM. Edited, with an Introduction and Notes, by H. C. BEECHING, M.A. *Pott 8vo. Cloth, 1s. 6d. net; leather, 2s. 6d. net.* [Little Library.

THE EARLY POEMS OF. Edited by J. C. COLLINS, M.A. *Pott 8vo. Cloth, 1s. 6d. net; leather, 2s. 6d. net.* [Little Library.

THE PRINCESS. Edited by ELIZABETH WORDSWORTH. *Pott 8vo. Cloth, 1s. 6d. net; leather, 2s. 6d. net.* [Little Library.

Alice Terton. LIGHTS AND SHADOWS IN A HOSPITAL. *Crown 8vo. 3s. 6d.*

W. M. Thackeray. VANITY FAIR. With an Introduction by S. GWYNN. *Three*

Volumes. *Pott 8vo. Each volume, cloth,* 1s. 6d. *net; leather,* 2s. 6d. *net.*
[Little Library.
PENDENNIS. Edited by S. GWYNN. *Three Volumes. Pott 8vo. Each volume, cloth,* 1s. 6d. *net · leather,* 2s. 6d. *net.*
[Little Library.
ESMOND. Edited by STEPHEN GWYNN. *Two volumes. Pott 8vo. Each Volume, cloth,* 1s. 6d. *net; leather,* 2s. 6d. *net.*
[Little Library.
F. W. Theobald, M.A. INSECT LIFE. Illustrated. *Crown 8vo.* 2s. 6d.
[University Extension Series.
A. H. Thompson. CAMBRIDGE AND ITS COLLEGES. Illustrated by E. H. NEW. *Pott 8vo. Cloth,* 3s.; *leather,* 3s. 6d. *net.* [Little Guides.
'It is brightly written and learned, and is just such a book as a cultured visitor needs.'—*Scotsman.*
Paget Toynbee, Litt.D., M.A. See Dante. DANTE STUDIES AND RESEARCHES. *Demy 8vo.* 10s. 6d. *net.*
THE LIFE OF DANTE ALIGHIERI. With 12 Illustrations. *Second Edition. Fcap. 8vo. Cloth,* 3s. 6d.; *leather,* 4s. *net.* [Little Biographies.
Herbert Trench. DEIRDRE WED: and Other Poems. *Crown 8vo.* 5s.
G. E. Troutbeck. WESTMINSTER ABBEY. Illustrated by F. D. BEDFORD. *Pott 8vo. Cloth,* 3s.; *leather,* 3s. 6d. *net.*
[Little Guides.
'In comeliness, and perhaps in completeness, this work must take the first place.'—*Academy.*
'A really first-rate guide-book.'—*Literature.*
Gertrude Tuckwell. THE STATE AND ITS CHILDREN. *Crown 8vo.* 2s. 6d.
[Social Questions Series.
Louisa Twining. WORKHOUSES AND PAUPERISM. *Crown 8vo.* 2s. 6d.
[Social Questions Series.
E. A. Tyler. A JUNIOR CHEMISTRY. With 73 Illustrations. *Crown 8vo.* 2s. 6d.
[Methuen's Junior School Books.
G. W. Wade, D.D. OLD TESTAMENT HISTORY. With Maps. *Second Edition. Crown 8vo.* 6s.
'Careful, scholarly, embodying the best results of modern criticism, and written with great lucidity.'—*Examiner.*
Izaak Walton. THE LIVES OF DONNE, WOTTON, HOOKER, HERBERT AND SANDERSON. With an Introduction by VERNON BLACKBURN, and a Portrait. 3s. 6d.
THE COMPLEAT ANGLER. Edited by J. BUCHAN. *Pott 8vo. Cloth.* 1s. 6d. *net; leather,* 2s. 6d. *net.* [Little Library.
D. S. Van Warmelo. ON COMMANDO. With Portrait. *Crown 8vo.* 3s. 6d.
'A fighting Boer's simple, straightforward story of his life on commando. . . . Full of entertaining incidents.'—*Pall Mall Gazette.*

Grace Warrack. See Lady Julian of Norwich.
Mrs. Alfred Waterhouse. A LITTLE BOOK OF LIFE AND DEATH. Edited by. *Second Edition. Pott 8vo. Cloth,* 1s. 6d. *net; leather,* 2s. 6d. *net.* [Little Library.
C. C. J. Webb, M.A. See St. Anselm.
F. C. Webber. CARPENTRY AND JOINERY. With many Illustrations. *Third Edition. Crown 8vo.* 3s. 6d.
'An admirable elementary text-book on the subject.'—*Builder.*
Sidney H. Wells. PRACTICAL MECHANICS. With 75 Illustrations and Diagrams. *Second Edition. Crown 8vo.* 3s. 6d. [Textbooks of Technology.
J. Wells, M.A., Fellow and Tutor of Wadham College. OXFORD AND OXFORD LIFE. By Members of the University. *Third Edition. Crown 8vo.* 3s. 6d.
A SHORT HISTORY OF ROME. *Fourth Edition.* With 3 Maps. *Cr. 8vo.* 3s. 6d.
This book is intended for the Middle and Upper Forms of Public Schools and for Pass Students at the Universities. It contains copious Tables, etc.
'An original work written on an original plan, and with uncommon freshness and vigour.'—*Speaker.*
OXFORD AND ITS COLLEGES. Illustrated by E. H. New. *Fifth Edition. Pott 8vo. Cloth,* 3s.; *leather,* 3s. 6d. *net.*
[Little Guides.
'An admirable and accurate little treatise, attractively illustrated.'—*World.*
Helen C. Wetmore. THE LAST OF THE GREAT SCOUTS ('Buffalo Bill'). With Illustrations. *Second Edition. Demy 8vo.* 6s.
'A narrative of one of the most attractive figures in the public eye.'—*Daily Chronicle.*
C. Whibley. See Henley and Whibley.
L. Whibley, M.A., Fellow of Pembroke College, Cambridge. GREEK OLIGARCHIES: THEIR ORGANISATION AND CHARACTER. *Crown 8vo.* 6s.
G. H. Whitaker, M.A. THE EPISTLE OF ST. PAUL THE APOSTLE TO THE EPHESIANS. Edited by. *Fcap. 8vo.* 1s. 6d. *net.* [Churchman's Bible.
Gilbert White. THE NATURAL HISTORY OF SELBORNE. Edited by L. C. MIALL, F.R.S., assisted by W. WARDE FOWLER, M.A. *Crown 8vo.* 6s.
[Methuen's Standard Library.
E. E. Whitfield. PRECIS WRITING AND OFFICE CORRESPONDENCE. *Second Edition. Crown 8vo.* 2s.
[Commercial Series.
COMMERCIAL EDUCATION IN THEORY AND PRACTICE. *Crown 8vo.* 5s.
An introduction to Methuen's Commercial Series treating the question of Commercial Education fully from both the point of view of the teacher and of the parent.
[Commercial Series.

Miss Whitley. See Lady Dilke.

W. H. Wilkins, B.A. THE ALIEN INVASION. *Crown 8vo.* 2s. 6d.
[Social Questions Series.

W. Williamson. THE BRITISH GARDENER. Illustrated. *Demy 8vo.* 10s. 6d.

W. Williamson, B.A. JUNIOR ENGLISH EXAMINATION PAPERS. *Fcap. 8vo.* 1s. [Junior Examination Series.

A JUNIOR ENGLISH GRAMMAR. With numerous passages for parsing and analysis, and a chapter on Essay Writing. *Crown 8vo.* 2s. [Methuen's Junior School Books.

A CLASS-BOOK OF DICTATION PASSAGES. *Seventh Edition. Crown 8vo.* 1s. 6d. [Methuen's Junior School Books.

EASY DICTATION AND SPELLING. *Second Edition. Fcap. 8vo.* 1s.

E. M. Wilmot-Buxton. THE MAKERS OF EUROPE. *Crown 8vo.* 3s. 6d.
A Text-book of European History for Middle Forms.
'A book which will be found extremely useful.'—*Secondary Education.*

Beckles Willson. LORD STRATHCONA: the Story of his Life. Illustrated. *Demy 8vo.* 7s. 6d.
'An admirable biography, telling in the happiest manner the wonderful career of this giant of empire.'—*Black and White.*
'We should be glad to see this work taken as a model for imitation. He has given us an excellent and quite adequate account of the life of the distinguished Scotsman.'—*World.*

Richard Wilton, M.A., Canon of York. LYRA PASTORALIS: Songs of Nature, Church, and Home. *Pott 8vo.* 2s. 6d.
A volume of devotional poems.

S. E. Winbolt, M.A., Assistant Master in Christ's Hospital. EXERCISES IN LATIN ACCIDENCE. *Crown 8vo.* 1s. 6d.
An elementary book adapted for Lower Forms to accompany the Shorter Latin Primer.

B. C. A. Windle, F.R.S., D.Sc. SHAKESPEARE'S COUNTRY. Illustrated by E. H. New. *Second Edition. Pott 8vo.* Cloth, 3s.; leather, 3s. 6d. net. [Little Guides.
'One of the most charming guide books. Both for the library and as a travelling companion the book is equally choice and serviceable.'—*Academy.*

THE MALVERN COUNTRY. Illustrated by E. H. New. *Pott 8vo.* Cloth, 3s.; leather, 3s. 6d. net. [Little Guides.

Canon Winterbotham, M.A., B.Sc., LL.B. THE KINGDOM OF HEAVEN HERE AND HEREAFTER. *Crown 8vo.* 3s. 6d. [Churchman's Library.

J. A. E. Wood. HOW TO MAKE A DRESS. Illustrated. *Second Edition. Crown 8vo.* 1s. 6d.
[Text Books of Technology.

Elizabeth Wordsworth. See Tennyson.

Arthur Wright, M.A., Fellow of Queen's College, Cambridge. SOME NEW TESTAMENT PROBLEMS. *Crown 8vo.* 6s. [Churchman's Library.

Sophie Wright. GERMAN VOCABULARIES FOR REPETITION. *Fcap. 8vo.* 1s. 6d.

A. B. Wylde. MODERN ABYSSINIA. With a Map and a Portrait. *Demy 8vo.* 15s. net.

G. Wyndham, M.P. THE POEMS OF WILLIAM SHAKESPEARE. With an Introduction and Notes. *Demy 8vo.* Buckram, gilt top. 10s. 6d.
'We have no hesitation in describing Mr. George Wyndham's introduction as a masterly piece of criticism, and all who love our Elizabethan literature will find a very garden of delight in it.'—*Spectator.*

W. B. Yeats. AN ANTHOLOGY OF IRISH VERSE. *Revised and Enlarged Edition. Crown 8vo.* 3s. 6d.

T. M. Young. THE AMERICAN COTTON INDUSTRY: A Study of Work and Workers. With an Introduction by Elijah Helm, Secretary to the Manchester Chamber of Commerce. *Crown 8vo.* Cloth, 2s. 6d.; paper boards, 1s. 6d.
'Thorough, comprehensive, disconcerting.'—*St. James's Gazette.*
'Able and interesting; a really excellent contribution.'—*Pilot.*

Methuen's Standard Library

Crown 8vo. 6s. each Volume.

'A series which, by the beauty and excellence of production as well as by the qualifications of its editors, is one of the best things now to be found in the book market.'—*Manchester Guardian.*

Memoirs of My Life and Writings. By Edward Gibbon. Edited by G. Birkbeck Hill, LL.D.

The Decline and Fall of the Roman Empire. By Edward Gibbon. Edited by J. B. Bury, LL.D. *In Seven Volumes. Also, Demy 8vo. Gilt top.* 8s. 6d. each.

The Natural History of Selborne. By Gilbert White. Edited by L. C. Miall, F.R.S., Assisted by W. Warde Fowler, M.A.

The History of the Life of Thomas Ellwood. Edited by C. G. Crump, M.A.

La Commedia Di Dante Alighieri. The Italian Text. Edited by Paget Toynbee, Litt.D., M.A. *Also, Demy 8vo. Gilt top.* 8s. 6d.

The Early Poems of Alfred, Lord Tennyson. Edited by J. Churton Collins, M.A.

In Memoriam, Maud, and The Princess. By Alfred, Lord Tennyson. Edited by J. Churton Collins, M.A.

The Journal to Stella. By Jonathan Swift. Edited by G. A. Aitken, M.A.

The Letters of Lord Chesterfield to his Son. Edited by C. Strachey, and Notes by A. Calthrop. *Two Volumes.*

Critical and Historical Essays. By Lord Macaulay. Edited by F. C. Montague, M.A. *Three Volumes.*

The French Revolution. By Thomas Carlyle. Edited by C. R. L. Fletcher, Fellow of Magdalen College, Oxford. *Three Volumes.*

General Literature

Byzantine Texts.

Edited by J. B. BURY, M.A., Litt.D.

ZACHARIAH OF MITYLENE. Translated by F. J. Hamilton, D.D., and E. W. Brooks. *Demy 8vo. 12s. 6d. net.*

EVAGRIUS. Edited by Léon Parmentier and M. Bidez. *Demy 8vo. 10s. 6d. net.*

THE HISTORY OF PSELLUS. Edited by C. Sathas. *Demy 8vo. 15s. net.*

ECTHESIS CHRONICA. Edited by Professor Lambros. *Demy 8vo. 7s. 6d. net.*

The Little Library

With Introductions, Notes, and Photogravure Frontispieces.

Pott 8vo. Each Volume, cloth, 1s. 6d. net; leather, 2s. 6d. net.

'Altogether good to look upon, and to handle.'—*Outlook.*
'A perfect series.'—*Pilot.*
'It is difficult to conceive more attractive volumes.'—*St. James's Gazette.*
'Very delicious little books.'—*Literature.*

VANITY FAIR. By W. M. Thackeray. Edited by S. Gwynn. *Three Volumes.*

PENDENNIS. By W. M. Thackeray. Edited by S. Gwynn. *Three Volumes.*

ESMOND. By W. M. Thackeray. Edited by Stephen Gwynn. *Two Volumes.*

JOHN HALIFAX, GENTLEMAN. By Mrs. Craik. Edited by Annie Matheson. *Two Volumes.*

PRIDE AND PREJUDICE. By Jane Austen. Edited by E. V. Lucas. *Two Volumes.*

NORTHANGER ABBEY. By Jane Austen. Edited by E. V. Lucas.

THE PRINCESS. By Alfred, Lord Tennyson. Edited by Elizabeth Wordsworth.

MAUD. By Alfred, Lord Tennyson. Edited by Elizabeth Wordsworth.

IN MEMORIAM. By Alfred, Lord Tennyson. Edited by H. C. Beeching, M.A.

THE EARLY POEMS OF ALFRED, LORD TENNYSON. Edited by J. C. Collins, M.A.

A LITTLE BOOK OF ENGLISH LYRICS. With Notes.

THE INFERNO OF DANTE. Translated by H. F. Cary. Edited by Paget Toynbee, Litt.D., M.A.

THE PURGATORIO OF DANTE. Translated by H. F. Cary. Edited by Paget Toynbee, Litt.D., M.A.

THE PARADISO OF DANTE. Translated by H. F. Cary. Edited by Paget Toynbee, Litt.D., M.A.

A LITTLE BOOK OF SCOTTISH VERSE. Edited by T. F. Henderson.

A LITTLE BOOK OF LIGHT VERSE. Edited by A. C. Deane.

A LITTLE BOOK OF ENGLISH SONNETS. Edited by J. B. B. Nichols.

SELECTIONS FROM WORDSWORTH. Edited by Nowell C. Smith.

SELECTIONS FROM THE EARLY POEMS OF ROBERT BROWNING. Edited by W. Hall Griffin, M.A.

THE ENGLISH POEMS OF RICHARD CRASHAW. Edited by Edward Hutton.

SELECTIONS FROM WILLIAM BLAKE. Edited by M. Perugini.

A LITTLE BOOK OF LIFE AND DEATH. Edited by Mrs. Alfred Waterhouse.

A LITTLE BOOK OF ENGLISH PROSE. Edited by Mrs. P. A. Barnett.

EOTHEN. By A. W. Kinglake. With an Introduction and Notes.

CRANFORD. By Mrs. Gaskell. Edited by E. V. Lucas.

LAVENGRO. By George Borrow. Edited by F. Hindes Groome. *Two Volumes.*

THE HISTORY OF THE CALIPH VATHEK. By William Beckford. Edited by E. Denison Ross.

THE COMPLEAT ANGLER. By Izaak Walton. Edited by J. Buchan.

MARRIAGE. By Susan Ferrier. Edited by Miss Goodrich-Freer and Lord Iddesleigh. *Two Volumes.*

THE INHERITANCE. By Susan Ferrier. Edited by Miss Goodrich-Freer and Lord Iddesleigh. *Two Volumes.*

ELIA, AND THE LAST ESSAYS OF ELIA. By Charles Lamb. Edited by E. V. Lucas.

A SENTIMENTAL JOURNEY. By Laurence Sterne. Edited by H. W. Paul.

MANSIE WAUCH. By D. M. Moir. Edited by T. F. Henderson.

THE INGOLDSBY LEGENDS. By R. H. Barham. Edited by J. B. Atlay. *Two Volumes.*

THE SCARLET LETTER. By Nathaniel Hawthorne.

The Little Guides

Pott 8vo, cloth, 3s.; leather, 3s. 6d. net.

OXFORD AND ITS COLLEGES. By J. Wells, M.A. Illustrated by E. H. New. *Fourth Edition.*

CAMBRIDGE AND ITS COLLEGES. By A. Hamilton Thompson. Illustrated by E. H. New.

THE MALVERN COUNTRY. By B. C. A. Windle, D.Sc., F.R.S. Illustrated by E. H. New.

SHAKESPEARE'S COUNTRY. By B. C. A. Windle, D.Sc., F.R.S. Illustrated by E. H. New. *Second Edition.*

SUSSEX. By F. G. Brabant, M.A. Illustrated by E. H. New.

WESTMINSTER ABBEY. By G. E. Troutbeck. Illustrated by F. D. Bedford.

NORFOLK. By W. A. Dutt. Illustrated by B. C. Boulter.

CORNWALL. By A. L. Salmon. Illustrated by B. C. Boulter.

BRITTANY. By S. Baring-Gould. Illustrated by J. Wylie.

THE ENGLISH LAKES. By F. G. Brabant, M.A. Illustrated by E. H. New. *4s.; leather, 4s. 6d. net.*

Little Biographies

Fcap. 8vo. Each volume, cloth, 3s. 6d. ; leather, 4s. net.

DANTE ALIGHIERI. By Paget Toynbee, Litt.D., M.A. With 12 Illustrations. *Second Edition.*

SAVONAROLA. By E. L. S. Horsburgh, M.A. With Portraits and Illustrations.

JOHN HOWARD. By E. C. S. Gibson, D.D., Vicar of Leeds. With 12 Illustrations.

TENNYSON. By A. C. Benson, M.A. With 12 Illustrations.

WALTER RALEIGH By Miss J. A. Taylor. With 12 Illustrations.

ERASMUS. By E. F. H. CAPEY. With 12 Illustrations.

The Little Blue Books

General Editor, E. V. LUCAS.

Illustrated. Square Fcap. 8vo. 2s. 6d.

'Very elegant and very interesting volumes.'—*Glasgow Herald.*
'A delightful series of diminutive volumes.'—*World.*
'The series should be a favourite among juveniles.'—*Observer.*

1. THE CASTAWAYS OF MEADOWBANK. By T. COBB.
2. THE BEECHNUT BOOK. By JACOB ABBOTT. Edited by E. V. LUCAS.
3. THE AIR GUN. By T. HILBERT.
4. A SCHOOL YEAR. By NETTA SYRETT.
5. THE PEELES AT THE CAPITAL. By T. HILBERT.
6. THE TREASURE OF PRINCEGATE PRIORY. By T. COBB.

The Library of Devotion

With Introductions and (where necessary) Notes.

Pott 8vo, cloth, 2s. ; leather, 2s. 6d. net.

'This series is excellent.'—THE LATE BISHOP OF LONDON.
'Well worth the attention of the Clergy.'—THE BISHOP OF LICHFIELD.
'The new "Library of Devotion" is excellent.'—THE BISHOP OF PETERBOROUGH.
'Charming.'—*Record.*   'Delightful.'—*Church Bells.*

THE CONFESSIONS OF ST. AUGUSTINE. Edited by C. Bigg, D.D. *Third Edition.*

THE CHRISTIAN YEAR. Edited by Walter Lock, D.D. *Second Edition.*

THE IMITATION OF CHRIST. Edited by C. Bigg, D.D. *Second Edition.*

A BOOK OF DEVOTIONS. Edited by J. W. Stanbridge, B.D.

LYRA INNOCENTIUM. Edited by Walter Lock, D.D.

A SERIOUS CALL TO A DEVOUT AND HOLY LIFE. Edited by C. Bigg, D.D. *Second Edition.*

THE TEMPLE. Edited by E. C. S. Gibson, D.D.

A GUIDE TO ETERNITY. Edited by J. W. Stanbridge, B.D.

THE PSALMS OF DAVID. Edited by B. W. Randolph, D.D.

LYRA APOSTOLICA. Edited by Canon Scott Holland and H. C. Beeching, M.A.

THE INNER WAY. Edited by A. W. Hutton, M.A.

THE THOUGHTS OF PASCAL. Edited by C. S. Jerram, M.A.

ON THE LOVE OF GOD. Edited by W. J. Knox Little, M.A.

A MANUAL OF CONSOLATION FROM THE SAINTS AND FATHERS. Edited by J. H. Burn, B.D.

THE SONG OF SONGS. Edited by B. Blaxland, M.A.

THE DEVOTIONS OF ST. ANSELM. Edited by C. C. J. Webb, M.A.

The Westminster Commentaries

General Editor, WALTER LOCK, D.D., Warden of Keble College,
Dean Ireland's Professor of Exegesis in the University of Oxford.

THE BOOK OF JOB. Edited by E. C. S. Gibson, D.D. *Demy 8vo.* 6s.

THE ACTS OF THE APOSTLES. Edited by R. B Rackham, M.A. *Demy 8vo.* 12s. 6d.

Handbooks of Theology

General Editor, A. ROBERTSON, D.D., Principal of King's College, London.

THE XXXIX. ARTICLES OF THE CHURCH OF ENGLAND. Edited by E. C. S. Gibson, D.D. *Third and Cheaper Edition in One Volume. Demy 8vo.* 12s. 6d.

AN INTRODUCTION TO THE HISTORY OF RELIGION. By F. B. Jevons, M.A., Litt.D. *Second Edition. Demy 8vo.* 10s. 6d.

THE DOCTRINE OF THE INCARNATION. By R. L. Ottley, M.A. *Second and Cheaper Edition. Demy 8vo.* 12s. 6d.

AN INTRODUCTION TO THE HISTORY OF THE CREEDS. By A. E. Burn, B.D. *Demy 8vo.* 10s. 6d.

THE PHILOSOPHY OF RELIGION IN ENGLAND AND AMERICA. By Alfred Caldecott, D.D. *Demy 8vo.* 10s. 6d.

The Churchman's Library

General Editor, J. H. BURN, B.D., F.R.S.E., Examining Chaplain to the Bishop of Aberdeen.

THE BEGINNINGS OF ENGLISH CHRISTIANITY. By W. E. Collins, M.A. With Map. *Crown 8vo. 3s. 6d.*

SOME NEW TESTAMENT PROBLEMS. By Arthur Wright, M.A. *Crown 8vo. 6s.*

THE KINGDOM OF HEAVEN HERE AND HEREAFTER. By Canon Winterbotham, M.A., B.Sc., LL.B. *Crown 8vo. 3s. 6d.*

THE WORKMANSHIP OF THE PRAYER BOOK: Its Literary and Liturgical Aspects. By J. Dowden, D.D. *Second Edition. Crown 8vo. 3s. 6d.*

EVOLUTION. By F. B. Jevons, M.A., Litt.D. *Crown 8vo. 3s. 6d.*

THE OLD TESTAMENT AND THE NEW SCHOLARSHIP. By J. W. Peters, D.D. *Crown 8vo. 6s.*

THE CHURCHMAN'S INTRODUCTION TO THE OLD TESTAMENT. Edited by A. M. Mackay, B.A. *Crown 8vo. 3s. 6d.*

THE CHURCH OF CHRIST By E. T. Green, M.A. *Crown 8vo. 6s.*

COMPARATIVE THEOLOGY. By J. A. MacCulloch. *Crown 8vo. 6s.*

The Churchman's Bible

General Editor, J. H. BURN, B.D., F.R.S.E.

The volumes are practical and devotional, and the text of the Authorised Version is explained in sections, which correspond as far as possible with the Church Lectionary.

THE EPISTLE TO THE GALATIANS. Explained by A. W. Robinson, M.A. *Fcap. 8vo. 1s. 6d. net.*

ECCLESIASTES. Explained by A. W. Streane, D.D. *Fcap. 8vo. 1s. 6d. net.*

THE EPISTLE TO THE PHILIPPIANS. Explained by C. R. D. Biggs, D.D. *Fcap. 8vo. 1s. 6d. net.*

THE EPISTLE OF ST. JAMES. Edited by H. W. Fulford, M.A. *Fcap. 8vo. 1s. 6d. net.*

ISAIAH. Edited by W. E. Barnes, D.D., Hulsaean Professor of Divinity. *Two Volumes. Fcap. 8vo. 2s. net each.* Vol. I. With Map.

THE EPISTLE OF ST. PAUL THE APOSTLE TO THE EPHESIANS. Edited by G. H. Whitaker, M.A. *Fcap. 8vo. 1s. 6d. net.*

Leaders of Religion

Edited by H. C. BEECHING, M.A. *With Portraits. Crown 8vo. 3s. 6d.*

A series of short biographies of the most prominent leaders of religious life and thought of all ages and countries.

CARDINAL NEWMAN. By R. H. Hutton.
JOHN WESLEY. By J. H. Overton, M.A.
BISHOP WILBERFORCE. By G. W. Daniell, M.A.
CARDINAL MANNING. By A. W. Hutton, M.A.
CHARLES SIMEON. By H. C. G. Moule, D.D.
JOHN KEBLE. By Walter Lock, D.D.
THOMAS CHALMERS. By Mrs. Oliphant.
LANCELOT ANDREWES. By R. L. Ottley, M.A.
AUGUSTINE OF CANTERBURY. By E. L. Cutts, D.D.
WILLIAM LAUD. By W. H. Hutton, M.A.
JOHN KNOX. By F. MacCunn.
JOHN HOWE. By R. F. Horton, D.D.
BISHOP KEN. By F. A. Clarke, M.A.
GEORGE FOX, THE QUAKER. By T. Hodgkin. D.C.L.
JOHN DONNE. By Augustus Jessopp, D.D.
THOMAS CRANMER. By A. J. Mason.
BISHOP LATIMER. By R. M. Carlyle and A. J. Carlyle, M.A.
BISHOP BUTLER. By W. A. Spooner, M.A.

Social Questions of To-day

Edited by H. DE B. GIBBINS, Litt.D., M.A.

Crown 8vo. 2s. 6d.

TRADE UNIONISM—NEW AND OLD. By G. Howell. *Third Edition.*
THE CO-OPERATIVE MOVEMENT TO-DAY. By G. J. Holyoake. *Second Edition.*
PROBLEMS OF POVERTY. By J. A. Hobson, M.A. *Fourth Edition.*
THE COMMERCE OF NATIONS. By C. F. Bastable, M.A. *Second Edition.*
THE ALIEN INVASION. By W. H. Wilkins, B.A.
THE RURAL EXODUS. By P. Anderson Graham.
LAND NATIONALIZATION. By Harold Cox, B.A.
A SHORTER WORKING DAY. By H. de B. Gibbins and R. A. Hadfield.
BACK TO THE LAND: An Inquiry into Rural Depopulation. By H. E. Moore.
TRUSTS, POOLS, AND CORNERS. By J. Stephen Jeans.
THE FACTORY SYSTEM. By R. W. Cooke-Taylor.
THE STATE AND ITS CHILDREN. By Gertrude Tuckwell.
WOMEN'S WORK. By Lady Dilke, Miss Bulley, and Miss Whitley.
SOCIALISM AND MODERN THOUGHT. By M. Kauffmann.
THE HOUSING OF THE WORKING CLASSES. By E. Bowmaker.
THE PROBLEM OF THE UNEMPLOYED. By J. A. Hobson, B.A.
LIFE IN WEST LONDON. By Arthur Sherwell, M.A. *Third Edition.*
RAILWAY NATIONALIZATION. By Clement Edwards.
WORKHOUSES AND PAUPERISM. By Louisa Twining.
UNIVERSITY AND SOCIAL SETTLEMENTS. By W. Reason, M.A.

University Extension Series

Edited by J. E. SYMES, M.A.,
Principal of University College, Nottingham.

Crown 8vo. Price (with some exceptions) 2s. 6d.

A series of books on historical, literary, and scientific subjects, suitable for extension students and home-reading circles. Each volume is complete in itself, and the subjects are treated by competent writers in a broad and philosophic spirit.

THE INDUSTRIAL HISTORY OF ENGLAND. By H. de B. Gibbins, Litt.D., M.A. *Eighth Edition.* Revised. With Maps and Plans. 3s.

A HISTORY OF ENGLISH POLITICAL ECONOMY. By L. L. Price, M.A. *Third Edition.*

PROBLEMS OF POVERTY. By J. A. Hobson, M.A. *Fourth Edition.*

VICTORIAN POETS. By A. Sharp.

THE FRENCH REVOLUTION. By J. E. Symes, M.A.

PSYCHOLOGY. By S. F. Granger, M.A. *Second Edition.*

THE EVOLUTION OF PLANT LIFE: Lower Forms. By G. Massee. Illustrated.

AIR AND WATER. By V. B. Lewes, M.A. Illustrated.

THE CHEMISTRY OF LIFE AND HEALTH. By C. W. Kimmins, M.A. Illustrated.

THE MECHANICS OF DAILY LIFE. By V. P. Sells, M.A. Illustrated.

ENGLISH SOCIAL REFORMERS. By H. de B. Gibbins, Litt.D., M.A. *Second Edition.*

ENGLISH TRADE AND FINANCE IN THE SEVENTEENTH CENTURY. By W. A. S. Hewins, B.A.

THE CHEMISTRY OF FIRE. By M. M. Pattison Muir, M.A. Illustrated.

A TEXT-BOOK OF AGRICULTURAL BOTANY. By M. C. Potter, M.A., F.L.S. Illustrated. *Second Edition.* 4s. 6d.

THE VAULT OF HEAVEN. A Popular Introduction to Astronomy. By R. A. Gregory. With numerous Illustrations.

METEOROLOGY. By H. N. Dickson, F.R.S.E., F.R. Met. Soc. Illustrated.

A MANUAL OF ELECTRICAL SCIENCE. By George J. Burch, M.A., F.R.S. Illustrated. 3s.

THE EARTH. An Introduction to Physiography. By Evan Small, M.A. Illustrated.

INSECT LIFE. By F. W. Theobald, M.A. Illustrated.

ENGLISH POETRY FROM BLAKE TO BROWNING. By W. M. Dixon, M.A. *Second Edition.*

ENGLISH LOCAL GOVERNMENT. By E. Jenks, M.A.

THE GREEK VIEW OF LIFE. By G. L. Dickinson. *Second Edition.*

Methuen's Commercial Series

Edited by H. DE B. GIBBINS, Litt.D., M.A.

COMMERCIAL EDUCATION IN THEORY AND PRACTICE. By E. E. Whitfield, M.A.
An introduction to Methuen's Commercial Series treating the question of Commercial Education fully from both the point of view of the teacher and of the parent.

BRITISH COMMERCE AND COLONIES FROM ELIZABETH TO VICTORIA. By H. de B. Gibbins, Litt.D., M.A. *Third Edition.* 2s.

COMMERCIAL EXAMINATION PAPERS. By H. de B. Gibbins, Litt.D., M.A. 1s. 6d.

THE ECONOMICS OF COMMERCE. By H. de B. Gibbins, Litt.D., M.A. 1s. 6d.

A GERMAN COMMERCIAL READER. By S. E. Bally. With Vocabulary. 2s.

A COMMERCIAL GEOGRAPHY OF THE BRITISH EMPIRE. By L. W. Lyde, M.A. *Third Edition.*

A PRIMER OF BUSINESS. By S. Jackson, M.A. *Third Edition.* 1s. 6d.

COMMERCIAL ARITHMETIC. By F. G. Taylor, M.A. *Third Edition.* 1s. 6d.

FRENCH COMMERCIAL CORRESPONDENCE. By S. E. Bally. With Vocabulary. *Third Edition.* 2s.

GERMAN COMMERCIAL CORRESPONDENCE. By S. E. Bally. With Vocabulary. 2s. 6d.

A FRENCH COMMERCIAL READER. By S. E. Bally. With Vocabulary. *Second Edition.* 2s.

PRECIS WRITING AND OFFICE CORRESPONDENCE. By E. E. Whitfield, M.A. *Second Edition.* 2s.

A GUIDE TO PROFESSIONS AND BUSINESS. By H. Jones. 1s. 6d.

THE PRINCIPLES OF BOOK-KEEPING BY DOUBLE ENTRY. By J. E. B. M'Allen, M.A. 2s.

COMMERCIAL LAW. By W. Douglas Edwards. 2s.

A COMMERCIAL GEOGRAPHY OF FOREIGN NATIONS. By F. C. Boon, B.A. 2s.

Classical Translations

Edited by H. F. FOX, M.A., Fellow and Tutor of Brasenose College, Oxford.

ÆSCHYLUS—Agamemnon, Choephoroe, Eumenides. Translated by Lewis Campbell, LL.D. 5s.

CICERO—De Oratore I. Translated by E. N. P. Moor, M.A. 3s. 6d.

CICERO—Select Orations (Pro Milone, Pro Mureno, Philippic II., in Catilinam). Translated by H. E. D. Blakiston, M.A. 5s.

CICERO—De Natura Deorum. Translated by F. Brooks, M.A. 3s. 6d.

CICERO—De Officiis. Translated by G. B. Gardiner, M.A. 2s. 6d.

HORACE—The Odes and Epodes. Translated by A. Godley, M.A. 2s.

LUCIAN—Six Dialogues (Nigrinus, Icaro-Menippus, The Cock, The Ship, The Parasite, The Lover of Falsehood). Translated by S. T. Irwin, M.A. 3s. 6d.

SOPHOCLES—Electra and Ajax. Translated by E. D. A. Morshead, M.A. 2s. 6d.

TACITUS—Agricola and Germania. Translated by R. B. Townshend. 2s. 6d.

General Literature

Methuen's Junior School-Books.
Edited by O. D. INSKIP, LL.D., and W. WILLIAMSON, B.A.

A CLASS-BOOK OF DICTATION PASSAGES. By W. Williamson, B.A. *Seventh Edition.* Crown 8vo. 1s. 6d.

THE GOSPEL ACCORDING TO ST. MARK. Edited by A. E. Rubie, M.A., Headmaster of the Royal Naval School, Eltham. With Three Maps. *Crown 8vo.* 1s. 6d.

A JUNIOR ENGLISH GRAMMAR. By W. Williamson, B.A. With numerous passages for parsing and analysis, and a chapter on Essay Writing. *Crown 8vo.* 2s.

A JUNIOR CHEMISTRY. By E. A. Tyler, B.A., F.C.S., Science Master at Framlingham College. With 73 Illustrations. *Crown 8vo.* 2s. 6d.

School Examination Series
Edited by A. M. M. STEDMAN, M.A. *Crown 8vo.* 2s. 6d.

FRENCH EXAMINATION PAPERS. By A. M. M. Stedman, M.A. *Twelfth Edition.*
A KEY, issued to Tutors and Private Students only, to be had on application to the Publishers. *Fifth Edition.* Crown 8vo. 6s. net.

LATIN EXAMINATION PAPERS. By A. M. M. Stedman, M.A. *Eleventh Edition.*
KEY (*Fourth Edition*) issued as above. 6s. net.

GREEK EXAMINATION PAPERS. By A. M. M. Stedman, M.A. *Sixth Edition.*
KEY (*Second Edition*) issued as above. 6s. net.

GERMAN EXAMINATION PAPERS. By R. J. Morich. *Fifth Edition.*
KEY (*Second Edition*) issued as above. 6s. net.

HISTORY AND GEOGRAPHY EXAMINATION PAPERS. By C. H. Spence, M.A., Clifton College. *Second Edition.*

PHYSICS EXAMINATION PAPERS. By R. E. Steel, M.A., F.C.S.

GENERAL KNOWLEDGE EXAMINATION PAPERS. By A. M. M. Stedman, M.A. *Fourth Edition.*
KEY (*Second Edition*) issued as above. 7s. net.

EXAMINATION PAPERS IN ENGLISH HISTORY. By J. Tait Plowden-Wardlaw, B.A. *Crown 8vo.* 2s. 6d.

Junior Examination Series.
Edited by A. M. M. STEDMAN, M.A. *Fcap. 8vo.* 1s.

JUNIOR FRENCH EXAMINATION PAPERS. By F. Jacob, B.A.

JUNIOR LATIN EXAMINATION PAPERS. By C. G. Botting, M.A.

JUNIOR ENGLISH EXAMINATION PAPERS. By W. Williamson, B.A., Headmaster West Kent Grammar School, Brockley.

JUNIOR ARITHMETIC EXAMINATION PAPERS. By W. S. Beard, Headmaster Modern School, Fareham.

JUNIOR ALGEBRA EXAMINATION PAPERS. By W. S. Finn, M.A.

Technology—Textbooks of
Edited by W. GARNETT, D.C.L., and PROFESSOR J. WERTHEIMER, F.I.C.
Fully Illustrated.

HOW TO MAKE A DRESS. By J. A. E Wood. *Second Edition.* Crown 8vo. 1s. 6d.

CARPENTRY AND JOINERY. By F. C. Webber. *Second Edition.* Crown 8vo. 3s. 6d.

PRACTICAL MECHANICS. By Sidney H. Wells. *Second Edition.* Crown 8vo. 3s. 6d.

PRACTICAL PHYSICS. By H. Stroud, D.Sc., M.A. Crown 8vo. 3s. 6d.

MILLINERY, THEORETICA AND PRACTICAL. By Clare Hill. *Crown 8vo.* 2s.

PRACTICAL CHEMISTRY. By W. French, M.A Crown 8vo. Part I. 1s. 6d.

PART II.—FICTION

Marie Corelli's Novels.
Crown 8vo. 6s. each.

A ROMANCE OF TWO WORLDS. *Twenty-Third Edition.*

VENDETTA. *Nineteenth Edition.*

THELMA. *Twenty-Eighth Edition.*

ARDATH: THE STORY OF A DEAD SELF. *Fourteenth Edition.*

THE SOUL OF LILITH. *Eleventh Edit.*

WORMWOOD. *Twelfth Edition.*

BARABBAS: A DREAM OF THE WORLD'S TRAGEDY. *Thirty-Eighth Edition.*

'The tender reverence of the treatment and the imaginative beauty of the writing have reconciled us to the daring of the conception. This "Dream of the World's Tragedy" is a lofty and not inadequate paraphrase of the supreme climax of the inspired narrative.'—*Dublin Review.*

THE SORROWS OF SATAN. *Forty-Sixth Edition.*

'A very powerful piece of work. . . . The conception is magnificent, and is likely to win an abiding place within the memory of man. . . . The author has immense command of language, and a limitless audacity. . . . This interesting and remarkable romance will live long after much of the ephemeral literature of the day is forgotten. . . . A literary phenomenon . . . novel, and even sublime.'—W. T. STEAD in the *Review of Reviews.*

THE MASTER CHRISTIAN.
[165*th Thousand.*

'It cannot be denied that "The Master Christian" is a powerful book; that it is one likely to raise uncomfortable questions in all but the most self-satisfied readers, and that it strikes at the root of the failure of the Churches—the decay of faith—in a manner which shows the inevitable disaster heaping up. . . . The good Cardinal Bonpré is a beautiful figure, fit to stand beside the good Bishop in "Les Misérables." It is a book with a serious purpose expressed with absolute unconventionality and passion . . . And this is to say it is a book worth reading.'—*Examiner.*

TEMPORAL POWER: A STUDY IN SUPREMACY.
[150*th Thousand.*

'It is impossible to read such a work as "Temporal Power" without becoming convinced that the story is intended to convey certain criticisms on the ways of the world and certain suggestions for the betterment of humanity. . . . The chief characteristics of the book are an attack on conventional prejudices and manners and on certain practices attributed to the Roman Church (the policy of M. Combes makes parts of the novel specially up to date), and the propounding of theories for the improvement of the social and political systems. . . . If the chief intention of the book was to hold the mirror up to shams, injustice, dishonesty, cruelty, and neglect of conscience, nothing but praise can be given to that intention.'—*Morning Post.*

Anthony Hope's Novels.
Crown 8vo. 6s. each.

THE GOD IN THE CAR. *Ninth Edition.*

'A very remarkable book, deserving of critical analysis impossible within our limit; brilliant, but not superficial; well considered, but not elaborated; constructed with the proverbial art that conceals, but yet allows itself to be enjoyed by readers to whom fine literary method is a keen pleasure.'—*The World.*

A CHANGE OF AIR. *Sixth Edition.*

'A graceful, vivacious comedy, true to human nature. The characters are traced with a masterly hand.'—*Times.*

A MAN OF MARK. *Fifth Edition.*

'Of all Mr. Hope's books, "A Man of Mark" is the one which best compares with "The Prisoner of Zenda."'—*National Observer.*

THE CHRONICLES OF COUNT ANTONIO. *Fifth Edition.*

'It is a perfectly enchanting story of love and chivalry, and pure romance. The Count is the most constant, desperate, and modest and tender of lovers, a peerless gentleman, an intrepid fighter, a faithful friend, and a magnanimous foe.'—*Guardian.*

PHROSO. Illustrated by H. R. MILLAR. *Sixth Edition.*

'The tale is thoroughly fresh, quick with vitality, stirring the blood.'—*St. James's Gazette.*

SIMON DALE. Illustrated. *Sixth Edition.*

'There is searching analysis of human nature, with a most ingeniously constructed plot. Mr. Hope has drawn the contrasts of his women with marvellous subtlety and delicacy.'—*Times.*

THE KING'S MIRROR. *Fourth Edition.*

'In elegance, delicacy, and tact it ranks with the best of his novels, while in the wide range of its portraiture and the subtilty of its analysis it surpasses all his earlier ventures.'—*Spectator.*

QUISANTE. *Third Edition.*

'The book is notable for a very high literary quality, and an impress of power and mastery on every page.'—*Daily Chronicle.*

W. W. Jacobs' Novels.
Crown 8vo. 3s. 6d. each.

MANY CARGOES. *Twenty-Sixth Edition.*
SEA URCHINS. *Ninth Edition.*
A MASTER OF CRAFT. Illustrated. *Fifth Edition.*

'Can be unreservedly recommended to all who have not lost their appetite for wholesome laughter.'—*Spectator.*

'The best humorous book published for many a day.'—*Black and White.*

LIGHT FREIGHTS. Illustrated. *Fourth Edition.*

'His wit and humour are perfectly irresistible. Mr. Jacobs writes of skippers, and mates, and seamen, and his crew are the jolliest lot that ever sailed.'—*Daily News.*

'Laughter in every page.'—*Daily Mail.*

FICTION

Lucas Malet's Novels.
Crown 8vo. 6s. each.

COLONEL ENDERBY'S WIFE. *Third Edition.*

A COUNSEL OF PERFECTION. *New Edition.*

LITTLE PETER. *Second Edition.* 3s. 6d.

THE WAGES OF SIN. *Thirteenth Edition.*

THE CARISSIMA. *Fourth Edition.*

THE GATELESS BARRIER. *Fourth Edition.*

'In "The Gateless Barrier" it is at once evident that, whilst Lucas Malet has preserved her birthright of originality, the artistry, the actual writing, is above even the high level of the books that were born before.'—*Westminster Gazette.*

THE HISTORY OF SIR RICHARD CALMADY. *Seventh Edition.* A Limited Edition in Two Volumes. *Crown 8vo.* 12s.

'A picture finely and amply conceived. In the strength and insight in which the story has been conceived, in the wealth of fancy and reflection bestowed upon its execution, and in the moving sincerity of its pathos throughout, "Sir Richard Calmady" must rank as the great novel of a great writer.'—*Literature.*

'The ripest fruit of Lucas Malet's genius. A picture of maternal love by turns tender and terrible.'—*Spectator.*

'A remarkably fine book, with a noble motive and a sound conclusion.'—*Pilot.*

Gilbert Parker's Novels.
Crown 8vo. 6s. each.

PIERRE AND HIS PEOPLE. *Fifth Edition.*

'Stories happily conceived and finely executed. There is strength and genius in Mr. Parker's style.'—*Daily Telegraph.*

MRS. FALCHION. *Fourth Edition.*

'A splendid study of character.'— *Athenæum.*

THE TRANSLATION OF A SAVAGE. *Second Edition.*

THE TRAIL OF THE SWORD. *Illustrated. Seventh Edition.*

'A rousing and dramatic tale. A book like this is a joy inexpressible.'— *Daily Chronicle.*

WHEN VALMOND CAME TO PONTIAC: The Story of a Lost Napoleon. *Fifth Edition.*

'Here we find romance—real, breathing, living romance. The character of Valmond is drawn unerringly.'—*Pall Mall Gazette.*

AN ADVENTURER OF THE NORTH: The Last Adventures of 'Pretty Pierre.' *Second Edition.*

'The present book is full of fine and moving stories of the great North.'—*Glasgow Herald.*

THE SEATS OF THE MIGHTY. *Illustrated. Twelfth Edition.*

'Mr. Parker has produced a really fine historical novel.'—*Athenæum.*

'A great book.'—*Black and White.*

THE BATTLE OF THE STRONG: a Romance of Two Kingdoms. *Illustrated. Fourth Edition.*

'Nothing more vigorous or more human has come from Mr. Gilbert Parker than this novel.'—*Literature.*

THE POMP OF THE LAVILETTES. *Second Edition.* 3s. 6d.

'Unforced pathos, and a deeper knowledge of human nature than he has displayed before.'—*Pall Mall Gazette.*

Arthur Morrison's Novels.
Crown 8vo. 6s. each.

TALES OF MEAN STREETS. *Fifth Edition.*

'A great book. The author's method is amazingly effective, and produces a thrilling sense of reality. The writer lays upon us a master hand. The book is simply appalling and irresistible in its interest. It is humorous also; without humour it would not make the mark it is certain to make.'—*World.*

A CHILD OF THE JAGO. *Fourth Edition.*

'The book is a masterpiece.'—*Pall Mall Gazette.*

TO LONDON TOWN. *Second Edition.*

'This is the new Mr. Arthur Morrison, gracious and tender, sympathetic and human.'—*Daily Telegraph.*

CUNNING MURRELL.

'Admirable. . . . Delightful humorous relief . . . a most artistic and satisfactory achievement.'—*Spectator.*

THE HOLE IN THE WALL. *Third Edition.*

'A masterpiece of artistic realism. It has a finality of touch that only a master may command.'—*Daily Chronicle.*

'An absolute masterpiece, which any novelist might be proud to claim.'—*Graphic.*

'"The Hole in the Wall" is a masterly piece of work. His characters are drawn with amazing skill. Extraordinary power.' —*Daily Telegraph.*

Eden Phillpotts' Novels.
Crown 8vo. 6s. each.

LYING PROPHETS.
CHILDREN OF THE MIST.
THE HUMAN BOY. With a Frontispiece. *Fourth Edition.*
  'Mr. Phillpotts knows exactly what school-boys do, and can lay bare their inmost thoughts; likewise he shows an all-pervading sense of humour.'—*Academy.*
SONS OF THE MORNING. *Second Edition.*
  'A book of strange power and fascination.'—*Morning Post.*
THE STRIKING HOURS. *Second Edition.*
  'Tragedy and comedy, pathos and humour, are blended to a nicety in this volume.'—*World.*
  'The whole book is redolent of a fresher and ampler air than breathes in the circumscribed life of great towns.'—*Spectator.*

FANCY FREE. Illustrated. *Second Edition.*
  'Of variety and racy humour there is plenty.'—*Daily Graphic.*

THE RIVER. *Third Edition.*
  '"The River" places Mr. Phillpotts in the front rank of living novelists.'—*Punch.*
  'Since "Lorna Doone" we have had nothing so picturesque as this new romance.' *Birmingham Gazette.*
  'Mr. Phillpotts's new book is a masterpiece which brings him indisputably into the front rank of English novelists.'—*Pall Mall Gazette.*
  'This great romance of the River Dart. The finest book Mr. Eden Phillpotts has written.'—*Morning Post.*

S. Baring-Gould's Novels.
Crown 8vo. 6s. each.

ARMINELL. *Fifth Edition.*
URITH. *Fifth Edition.*
IN THE ROAR OF THE SEA. *Seventh Edition.*
MRS. CURGENVEN OF CURGENVEN. *Fourth Edition.*
CHEAP JACK ZITA. *Fourth Edition.*
THE QUEEN OF LOVE. *Fifth Edition.*
MARGERY OF QUETHER. *Third Edition.*
JACQUETTA. *Third Edition.*
KITTY ALONE. *Fifth Edition.*
NOÉMI. Illustrated. *Fourth Edition.*

THE BROOM-SQUIRE. Illustrated. *Fourth Edition.*
THE PENNYCOMEQUICKS. *Third Edition.*
DARTMOOR IDYLLS.
GUAVAS THE TINNER. Illustrated. *Second Edition.*
BLADYS. Illustrated. *Second Edition.*
DOMITIA. Illustrated. *Second Edition.*
PABO THE PRIEST.
WINIFRED. Illustrated. *Second Edition.*
THE FROBISHERS.
ROYAL GEORGIE. Illustrated.
MISS QUILLET. Illustrated.

Robert Barr's Novels.
Crown 8vo. 6s. each.

IN THE MIDST OF ALARMS. *Third Edition.*
  'A book which has abundantly satisfied us by its capital humour.'—*Daily Chronicle.*
THE MUTABLE MANY. *Second Edition.*
  'There is much insight in it, and much excellent humour.'—*Daily Chronicle.*
THE COUNTESS TEKLA. *Third Edition.*
  'Of these mediæval romances, which are now gaining ground "The Countess Tekla" is the very best we have seen.'—*Pall Mall Gazette.*

THE STRONG ARM. Illustrated. *Second Edition.*

THE VICTORS.
  'Mr. Barr has a rich sense of humour.'—*Onlooker.*
  'A very convincing study of American life in its business and political aspects.'—*Pilot.*
  'Good writing, illuminating sketches of character, and constant variety of scene and incident.'—*Times.*

F. Anstey, Author of 'Vice Versa.' A BAYARD FROM BENGAL. Illustrated by BERNARD PARTRIDGE. *Third Edition.* Crown 8vo. 3s. 6d.
  'A highly amusing story.'— *Pall Mall Gazette.*
  'A volume of rollicking irresponsible fun.'— *Outlook.*
  'This eminently mirthful narrative.'— *Globe.*
  'Immensely diverting.'—*Glasgow Herald.*

Richard Bagot. A ROMAN MYSTERY. *Third Edition.* Crown 8vo. 6s.
  'An admirable story. The plot is sensational and original, and the book is full of telling situations.'—*St. James's Gazette.*

FICTION

Andrew Balfour. BY STROKE OF SWORD. Illustrated. *Fourth Edition.* Crown 8vo. 6s.

'A recital of thrilling interest, told with unflagging vigour.'—*Globe.*

VENGEANCE IS MINE. Illustrated. Crown 8vo. 6s.

See also Fleur de Lis Novels.

M. C. Balfour. THE FALL OF THE SPARROW. Crown 8vo. 6s.

S. Baring Gould. See page 34.

Jane Barlow. THE LAND OF THE SHAMROCK. Crown 8vo. 6s.

FROM THE EAST UNTO THE WEST. Crown 8vo. 6s.

THE FOUNDING OF FORTUNES. Crown 8vo. 6s.

'This interesting and delightful book. Its author has done nothing better, and it is scarcely an exaggeration to say that it would be an injustice to Ireland not to read it.'—*Scotsman.*

See also Fleur de Lis Novels.

Robert Barr. See page 34.

J. A. Barry. IN THE GREAT DEEP. Crown 8vo. 6s.

George Bartram, Author of 'The People of Clopton.' THE THIRTEEN EVENINGS. Crown 8vo. 6s.

Harold Begbie. THE ADVENTURES OF SIR JOHN SPARROW. Crown 8vo. 6s.

'Mr. Begbie often recalls Stevenson's manner and makes "Sir John Sparrow" most diverting writing. Sir John is inspired with the idea that it is his duty to reform the world, and launches into the vortex of faddists. His experiences are traced with spacious and Rabelaisian humour. Every character has the salience of a type. Entertainingly and deftly written.'— *Daily Graphic.*

E. F. Benson. DODO: A Detail of the Day. Crown 8vo. 6s.

THE CAPSINA. Crown 8vo. 6s.

See also Fleur de Lis Novels.

Margaret Benson. SUBJECT TO VANITY. Crown 8vo. 3s. 6d.

Sir Walter Besant. A FIVE YEARS' TRYST, and Other Stories. Crown 8vo. 6s.

J. Bloundelle Burton, Author of 'The Clash of Arms.' THE YEAR ONE: A Page of the French Revolution. Illustrated. Crown 8vo. 6s.

DENOUNCED. Crown 8vo. 6s.

THE CLASH OF ARMS. Crown 8vo. 6s.

ACROSS THE SALT SEAS. Crown 8vo. 6s.

SERVANTS OF SIN. Crown 8vo. 6s.

THE FATE OF VALSEC. Crown 8vo. 6s.

'The characters are admirably portrayed. The book not only arrests and sustains the attention, but conveys valuable information in the most pleasant guise.'—*Morning Post.*

See also Fleur de Lis Novels.

Ada Cambridge. THE DEVASTATORS. Crown 8vo. 6s.

PATH AND GOAL. Crown 8vo. 6s.

Bernard Capes, Author of 'The Lake of Wine.' PLOTS. Crown 8vo. 6s.

'The stories are excellently fanciful and concentrated and quite worthy of the author's best work.'—*Morning Leader.*

Weatherby Chesney. JOHN TOPP: PIRATE. *Second Edition.* Crown 8vo. 6s.

THE FOUNDERED GALLEON. Crown 8vo. 6s.

THE BRANDED PRINCE. Crown 8vo. 6s.

'Always highly interesting and surprising.'—*Daily Express.*

'An ingenious, cleverly-contrived story.'— *Outlook.*

Mrs. W. K. Clifford. A WOMAN ALONE. Crown 8vo. 3s. 6d.

See also Fleur de Lis Novels.

J. Maclaren Cobban. THE KING OF ANDAMAN: A Saviour of Society. Crown 8vo. 6s.

WILT THOU HAVE THIS WOMAN? Crown 8vo. 6s.

THE ANGEL OF THE COVENANT. Crown 8vo. 6s.

E. H. Cooper, Author of 'Mr. Blake of Newmarket.' A FOOL'S YEAR. Crown 8vo. 6s.

Julian Corbett. A BUSINESS IN GREAT WATERS. Crown 8vo. 6s.

Marie Corelli. See page 31.

L. Cope Cornford. CAPTAIN JACOBUS: A Romance of the Road. Cr. 8vo. 6s.

See also Fleur de Lis Novels.

Stephen Crane. WOUNDS IN THE RAIN. Crown 8vo. 6s.

S. R. Crockett, Author of 'The Raiders,' etc. LOCHINVAR. Illustrated. *Second Edition.* Crown 8vo. 6s.

'Full of gallantry and pathos, of the clash of arms, and brightened by episodes of humour and love.'—*Westminster Gazette.*

THE STANDARD BEARER. Cr. 8vo. 6s.

'Mr. Crockett at his best.'—*Literature.*

B. M. Croker, Author of 'Peggy of the Bartons.' ANGEL. *Third Edition.* Crown 8vo. 6s.

'An excellent story. Clever pictures of Anglo-Indian life abound. The heroine is delightful.'—*Manchester Guardian.*

PEGGY OF THE BARTONS. Crown 8vo. 6s.

A STATE SECRET. Crown 8vo. 3s. 6d.

Hope Dawlish. A SECRETARY OF LEGATION. Crown 8vo. 6s.

A. J. Dawson. DANIEL WHYTE. Crown 8vo. 6s.

C. E. Denny. THE ROMANCE OF UPFOLD MANOR. Crown 8vo. 6s.

Evelyn Dickinson. A VICAR'S WIFE. Crown 8vo. 6s.

THE SIN OF ANGELS. Crown 8vo. 3s. 6d.

Harris Dickson. THE BLACK WOLF'S BREED. Illustrated. *Second Edition. Crown 8vo. 6s.*

A. Conan Doyle, Author of 'Sherlock Holmes,' 'The White Company,' etc. ROUND THE RED LAMP. *Eighth Edition. Crown 8vo. 6s.*

'The book is far and away the best view that has been vouchsafed us behind the scenes of the consulting-room.'—*Illustrated London News.*

Sara Jeannette Duncan (Mrs. Everard Cotes), Author of 'A Voyage of Consolation.' THOSE DELIGHTFUL AMERICANS. Illustrated. *Third Edition. Crown 8vo. 6s.*

'A rattling picture of American life, bright and good-tempered throughout.'—*Scotsman.*

THE PATH OF A STAR. Illustrated. *Second Edition. Crown 8vo. 6s.*

See also Fleur de Lis Novels.

C. F. Embree. A HEART OF FLAME. *Crown 8vo. 6s.*

G. Manville Fenn. AN ELECTRIC SPARK. *Crown 8vo. 6s.*

ELI'S CHILDREN. *Crown 8vo. 2s. 6d.*

A DOUBLE KNOT. *Crown 8vo. 2s. 6d.*

See also Fleur de Lis Novels.

J. H. Findlater. THE GREEN GRAVES OF BALGOWRIE. *Fourth Edition. Crown 8vo. 6s.*

'A powerful and vivid story.'—*Standard.*

'A beautiful story, sad and strange as truth itself.'—*Vanity Fair.*

'A singularly original, clever, and beautiful story.'—*Guardian.*

A DAUGHTER OF STRIFE. *Crown 8vo. 6s.*

See also Fleur de Lis Novels.

Mary Findlater. OVER THE HILLS. *Second Edition. Crown 8vo. 6s.*

BETTY MUSGRAVE. *Second Edition. Crown 8vo. 6s.*

A NARROW WAY. *Third Edition. Crown 8vo. 6s.*

J. S. Fletcher. THE BUILDERS. *Crown 8vo. 6s.*

See also Fleur de Lis Novels.

M. E. Francis. MISS ERIN. *Second Edition. Crown 8vo. 6s.*

Tom Gallon, Author of 'Kiddy.' RICKERBY'S FOLLY. *Crown 8vo. 6s.*

Mary Gaunt. DEADMAN'S. *Crown 8vo. 6s.*

THE MOVING FINGER. *Crown 8vo. 3s. 6d.*

See also Fleur de Lis Novels.

Dorothea Gerard, Author of 'Lady Baby.' THE MILLION. *Crown 8vo. 6s.*

THE CONQUEST OF LONDON. *Second Edition. Crown 8vo. 6s.*

THE SUPREME CRIME. *Cr. 8vo. 6s.*

HOLY MATRIMONY. *Second Edition. Crown 8vo. 6s.*

'The love story which it enshrines is a very pretty and tender one.'—*Morning Leader.*

'Distinctly interesting.'—*Athenæum.*

THINGS THAT HAVE HAPPENED. *Crown 8vo. 6s.*

R. Murray Gilchrist. WILLOWBRAKE. *Crown 8vo. 6s.*

Algernon Gissing. THE KEYS OF THE HOUSE. *Crown 8vo. 6s.*

George Gissing, Author of 'Demos,' 'In the Year of Jubilee,' etc. THE TOWN TRAVELLER. *Second Edition. Crown 8vo. 6s.*

THE CROWN OF LIFE. *Crown 8vo. 6s.*

Ernest Glanville. THE KLOOF BRIDE. *Crown 8vo. 3s. 6d.*

THE LOST REGIMENT. *Crown 8vo. 3s. 6d.*

THE DESPATCH RIDER. *Crown 8vo. 3s. 6d.*

THE INCA'S TREASURE. Illustrated. *Crown 8vo. 3s. 6d.*

'No lack of exciting incident.'—*Scotsman.*

'Most thrilling and exciting.'—*Glasgow Herald.*

Charles Gleig. BUNTER'S CRUISE. Illustrated. *Crown 8vo. 3s. 6d.*

Julien Gordon. MRS. CLYDE. *Crown 8vo. 6s.*

'A clever picture of many phases of feminine and American life.'—*Daily Express.*

'Full of vivacity, with many excruciatingly clever and entertaining scenes.'—*Pilot.*

S. Gordon. A HANDFUL OF EXOTICS. *Crown 8vo. 3s. 6d.*

C. F. Goss. THE REDEMPTION OF DAVID CORSON. *Third Edition. Crown 8vo. 6s.*

E. M'Queen Gray. ELSA. *Crown 8vo. 6s.*

MY STEWARDSHIP. *Crown 8vo. 2s. 6d.*

A. G. Hales. JAIR THE APOSTATE. Illustrated. *Crown 8vo. 6s.*

'An extraordinarily vivid story.'—*World.*

'Mr. Hales has a vivid pen, and the scenes are described with vigour and colour.'—*Morning Post.*

Lord Ernest Hamilton. MARY HAMILTON. *Third Edition. Crown 8vo. 6s.*

Mrs. Burton Harrison. A PRINCESS OF THE HILLS. Illustrated. *Crown 8vo. 6s.*

'Vigorous, swift, exciting.'—*Outlook.*

'A singularly pleasant story of the Tyrol.'—*Morning Post.*

Robert Hichens, Author of 'Flames,' etc. THE PROPHET OF BERKELEY SQUARE. *Second Edition. Crown 8vo. 6s.*

'One continuous sparkle. Mr. Hichens is witty, satirical, caustic, irresistibly humorous.'—*Birmingham Gazette.*

TONGUES OF CONSCIENCE. *Second Edition. Crown 8vo. 6s.*

FELIX. *Fourth Edition. Crown 8vo. 6s.*

'Firm in texture, sane, sincere, and

FICTION

natural. "Felix" is a clever book, and in many respects a true one.'—*Daily Chronicle.*

'A really powerful book.'—*Morning Leader.*

'The story is related with unflagging spirit.'—*World.*

'"Felix" will undoubtedly add to a considerable reputation.'—*Daily Mail.*

See also Fleur de Lis Novels.

John Oliver Hobbes, Author of 'Robert Orange.' THE SERIOUS WOOING. *Crown 8vo. 6s.*

'Mrs. Craigie is as brilliant as she ever has been; her characters are all illuminated with sparkling gems of description, and the conversation scintillates with an almost bewildering blaze.'—*Athenæum.*

Anthony Hope. See page 32.

I. Hooper. THE SINGER OF MARLY. *Crown 8vo. 6s.*

Violet Hunt. THE HUMAN INTEREST. *Crown 8vo. 6s.*

C. J. Cutcliffe Hyne, Author of 'Captain Kettle.' PRINCE RUPERT THE BUCCANEER. With 8 Illustrations. *Second Edition. Crown 8vo. 6s.*
MR. HORROCKS, PURSER. *Crown 8vo. 6s.*

W. W. Jacobs. See page 32.

Henry James, Author of 'What Maisie Knew.' THE SACRED FOUNT. *Crown 8vo. 6s.*
THE SOFT SIDE. *Second Edition. Crown 8vo. 6s.*

C. F. Keary. THE JOURNALIST. *Crown 8vo. 6s.*

Florence Finch Kelly. WITH HOOPS OF STEEL. *Crown 8vo. 6s.*

Hon. Emily Lawless. TRAITS AND CONFIDENCES. *Crown 8vo. 6s.*
WITH ESSEX IN IRELAND. *New Edition. Crown 8vo. 6s.*
See also Fleur de Lis Novels.

Harry Lawson, Author of 'When the Billy Boils.' CHILDREN OF THE BUSH. *Crown 8vo. 6s.*

'Full of human sympathy and the genuine flavour of a wild, untrammelled, unsophisticated life.'—*Morning Leader.*

'The author writes of the wild, picturesque life "out back," with all the affection of a native and the penetrating insight of long observation.'—*Daily Telegraph.*

E. Lynn Linton. THE TRUE HISTORY OF JOSHUA DAVIDSON, Christian and Communist. *Eleventh Edition. Crown 8vo. 1s.*

Norma Lorimer. MIRRY ANN. *Crown 8vo. 6s.*
JOSIAH'S WIFE. *Crown 8vo. 6s.*

Charles K. Lush. THE AUTOCRATS. *Crown 8vo. 6s.*

Edna Lyall. DERRICK VAUGHAN, NOVELIST. *42nd thousand. Crown 8vo. 3s. 6d.*

S. Macnaughtan. THE FORTUNE OF CHRISTINA MACNAB. *Second Edition. Crown 8vo. 6s.*

A. Macdonell. THE STORY OF TERESA. *Crown 8vo. 6s.*

Harold Macgrath. THE PUPPET CROWN. Illustrated. *Crown 8vo. 6s.*

Lucas Malet. See page 33.

Mrs. M. E. Mann. OLIVIA'S SUMMER. *Second Edition. Crown 8vo. 6s.*

'An exceptionally clever book, told with consummate artistry and reticence.'—*Daily Mail.*

'Full of shrewd insight and quiet humour.'—*Academy.*

'Wholly delightful; a very beautiful and refreshing tale.'—*Pall Mall Gazette.*

'The author touches nothing that she does not adorn, so delicate and firm is her hold.'—*Manchester Guardian.*

'A powerful story.'—*Times.*

Richard Marsh. BOTH SIDES OF THE VEIL. *Second Edition. Crown 8vo. 6s.*
THE SEEN AND THE UNSEEN. *Crown 8vo. 6s.*
MARVELS AND MYSTERIES. *Crown 8vo. 6s.*
THE TWICKENHAM PEERAGE. *Second Edition. Crown 8vo. 6s.*

'It is a long time since my Baronite read a novel of such entrancing interest as "The Twickenham Peerage." He recommends the gentle reader to get the book. In addition to its breathless interest, it is full of character and bubbling with fun.'—*Punch.*

A. E. W. Mason, Author of 'The Courtship of Morrice Buckler,' 'Miranda of the Balcony,' etc. CLEMENTINA. Illustrated. *Crown 8vo. 6s.*

'A romance of the most delicate ingenuity and humour ... the very quintessence of romance.'—*Spectator.*

Helen Mathers, Author of 'Comin' thro' the Rye.' HONEY. *Fourth Edition. Crown 8vo. 6s.*

'Racy, pointed, and entertaining.'—*Vanity Fair.*

'Honey is a splendid girl.'—*Daily Express.*

'A vigorously written story, full of clever things, a piquant blend of sweet and sharp.' *Daily Telegraph.*

L. T. Meade. DRIFT. *Crown 8vo. 6s.*

Bertram Mitford. THE SIGN OF THE SPIDER. Illustrated. *Fifth Edition. Crown 8vo. 3s. 6d.*

F. F. Montresor, Author of 'Into the Highways and Hedges.' THE ALIEN. *Second Edition. Crown 8vo. 6s.*

'Fresh, unconventional, and instinct with human sympathy.'—*Manchester Guardian.*

'Miss Montresor creates her tragedy out of passions and necessities elementarily human. Perfect art.'—*Spectator.*

Arthur Morrison. See page 33.

W. E. Norris. THE CREDIT OF THE COUNTY. Illustrated. *Second Edition.* Crown 8vo. 6s.

'A capital novel it is, deftly woven together of the comedy and tragedy of life.'—*Yorkshire Post.*

'It is excellent—keen, graceful, diverting.'—*Times.*

THE EMBARRASSING ORPHAN. Crown 8vo. 6s.

HIS GRACE. *Third Edition.* Crown 8vo. 6s.

THE DESPOTIC LADY. Crown 8vo. 6s.

CLARISSA FURIOSA. Crown 8vo. 6s.

GILES INGILBY. *Illustrated. Second Edition.* Crown 8vo. 6s.

AN OCTAVE. *Second Edition.* Crown 8vo. 6s.

A DEPLORABLE AFFAIR. Crown 8vo. 3s. 6d.

JACK'S FATHER. Crown 8vo. 2s. 6d.

See also Fleur de Lis Novels.

Mrs. Oliphant. THE TWO MARYS. Crown 8vo. 6s.

THE LADY'S WALK. Crown 8vo. 6s.

THE PRODIGALS. Crown 8vo. 3s. 6d.

See also Fleur de Lis Novels.

Alfred Ollivant. OWD BOB, THE GREY DOG OF KENMUIR. *Fifth Edition.* Crown 8vo. 6s.

'Weird, thrilling, strikingly graphic.'—*Punch.*

'We admire this book . . . It is one to read with admiration and to praise with enthusiasm.'—*Bookman.*

'It is a fine, open-air, blood-stirring book, to be enjoyed by every man and woman to whom a dog is dear.'—*Literature.*

E. Phillips Oppenheim. MASTER OF MEN. *Second Edition.* Crown 8vo. 6s.

Gilbert Parker. See page 33.

James Blythe Patton. BIJLI, THE DANCER. Crown 8vo. 6s.

Max Pemberton. THE FOOTSTEPS OF A THRONE. Illustrated. *Second Edition.* Crown 8vo. 6s.

'A story of pure adventure, with a sensation on every page.'—*Daily Mail.*

I CROWN THEE KING. With Illustrations by Frank Dadd and A. Forrestier. Crown 8vo. 6s.

'A romance of high adventure, of love and war.'—*Daily News.*

Mrs. F. E. Penny. A FOREST OFFICER. Crown 8vo. 6s.

Eden Phillpotts. See page 34.

'Q,' Author of 'Dead Man's Rock.' THE WHITE WOLF. *Second Edition.* Crown 8vo. 6s.

'Every story is an accomplished romance in its own way.'—*Scotsman.*

'The poet's vein, the breadth of vision, the touch of mysticism are plain in all.'—*Times.*

R. Orton Prowse. THE POISON OF ASPS. Crown 8vo. 3s. 6d.

Richard Pryce. TIME AND THE WOMAN. Crown 8vo. 6s.

THE QUIET MRS. FLEMING. Crown 8vo. 3s. 6d.

Walter Raymond, Author of 'Love and Quiet Life.' FORTUNE'S DARLING. Crown 8vo. 6s.

Edith Rickert. OUT OF THE CYPRESS SWAMP. Crown 8vo. 6s.

W. Pett Ridge. LOST PROPERTY. *Second Edition.* Crown 8vo. 6s.

'The story is an interesting and animated picture of the struggle for life in London, with a natural humour and tenderness of its own.'—*Scotsman*

'A simple, delicate bit of work, which will give pleasure to many. Much study of the masses has made him, not mad, but strong, and—wonder of wonders—cheerful.'—*Times.*

A SON OF THE STATE. Crown 8vo. 3s. 6d.

SECRETARY TO BAYNE, M.P. Crown 8vo. 6s.

C. G. D. Roberts. THE HEART OF THE ANCIENT WOOD. Crown 8vo. 3s. 6d.

Mrs. M. H. Roberton. A GALLANT QUAKER. Illustrated. Crown 8vo. 6s.

W. Clark Russell. MY DANISH SWEETHEART. Illustrated. *Fourth Edition.* Crown 8vo. 6s.

Grace Rhys. THE WOOING OF SHEILA. *Second Edition.* Crown 8vo. 6s.

'A really fine book. A book that deserves to live. Sheila is the sweetest heroine who has lived in a novelist's pages for many a day. Every scene and every incident has the impress of truth. It is a masterly romance, and one that should be widely read and appreciated.'—*Morning Leader.*

W. Satchell. THE LAND OF THE LOST. Crown 8vo. 6s.

Marshall Saunders. ROSE A CHARLITTE. Crown 8vo. 6s.

W. C. Scully. THE WHITE HECATOMB. Crown 8vo. 6s.

BETWEEN SUN AND SAND. Crown 8vo. 6s.

A VENDETTA OF THE DESERT. Crown 8vo. 3s. 6d.

Adeline Sergeant, Author of 'The Story of a Penitent Soul.' A GREAT LADY. Crown 8vo. 6s.

THE MASTER OF BEECHWOOD. Crown 8vo. 6s.

BARBARA'S MONEY. *Second Edition.* Crown 8vo. 6s.

'Full of life and incident, and Barbara is a delightful heroine.'—*Daily Express.*

'An unusually entertaining story.'—*World.*

W. F. Shannon. THE MESS DECK. Crown 8vo. 3s. 6d.

JIM TWELVES. *Second Edition.* Crown 8vo. 3s. 6d.

FICTION

'Full of quaint humour, wise saws, and deep-sea philosophy.'—*Morning Leader*.

'In "Jim Twelves" Mr. Shannon has created a delightful character.'—*Punch*.

'Bright and lively reading throughout.'—*Telegraph*.

Helen Shipton. THE STRONG GOD CIRCUMSTANCE. *Crown 8vo. 6s.*

R. N. Stephens. A GENTLEMAN PLAYER. *Crown 8vo. 6s.*

See also Fleur de Lis Novels.

E. H. Strain. ELMSLIE'S DRAG-NET. *Crown 8vo. 6s.*

Esmé Stuart. A WOMAN OF FORTY. *Crown 8vo. 3s. 6d.*

CHRISTALLA. *Crown 8vo. 6s.*

Duchess of Sutherland. ONE HOUR AND THE NEXT. *Third Edition. Crown 8vo. 6s.*

Annie Swan. LOVE GROWN COLD. *Second Edition. Crown 8vo. 5s.*

Benjamin Swift. SIREN CITY. *Crown 8vo. 6s.*

SORDON. *Crown 8vo. 6s.*

R. B. Townshend. LONE PINE: A Romance of Mexican Life. *Crown 8vo. 6s.*

Paul Waineman. A HEROINE FROM FINLAND. *Crown 8vo. 6s.*

'A lovely tale.'—*Manchester Guardian*.

'A vivid picture of pastoral life in a beautiful and too little known country.'—*Pall Mall Gazette*.

Victor Waite. CROSS TRAILS. *Crown 8vo. 6s.*

H. B. Marriott Watson. THE SKIRTS OF HAPPY CHANCE. Illustrated. *Second Edition. Crown 8vo. 6s.*

H. G. Wells. THE STOLEN BACILLUS, and other Stories. *Second Edition. Crown 8vo. 3s. 6d.*

THE PLATTNER STORY AND OTHERS. *Second Edition. Crown 8vo. 3s. 6d.*

THE SEA LADY. *Crown 8vo. 6s.*

'A strange, fantastic tale, a really beautiful idyll.'—*Standard*.

'In literary charm, in inventiveness, in fun and humour, it is equal to the best of Mr. Wells' stories.'—*Daily News*.

'Highly successful farce and plenty of polished satire.'—*Daily Mail*.

TALES OF SPACE AND TIME. *Crown 8vo. 6s.*

WHEN THE SLEEPER WAKES. *Crown 8vo. 6s.*

THE INVISIBLE MAN. *Crown 8vo. 6s.*

LOVE AND MR. LEWISHAM. *Crown 8vo. 6s.*

Stanley Weyman, Author of 'A Gentleman of France.' UNDER THE RED ROBE. With Illustrations by R. C. WOODVILLE. *Seventeenth Edition. Crown 8vo. 6s.*

'Every one who reads books at all must read this thrilling romance, from the first page of which to the last the breathless reader is haled along. An inspiration of manliness and courage.'—*Daily Chronicle*.

Mrs. C. N. Williamson, Author of 'The Barnstormers.' PAPA. *Second Edition. Crown 8vo. 6s.*

'Full of startling adventures and sensational episodes.'—*Daily Graphic*.

THE ADVENTURE OF PRINCESS SLYVIA. *Crown 8vo. 3s. 6d.*

C. N. and A. M. Williamson. THE LIGHTNING CONDUCTOR: Being the Romance of a Motor Car. Illustrated. *Crown 8vo. 6s.*

'A very ingenious and diverting book.'—*Morning Leader*.

Zack, Author of 'Life is Life.' TALES OF DUNSTABLE WEIR. *Crown 8vo. 6s.*

X.L. AUT DIABOLUS AUT NIHIL. *Crown 8vo. 3s. 6d.*

The Fleur de Lis Novels

Crown 8vo. 3s. 6d.

MESSRS. METHUEN are now publishing a cheaper issue of some of their popular Novels in a new and most charming style of binding.

Andrew Balfour.
TO ARMS!

Jane Barlow.
A CREEL OF IRISH STORIES.

E. F. Benson.
THE VINTAGE.

J. Bloundelle-Burton.
IN THE DAY OF ADVERSITY.

Mrs. Caffyn (Iota).
ANNE MAULEVERER.

Mrs. W. K. Clifford.
A FLASH OF SUMMER.

L. Cope Cornford.
SONS OF ADVERSITY.

Menie Muriel Dowie.
THE CROOK OF THE BOUGH.

Mrs. Dudeney.
THE THIRD FLOOR.

Sara Jeannette Duncan.
A VOYAGE OF CONSOLATION.

G. Manville Fenn.
THE STAR GAZERS.

Jane H. Findlater.
RACHEL.

Jane H. and Mary Findlater.
TALES THAT ARE TOLD.

J. S. Fletcher.
THE PATHS OF THE PRUDENT.

Mary Gaunt.
KIRKHAM'S FIND.

Robert Hichens.
BYEWAYS.

Emily Lawless.
HURRISH.
MAELCHO.

W. E. Norris.
MATTHEW AUSTIN.

Mrs. Oliphant.
SIR ROBERT'S FORTUNE.

Mary A. Owen.
THE DAUGHTER OF ALOUETTE.

Mary L. Pendered.
AN ENGLISHMAN.

Morley Roberts.
THE PLUNDERERS.

R. N. Stephens.
AN ENEMY TO THE KING.

Mrs. Walford.
SUCCESSORS TO THE TITLE.

Percy White.
A PASSIONATE PILGRIM.

Books for Boys and Girls
Crown 8vo. 3s. 6d.

THE ICELANDER'S SWORD. By S. Baring-Gould.
TWO LITTLE CHILDREN AND CHING. By Edith E. Cuthell.
TODDLEBEN'S HERO. By M. M. Blake.
ONLY A GUARD-ROOM DOG. By Edith E. Cuthell.
THE DOCTOR OF THE JULIET. By Harry Collingwood.
MASTER ROCKAFELLAR'S VOYAGE. By W. Clark Russell.
SYD BELTON : Or, the Boy who would not go to S By G. Manville Fenn.
THE RED GRANGE. By Mrs. Molesworth.
THE SECRET OF MADAME DE MONLUC. By Author of ' Mdle. Mori.'
DUMPS. By Mrs. Parr.
A GIRL OF THE PEOPLE. By L. T. Meade.
HEPSY GIPSY. By L. T. Meade. 2s. 6d.
THE HONOURABLE MISS. By L. T. Meade.

The Novelist

MESSRS. METHUEN are issuing under the above general title a Monthly Seri of Novels by popular authors at the price of Sixpence. Each number is as long the average Six Shilling Novel. The first numbers of 'THE NOVELIST' are follows :—

I. DEAD MEN TELL NO TALES. By E. W. Hornung.
II. JENNIE BAXTER, JOURNALIST. By Robert Barr.
III. THE INCA'S TREASURE. By Ernest Glanville.
IV. A SON OF THE STATE. By W. Pett Ridge.
V. FURZE BLOOM. By S. Baring-Gould.
VI. BUNTER'S CRUISE. By C. Gleig.
VII. THE GAY DECEIVERS. By Arthur Moore.
VIII. PRISONERS OF WAR. By A. Boyson Weekes.
IX. *Out of print.*
X. VELDT AND LAAGER: Tales of the Transvaal. By E. S. Valentine.
XI. THE NIGGER KNIGHTS. By F. Norreys Connel.
XII. A MARRIAGE AT SEA. By W. Clark Russell.
XIII. THE POMP OF THE LAVILETTES. By Gilbert Parker.
XIV. A MAN OF MARK. By Anthony Hope.
XV. THE CARISSIMA. By Lucas Malet.
XVI. THE LADY'S WALK. By Mrs. Oliphant.
XVII. DERRICK VAUGHAN. By Edna Lyall.
XVIII. IN THE MIDST OF ALARMS. By Robert Barr.
XIX. HIS GRACE. By W. E. Norris.
XX. DODO. By E. F. Benson.
XXI. CHEAP JACK ZITA. By S. Baring-Goul
XXII. WHEN VALMOND CAME TO PONTIAC. Gilbert Parker.
XXIII. THE HUMAN BOY. By Eden Phillpott
XXIV. THE CHRONICLES OF COUNT ANTON By Anthony Hope.
XXV. BY STROKE OF SWORD. By Andr Balfour.
XXVI. KITTY ALONE. By S. Baring-Gould.
XXVII. GILES INGILBY. By W. E. Norris.
XXVIII. URITH. By S. Baring-Gould.
XXIX. THE TOWN TRAVELLER. By Geor Gissing.
XXX. MR. SMITH. By Mrs. Walford.
XXXI. A CHANGE OF AIR. By Anthony Ho
XXXII. THE KLOOF BRIDE. By Ernest Glanvi
XXXIII. ANGEL. By B. M. Croker.
XXXIV. A COUNSEL OF PERFECTION. By Lu Malet.
XXXV. THE BABY'S GRANDMOTHER. By M L. B. Walford.
XXXVI. THE COUNTESS TEKLA. By Robert Ba

Methuen's Sixpenny Library

THE MATABELE CAMPAIGN. By Major-General Baden-Powell.
THE DOWNFALL OF PREMPEH. By Major-General Baden-Powell.
MY DANISH SWEETHEART. By W. Clark Russell.
IN THE ROAR OF THE SEA. By S. Baring-Gould.
PEGGY OF THE BARTONS. By B. M. Croker.
THE GREEN GRAVES OF BALGOWRIE. By Jane H. Findlater.
THE STOLEN BACILLUS. By H. G. Wells.
MATTHEW AUSTIN. By W. E. Norris.
THE CONQUEST OF LONDON. By Dorothea Gerard.
A VOYAGE OF CONSOLATION. By Sara J. Duncan.
THE MUTABLE MANY. By Robert Barr.
BEN HUR. By General Lew Wallace.
SIR ROBERT'S FORTUNE. By Mrs. Oliphant.
THE FAIR GOD. By General Lew Wallace.
CLARISSA FURIOSA. By W. E. Norris.
CRANFORD. By Mrs. Gaskell.
NOEMI. By S. Baring-Gould.
THE THRONE OF DAVID. By J. H. Ingraham.
ACROSS THE SALT SEAS. By J. Blounde Burton.
THE MILL ON THE FLOSS. By George Eliot.
PETER SIMPLE. By Captain Marryat.
MARY BARTON. By Mrs. Gaskell.
PRIDE AND PREJUDICE. By Jane Austen.
NORTH AND SOUTH. By Mrs. Gaskell.
JACOB FAITHFUL. By Captain Marryat.
SHIRLEY. By Charlotte Bronte.
FAIRY TALES RE-TOLD. By S. Baring Gould.
THE TRUE HISTORY OF JOSHUA DAVIDSON. Mrs. Lynn Linton.

www.ingramcontent.com/pod-product-compliance
Lightning Source LLC
Chambersburg PA
CBHW080548090426

42735CB00016B/3189